The American Political Process

The American Political Process

Richard Maidment
Senior Lecturer in Government, The Open University
Anthony McGrew
Senior Lecturer in Government, The Open University

SAGE PUBLICATIONS
in association with
The Open University

© The Open University 1986, 1991
First Published 1986
Second Edition 1991

 SAGE Publications Ltd
6 Bonhill Street
London EC2A 4PU

SAGE Publications Inc
2455 Teller Road
Newbury Park, California 91320

SAGE Publications India Pvt Ltd
32, M-Block Market
Greater Kailash–I
New Delhi 110 048

ISBN 0 8039 8525 8
ISBN 0 8039 8434 0 Pbk

Typeset by Text Processing Services, Operations Division, The Open University, Walton Hall, Milton Keynes, MK7 6AA
Printed in Great Britain by Billing and Sons Ltd, Worcester

Contents

Preface to the First Edition

The literature on the politics and government of the United States is extensive. There is no shortage of academic material on this subject. Indeed, if anything, there is an overabundance. So the appearance of a new introductory book on American government requires an explanation. It is unlikely to be welcomed unless it offers a different perspective. *The American Political Process* seeks to provide just such a degree of difference by giving prominence to the notion of democracy, a notion that is central to the political culture of the United States. The language of American politics can leave little doubt that Americans and their political representatives see themselves as democrats and the United States as the pre-eminent liberal democracy in the world. Politicians, from Presidents to those holding more humble offices, take this for granted. They often assert it but hardly ever feel the need to justify it. But how democratic, in fact, is the American polity? How representative are its institutions? To what extent is the public policy-making process open and accessible? These are some of the key questions asked in this book, and the attempt to answer them is its central concern.

The prominence of the notion of democracy in *The American Political Process* has consequences both for the content and structure of the book. Those characteristics of the political system that illuminate the answers to the questions are dealt with at length. In Part 1, which is written by Richard Maidment, the key constituent elements of the political process are described, analysed and placed within a historical context. These are the political culture, the Constitution, the institutions of the federal government, the political parties, and the multiplicity of interest groups.

Chapter 1 discusses a political culture that is and has been almost exclusively wedded to democratic values – values which have nevertheless been frequently ignored or violated in practice. For instance, and most dramatically, the idea of equality, a belief enshrined in the Declaration of Independence and to which homage has been paid throughout American history, has had to coexist with slavery, segregation and racial discrimination. How can this contradiction be explained? Does it mean that the proclaimed belief in equality is at best a veneer and at worst a charade, or does it suggest a political culture committed to equality but wrought with a significant degree of internal tension?

Chapter 2 on the Constitution also notes the tension in the democratic fabric of the American polity. The profound antipathy towards the 'majority faction' felt by the Founding Fathers in 1787 had an enormous impact on the Constitution. Although this antipathy was diluted within a few decades and ultimately disappeared, it was institutionalized in the constitutional arrangements, a fact which is perhaps most readily apparent in the role and importance of the federal judiciary. In no other liberal democracy do the courts have quite such an influence on the making of public policy. How does a democratic polity accommodate itself to the nine unelected judges of the United States Supreme Court making so many critical policy decisions? Chapter 3 investigates these and other issues.

The remaining chapters of Part 1 discuss the presidency, the Congress, political parties and interest groups and raise the difficult questions of power and representation. Is the President too powerful or not powerful enough? Is the Congress a representative legislative body or has its desire to reflect and respond to the views of its constituents made it a rather ineffective legislative institution? What is the significance for the American polity of the decline of the party system and the proliferation of interest group activity?

Part 2 of the book, written by Anthony McGrew, examines the public policy-making process. Chapter 7 provides a detailed analysis of how foreign policy is made, which highlights the dilemmas and perhaps the paradox of American democracy. Who are the important actors in the foreign policy process? Are there just a handful of individuals and interests involved or is the process open and accessible? Should American foreign policy seek to promote democracy abroad or should it be based on a harder notion of American interests? Which of the many competing explanations of the policy-making process provides the most convincing account? These questions are also discussed in Chapter 8, which offers a case study in US–Latin American relations, an area which vividly illustrates the complexity and tensions of American foreign policy.

The American Political Process cannot be comprehensive. There is, for instance, no substantial discussion of state and city politics, and federalism has a lower profile in this book than in many others. However, it is hoped that the book will provide both a distinctive introduction to the institutions and processes of American politics as well as raising, and to some degree resolving, questions on the *democratic* character of US government.

We owe a considerable obligation to our colleagues in the Faculty of Social Sciences of the Open University and especially to all the members of the D308 *Democratic Government and Politics* course team, whose advice, both individual and collective, has been invaluable. We also owe a great debt to Christopher Pollitt, chair of the course team, whose good sense, encouragement and patience has been above and beyond the call of duty. This book has benefited from the comments and suggestions of our colleagues in the 'Americanist' community. In particular, we wish to thank the late John D. Lees of the University of Keele, who will be sorely missed by his many friends, and Robert Garson, also of the University of Keele, for reading and, more importantly, for improving the manuscript. Of course, the manuscript would not even have existed without the skills of Mary Dicker, Sue How and Anne Hunt, who have typed successive drafts at great speed and with even greater good humour. Finally, we would like to thank Christine McGrew and Susan Maidment for their support and assistance in seeing this project to fruition.

RICHARD MAIDMENT
TONY MCGREW
June 1986

Preface to the Second Edition

Our principal objective in writing *The American Political Process* was to provide students of American politics with an understanding of what is perhaps the most complex governmental system in the world by placing it within a broad historical and cultural context. We were not primarily concerned with chronicling the latest events or the most up-to-date facts, many of which surface fleetingly and are then rightly forgotten. Nevertheless, in the four years since the first edition there have been several momentous developments, particularly the dramatic change that has occurred in the relationship between the Soviet Union and the United States. The beginning of the end of the Cold War and other developments, of not quite such global significance but nonetheless important, required to be noted and assessed in the book. Accordingly we have revised *The American Political Process* extensively while adhering to the existing structure. We have attempted to incorporate the major developments of the past four years, while maintaining the perspective on democracy which we hope gave this book its distinctive character. All the chapters have been carefully reexamined in the light of these events and the most appropriate and pertinent developments have been noted. Some chapters more than others have been modified by our review of events. In particular, Chapters 3–8 have been revised substantially and will, we hope, provide our readers with an understanding of recent events and developments.

We certainly have not sought to alter the character of *The American Political Process* after its very enthusiastic reception. It hardly needs to be recorded, but we have been both extremely grateful for and pleased with the response to the first edition of the book. We have enjoyed and been flattered by the reviews, but our greatest pleasure has derived from the knowledge that the book has been helpful to students, and in particular those students on the Open University course D308 *Democratic Government and Politics*. Of course, the success of the first edition was not solely due to us and we have acknowledged our considerable obligation to the contribution of our colleagues in the Faculty of Social Sciences at the Open University. We owe a similar debt to them in the preparation of this edition. In addition, we are in debt to all those students who have written to us with their comments and suggestions; we have found them extremely helpful and have taken them into account wherever possible. We are enormously grateful to Michael Dawson, who has made our life a great deal easier by dealing with all the administrative and production problems with his meticulous efficiency, good cheer and unflappability. Nigel Draper edited the first edition exceptionally well and has maintained that standard on this edition. Once again, the manuscript has been prepared by Anne Hunt and Mary Dicker, who have coped with all the difficulties with their usual efficiency, but also with patience and understanding that goes beyond the call of duty.

RICHARD MAIDMENT
TONY MCGREW
June 1990

Part 1
The Nature of the Political Process

1   The American Political Culture

1.1   American exceptionalism

'What is an American?', asked John de Crèvecœur at the time of the American Revolution. 'The American', wrote de Crèvecœur in answer to his own question, 'is a new man, who acts upon new principles; he must therefore entertain new ideas and form new opinions'. De Crèvecœur's 'new man' was neither a European nor the descendant of a European: 'He is an American, who leaving behind him all his ancient prejudices and manners, receives new ones from the new mode of life he has embraced, the new government he obeys' (de Crèvecœur, 1963, pp. 63–4). Two hundred years later, Ronald Reagan, in a speech accepting his party's presidential nomination in 1980, echoed these same sentiments: 'There are no words to express the extraordinary strength and character of this breed of people we call Americans... They are the kinds of men and women Tom Paine had in mind when he wrote during the darkest days of the American Revolution, "we have it in our power to begin the world over again" '.

In those intervening two centuries, countless other observers of American life, both foreign and American, asked and answered the same question: what is an American? Overwhelmingly, they shared de Crèvecœur's view of a new man in a new society, unencumbered by the past. America and Americans were not governed by the rules that controlled the Old World. The traditions and customs of Europe developed over several centuries and were of little concern to the New World. Americans were free to forge their own destiny. Unsurprisingly, most Americans, since the creation of the Republic, have endorsed this belief in their own uniqueness. They have accepted and continued to accept that the American historical experience is distinctive and different to all others. They believe, in other words, in American exceptionalism.

Has the American historical experience been quite so different from that of any other nation? Is this idea of American exceptionalism justified? To some extent, it does not matter as long as it is believed. The belief, by itself, has considerable political and cultural importance. If Americans conceive of themselves as being set apart, then that sense will have consequences; and some of these consequences, particularly in the area of foreign policy, have been very significant.[1]

Nevertheless, why do Americans believe in their distinctiveness? Ironically, as the twentieth century draws to a close, the United States increasingly resembles other Western democracies. It sufferes from a list of ailments which affect most nations of the West. Inflation, unemployment, the decline of traditional manufacturing industries, to name but a few problems, are as intractable in the United States as elsewhere. The United States does not appear to be especially advantaged today, but that was not always the case. Initially, there was an abundance of fertile land which, of course, distinguished the American settlements from contemporaneous European societies. The thirteen states which formed the United States in 1787 were located on the Atlantic seaboard, but by 1912, when Arizona joined, the Union had grown to forty-eight states and spanned the entire continent.[2]

The opening up of the West and the pushing back of the frontier increased the availability of land, which was extremely attractive to landless Europeans. However, the United States was not only well-endowed with land, but it also possessed a disproportionate percentage of other national resources, which were enormously helpful in the transition to industrialization. Although the United States started the process of industrialization after several European countries, it was the pre-eminent industrial society by the early decades of the twentieth century. As a consequence of this combination of abundant fertile agricultural land, a wealth of natural resources and subsequent industrial development, Americans have had a consistently high per capita income – in fact the highest, by most indicators, in the industrialized world for the past fifty years. The economy of the United States, as measured in gross national product, has been the largest in the world by a considerable margin for most of this century. So while it must not be forgotten that significant minorities, particularly racial ones, have not fully participated in the general prosperity, most Americans, throughout their history, have had a sense of economic well-being. Americans have been, in David Potter's memorable phrase, a 'people of plenty' (Potter, 1954).

The wealth of the United States, plus the confidence and optimism that flowed from it, certainly helped to form and sustain the notion of American exceptionalism. The belief in a secure and prosperous future encouraged the American sense of being a society apart, a sense which was reinforced by other factors.

The extraordinary heterogeneity of the American population is undoubtedly one of these factors. As early as the 1770s, de Crèvecœur noticed the diversity of the population: 'I could point out to you a family whose grandfather was an Englishman, whose wife was Dutch, whose son married a French woman and whose present four sons have now four wives of different nations' (de Crèvecœur, 1963, p. 63). Ironically, de Crèvecœur was writing at a time when the population was relatively homogeneous, at least by current American standards. It has been estimated that by the end of the eighteenth century, approximately 70 per cent of the five and a quarter million Americans were descendants of English or Welsh immigrants. Another 15 per cent were of Scottish or Irish ancestry, with Germans accounting for the only substantial group of non-British immigrants. By the end of the nineteenth century, the composition of the population had dramatically changed. Particularly after the end of the Civil War in 1865, the tempo of immigration rapidly increased. Some ten million people entered the country in the thirty years up to 1890, and a further fifteen million between 1890 and 1910. Although a percentage of these new immigrants came from Northern Europe, the great majority, especially in the second wave after 1890, originated in Southern and Eastern Europe. Thus, by the end of the first few decades of the twentieth century, there were substanital communities of Scandinavians, Russians, Poles, Italians and Greeks, to name but a few of the European groups, resident in the United States. Furthermore, there was a sprinkling of Chinese and Japanese who settled in the states on the Pacific coast. In recent years there has been substantial emigration from Puerto Rico, Mexico and Asian countries such as the Philippines and Korea. Apart from those who emigrated voluntarily, there were those who were brought in servitude from Africa. Black slaves and their descendants have always constituted a significant percentage of the population and have been an important element in the construction of the unique racial mosaic.

Racial heterogeneity has had a parallel religious diversity. The first colonists, who came in search of religious freedom, were Protestant, and more Americans today would consider themselves Protestant than the adherents of any other religion. However, the label Protestant does not convey the extraordinary array of churches and religious doctrines that exist within Protestantism, at least in the United States. As a result, there is no single Protestant voice, which, on occasion, can make those religions with fewer followers appear more influential. This is certainly true of American Catholicism which, apart from the last few decades, has spoken with one voice and as a consequence has wielded considerable influence, despite the fact that less than 25 per cent of Americans are Catholic. Jews, who constitute a mere 3 per cent of the population, are particularly well organized and articulate on certain issues. Apart from the main Judeo-Christian religions, there is an enormous variety of religions and sects which have found the United States a particularly fertile ground in which to flourish.

What, then, are the consequences of this racial and religious heterogeneity? The principal one is, paradoxically, that the 'new man' spoken of by de Crèvecœur and others has taken longer to emerge or has emerged in a somewhat different form, because Americans have clung to their national origins tenaciously. Racial or ethnic and religious loyalties have been far more long-lived than anticipated. The American 'melting pot', which was supposed to blend the varied and disparate ingredients into a new and uniform mixture, has not worked in quite that way. For instance, new immigrants, when they arrived in the large cities of the North East, were bewildered by their new and threatening surroundings and crowded together in the inner city. They formed ghettos, partly out of economic circumstance, partly due to racial and religious prejudice, but also because they found considerable security and comfort from a collective presence. The strength of their desire is evident from the fact that these enclaves have proved remarkably resilient, even when the economic constraints diminished and the prejudices abated. Geographically, the enclaves may have moved from the inner city to the suburbs, but the need for a community based on race, ethnicity and religion continued. This, of course, does not mean that immigrants were reluctant to become Americans, or that there was no attempt to integrate them. Quite to the contrary, immigrants were only too anxious to speak English, to be naturalized citizens and proclaim their Americanism; and they were encouraged to do so. Through their children, immigrants willingly participated in the various methods of socialization, notably the education system, to develop an American identity. However, as far as they were concerned, becoming an American did not negate their ancestry. They wanted and needed both. Their wish to be American simply had to coexist with their desire to retain and, indeed, parade their social and religious heritage. The immigrants' new American identity had to incorporate their history.

The strength of racial, ethnic and religious attachments in the United States have enormous implications. The most important is the effect on social class, because if Americans have traditionally looked, as it were, to their roots, what role has class played in American society? If the ties that bind are racial, what is the impact on class connections? It is certainly true that the United States is not, nor has it been, a classless society. It hardly needs to be said that there are inequalities of wealth and income. The patterns of income distribution and ownership of wealth are not that dramatically different from the other Western industrialized societies. Furthermore, a significant percentage of the American population is locked into a cycle of poverty. Nevertheless, it is readily apparent that a strong class consciousness has never developed in the United States. The signs of such a consciousness are absent.

The union movement, for example, is one of the least powerful in the Western world. It has never been particularly attractive to Americans: by 1984, barely 20 per cent of the non-agricultural labour force was unionized. The American union movement was also based on a very different set of assumptions and beliefs, by comparison with most European trade union movements. The American Federation of Labor (AFL), which was formed in 1886 to represent the craft occupations, enthusiastically supported capitalism. Even the more radical Congress of Industrial Organizations (CIO), established in 1938 during the worst economic depression this century and representing employees in mass-production industries, did not seek to overthrow the established economic order. Neither the AFL nor the CIO embraced socialism and, consequently, neither organization felt the need to establish their own party. Instead, they have individually and, since 1955 when they merged, jointly endorsed those candidates of both major parties whom they believe are helpful to the interests of unionism. The overwhelming majority of endorsements have in fact, during the twentieth century, gone to the Democratic Party. However, the value of these endorsements is questionable, because the rank-and-file members do not necessarily vote for the supported candidates. Indeed, class considerations in general do not appear to have a significant impact on American voting behaviour. In the 1988 presidential election, for instance, George Bush, the Republican candidate, received the support of approximately 50 per cent of the blue-collar or manual workers' vote, and 40 per cent of the vote of union members. Nor was 1988 an unusual year, for Republican candidates had achieved similar percentages in 1952, 1956, 1972, 1980 and 1984. Class is not as important a consideration in the United States as it is in most European societies.

What accounts for this lack of class consciousness? Race and ethnicity are a part of the answer, because they cut across economic and social divisions and consequently diminish class consciousness. Ethnicity, however, provides only one element of the explanation. An equally compelling factor, and one which re-emphasizes the distinctiveness of the American historical experience, was the absence of an *ancien régime* (Hartz, 1955). Feudalism, with its meticulously structured hierarchy, did not exist in America. There were no lords and no peasants. There was no aristocracy, no landless serfs and no carefully nurtured sense of where each and every per-

son was located in the immobile socio-economic hierarchy of a feudal society. Americans, therefore, unlike Europeans, did not spend several centuries
developing a collective consciousness derived from the experience of feudalism. They were not imprisoned by feudalism and its heritage in the way
that Europeans were. By contrast, Americans, in the words of Alexis de
Tocqueville in the 1830s, were 'born equal' (de Tocqueville, 1966, p. 123).
By the middle of the eighteenth century, when the vast majority of Europeans were landless, the ownership of land in America 'was almost universal among the white population' (Bailyn, 1968, p. 86). So America, unlike
most European societies, did not require a revolution to liberate itself from
the oppression of feudalism. Of course, there was a revolution in 1776 to
remove the existing political order, but there was little desire on the part of
American colonists to refashion the existing social and economic order.

There can be little doubt that the American historical experience is distinctive. The wealth of the country, its social and religious heterogeneity,
lack of class consciousness and the absence of a feudal heritage does distinguish the United States from other societies. However, there are other states
which possess some of these characteristics. Nevertheless, Americans see
themselves and speak of themselves as a people apart, possessing a unique
past and a 'rendezvous with destiny' (Goldman, 1952). In that sense, American exceptionalism is a reality. It is an important component of how
Americans see themselves and is a significant element of the American
political culture – those values and beliefs that establish the reference and
context within which everyday political activity is conducted. If American
exceptionalism is one element, what are the others?

1.2 Liberal democracy

The language of current American politics can leave little doubt that the
American electorate and their political representatives see themselves as
democrats and the United States as the pre-eminent liberal democracy in
the world. Politicians, like presidents or others holding more humble
offices, take this for granted. They often proclaim it, but rarely feel it
incumbent on them to justify it. Democracy, they assert, is an American
value, and their constituents agree. But is, and was, democracy a key American value, and if so, what precisely is meant by it?

Part of the difficulty in answering these questions is that the concept of
democracy is fluid and difficult to grasp. It is protean and can be interpreted in different ways within the same generation, let alone between generations. For example, currently the right to vote is crucial to the concept
of democracy. No political system would be recognized as a democracy if it
legally restricted the franchise and prevented specified broad categories of
its citizens from possessing it. Of course, the United States today would
have little difficulty in passing this test, but it would not have done so
earlier. It was not until 1920 that women were guaranteed the vote by an
amendment to the US Constitution.[3] Black men did not have the right to
vote until slavery was abolished in 1865, and even then they were prevented from voting by a combination of illegal devices and laws of dubious
constitutionality until well into the twentieth century. Furthermore, in the
early days of the Republic, the franchise was restricted by property qualifications, which varied from state to state.

So did these limitations on the franchise mean that while the United States today would qualify as a democracy, at least on the universal suffrage test, it was not a democracy previously? That is one possible conclusion, but it is a conclusion which conceals a strong and persistent impulse that has existed throughout the history of the United States to encourage and extend mass participation in the political process. It is, in essence, a majoritarian impulse, which not only ensured that the limitations on the franchise were swept aside, but also that the limitations were never as restrictive as those in Europe. The property qualifications which were so restrictive in England, for instance, had far less impact in America, where the ownership of land was much more widespread. By the end of the eighteenth century, by most estimates, at least 50 per cent of the white male population were eligible to vote, and within two or three decades, when property qualifications were abolished, some 80 per cent of those eligible were voting in presidential elections (Williamson, 1960). Admittedly, those eligible were only white males, but by no stretch of the imagination could the American political system, by the 1830s, be described as elite. It was a mass political process at a much earlier date than most European societies. This same impulse to extend participation not only led to the enfranchisement of women and blacks, but also to the introduction of such distinctively American electoral procedures as the primary election and the referendum. They were devised to end the control of the political bosses and special interests, who exercised their power and made deals, allegedly in smoke-filled rooms, and to give control to the electorate. Whether the primary election and the referendum succeeded in achieving these objectives is immaterial at this point, but what is significant is that they indicate the strength of the majoritarian impulse.

So how should the restrictions on the franchise that did exist in the United States be evaluated? What do they inform us of American attitudes towards democracy in general and popular suffrage in particular? One response is to suggest that it is ahistorical to impose the weight of twentieth-century notions of universal suffrage on the eighteenth and nineteenth centuries. On most contemporaneous criteria of popular suffrage, the United States emerges rather well, because popular participation grew faster there than in other countries.

Does that then imply that American attitudes towards democracy were consistently positive, because the suffrage was constantly being expanded to the limit of what was acceptable at the time? The answer is no. American attitudes towards democracy in general and popular suffrage in particular cannot be characterized quite so easily. The United States did not purposefully travel down an open road, removing the occasional obstacle, towards the goal of universal suffrage. The position is more complex, for alongside the desire to expand the perimeters of political participation, there has also existed concern over mass participation. Indeed, the gravity of that concern is central to the constitutional structure that was created in 1787. It is articulated most forcefully by James Madison, who is often referred to as the father of the American Constitution, in the *Federalist Papers*, those tracts written by Madison, Alexander Hamilton and John Jay after the Federal Convention in support of the ratification of the American Constitution by the individual state assemblies. It is reiterated by many others such as Chancellor Kent and John Calhoun over the next two hundred years. The majoritarian impulse and the fear of mass participation have lived together uncomfortably throughout American history. It is true that with the passage of time, the fear of majorities has receded, but the institutions and practices of American politics continue, at the very least, to reflect past worries and concerns over majoritarianism. These two contradictory instincts are very important and central to a political culture which incorporates them both and are indicative of the tensions that exist in American notions of democracy.

Minority rights

The worry about majorities is that they will abuse their power. If the majority faction, to use Madison's words, controls the institutions of government, there is a grave danger that it will ride roughshod over the interests of minorities. But why was Madison concerned that a majority faction would behave in an improper manner? To a large extent, Madison's fear of majorities derived from the Calvinist perception that all human beings were fully capable of behaving in an avaricious and rapacious manner, whether they were acting in the interests of a minority or even in an individual capacity. A majority faction was simply more dangerous than an individual or a minority because, by definition, it was more numerous and thus had a greater ability to gain power and enforce its interests. Consequently, it had to be feared, and minorities had to be protected.

The protection of minorities is also a significant indicator of whether a political system can be deemed to be a democracy, and there can be little doubt that the American political system emerges rather well from this test. The Madisonian fears are reflected in the American Constitution. Apart from the elaborate institutional arrangements in the Constitution which were intended to prevent the majority faction from gaining total control over the levers of government, there are certain crucial civil liberties that are protected by the Constitution. In the Bill of Rights, which is the first ten amendments to the Constitution, freedom of speech, freedom of religion and the freedom of the press, among other civil liberties, are constitutionally protected. They cannot be modified or limited other than by an amendment to the Constitution. No transient or marginal majority can remove these civil liberties. Therefore, there can be little doubt that the protection of minority rights is an important constituent element of the American political culture. However, once again, there is no easy unanimity.

It is inescapable, even to the most casual observer of American society, that there have been several episodes when the constitutionally protected civil liberties of minorities have been violated. For instance, in the aftermath of both the First and Second World Wars, there were episodes of anti-communist hysteria which resulted in numerous investigations of alleged communist infiltration into American public life. In both of these periods, but especially in the latter, there were the most serious abuses of civil liberties.

The initial investigations into communist activity after the Second World War were conducted by the House Un-American Activities Committee, a committee of the House of Representatives, but the most notorious were carried out by a United States Senate committee under the chairmanship of Senator Joseph McCarthy. McCarthy's techniques of investigation, which at best were barely legal and frequently relied on slander and innuendo, undoubtedly violated the civil liberties of those unfortunate individuals who were investigated by his committee. Even more disturbingly, McCarthy and his followers, at the apogee of their power in the early 1950s, were able, albeit for a brief period, to create an atmosphere of unease and disquiet which limited freedom of speech and the freedom of the press. Newspapers, the television networks and the major news magazines, to name but a few organizations, became extremely cautious over what they wrote or said and whom they employed, because they did not wish to incur the wrath of McCarthy and his allies. Any sentiment or any person that could be considered un-American was given a wide berth.

So how could such a situation arise in a political culture which extolled the protection of minority rights? One answer is that in the United States, as elsewhere, a discrepancy exists between the ideal and that which is practised. However, this is not an entirely satisfactory answer, because it ignores a crucial factor: the enormous desire for conformity in American society. The society that cherishes the rights of minorities nevertheless has felt uncomfortable, throughout its existence, with individuals or groups that deviated from the mainstream. On several occasions, of which McCarthyism is only one, this sense of discomfort has turned sour and degenerated into harassment of these groups with all the consequent infringements of their civil liberties. Why has there been this continuous desire for conformity? The explanation may be that there has been, and to some extent still is, a need to forge a new American identity out of a diverse social and religious heritage. De Crèvecœur's new man did not just emerge, he had to be created. An American identity self-consciously needed to be developed and proclaimed. What should an American believe or desire? What did an American stand for? These have always been important questions and carefully considered. The answers to them have been varied and have permitted a considerable element of diversity. Nevertheless, there have been boundaries of acceptability, and crossing these boundaries led into the terrain of un-Americanism, which has never been easily tolerated. The very notion of un-American activity, and the seriousness with which it is taken, is an indication of the power of the desire for conformity, a desire which does not diminish or deny the importance of minority rights to the political culture. The political culture simply incorporates them both with all the consequent disharmony and tension.

Equality

Another key characteristic of twentieth-century democracy is equality, and there can be little doubt of American commitment to it. 'We hold these truths to be self-evident', wrote Thomas Jefferson in the Declaration of Independence, 'that all men are created equal'. Abraham Lincoln, during the middle of the Civil War, declared at Gettysburg: 'Four score and seven years ago, our fathers brought forth on this continent a new nation conceived in liberty and dedicated to the proposition that all men are created equal'. These testaments of the American commitment to equality are two among many, although few have been as eloquent.

Speeches and declarations have not been the only occasions when the importance of equality has been proclaimed. Legal equality is enshrined in the Fourteenth Amendment to the Constitution. The desire for political equality is evident in the movement to extend the franchise. The commitment to social equality is indicated by the pervasive belief that no one is barred from any position, however eminent, as a consequence of birth. The notion that the journey from log cabin to the White House can be made is crucial to the political culture. For example, a recurrent theme of popular fiction in the nineteenth century is the rise of the hero from poverty to wealth. Wealth and success are available to anyone as long as they have ability and work hard. The frontier, after all, had been opened and settled by the dedication of ordinary men and women. They had held their destiny in their own hands; their future was not pre-ordained by class or birthright.

There is much in the American historical experience that sustains this belief in equality. From the outset the American colonies were hospitable to European immigrants. They were liberated from the rigidities of European society. Certainly, by the 1830s American society was swept up with an egalitarian fervour where privilege and rank no longer had any place in the American order. Furthermore, there were numerous instances in real life of men making a fortune on the back of their own ability and industry. The social and economic order was far more fluid and mobile in the United States.

But if there is much in the historical experience that sustains the belief that Americans are dedicated to equality, there is much else that contradicts it. The most dramatic contradiction concerns the position of black Americans. At the moment that Jefferson was claiming that all men were created equal, there were almost a million negro slaves who were decidedly unequal, some of whom, of course, belonged to Jefferson. They had neither social and economic nor political and legal equality – a position that was not constitutionally rectified until the end of the Civil War. However, the abolition of slavery did not resolve the problems of black Americans. The end of the Civil War saw the removal of the former slave owners from positions of power and influence in the southern states. However, their removal was only temporary; by the end of Reconstruction in the middle of the 1870s they were back in control, and with the restoration of the old order the ex-slaves were effectively returned to servitude. The passage of the Thirteenth, Fourteenth and Fifteenth Amendments to the Constitution, to end slavery and establish constitutional protections for former slaves, was nullified by a variety of devices to remove the political and legal equality of blacks.

It was not until the Civil Rights Act of 1964 and the 1965 Voting Rights Act that political and legal equality became a reality in the South. Even in the states of the North and West to which blacks had migrated in ever increasing numbers after the First World War, racial discrimination was the norm. Blacks were not disfranchised as they were in the South, nor did they suffer from legally enforced racial segregation. However, *de facto* segregation existed, and there can be little doubt that they were a deeply disadvantaged minority in the large cities of the North. Admittedly, over the past twenty years, their position, as reflected in most indicators, e.g. education, income, housing, etc., has improved significantly, but the residue of slavery and segregation, plus the continuance of discrimination in the North and South, albeit at a diminished level, has meant that black Americans are not fully equal citizens. So how is it that one of the first groups to arrive in America has not achieved equality in a political culture that values equality so highly?

There is no simple answer to this question, and it certainly will not be found by disparaging the American commitment to equality. The status of blacks has always been problematic, but it has been problematic because of the importance of equality in the American mind. In other words, Americans collectively have been, and still are, profoundly uneasy about the treatment of their fellow Americans, and the source of their unease is the self-evident disparity between the Jeffersonian belief in the rights of man and the status of blacks. Slavery and equality do not readily coexist. Indeed, American society could not easily accept slavery, and it is enormously significant that the only total breakdown in the political process arose out of slavery. Nor could the political culture easily accommodate segregation, disfranchisement and legal inequality, just as today it cannot readily accept racial discrimination. But these practices existed or continue to exist, so how were and are they justified?

Interestingly, apart from a few voices who hovered on the extreme fringes of American political life, there was no attempt to argue that blacks should not be allowed to vote or permitted to sit on juries. There was never a hint of an argument that blacks should be excluded from living in certain neighbourhoods, or any justification offered for discriminatory employment practices. Indeed, not only was there no effort to justify these practices, but they were deliberately concealed. For example, several southern states introduced literacy tests, which had to be passed before a citizen could be registered as a voter. The overt rationale for the introduction of the literacy test was that the right to vote should not be handed out indiscriminately but only granted to those who could understand and evaluate the issues and make sensible decisions. A literacy test would give at least a minimal indication of whether a voter possessed these qualities. Now the case for literacy tests is not overwhelming, but even if the arguments in favour of them are rejected, there is at least a discernible rationale present. The application of these tests, however, bore little relation to the formal rationale. It was blatantly discriminatory. Blacks across the South, regardless of their education, failed to pass these tests in any substantial numbers and consequently were unable to register to vote. But just in case some blacks did pass, another device, the white primary, and another argument, the sanctity of private arrangements, were brought into play.

The few blacks who did succeed in passing a literacy test did gain the vote but, until the 1940s, they had gained only the right to vote in the November general election. They had no right to vote in the primary election of the Democratic Party. Unfortunately for blacks, the South, until three decades ago, was dominated by one party. The Democratic Party had an all but monolithic hold on the voting allegiance of southerners. The Republican Party, by contrast, was an inconsequential force in southern political life. The candidates for the Democratic Party at presidential, congressional or state level had little difficulty in winning in normal circumstances. As a result, the Democratic primary was the election that mattered; the general election was a mere formality. The right to vote, if it was to be meaningful in the conditions that prevailed in the South, had to include the right to vote in the Democratic primary. Blacks, of course, were excluded from it. Once again the act of discrimination was not confronted centrally. Instead, the exclusion of blacks, which could not be fully disguised, was subordinated to another issue: the right of a private organization, in this case the Democratic Party, to set its own rules. Any proposed reform which would have imposed non-discriminatory practices on the Democratic Party was resisted and deflected by an appeal to the fear of governmental interference in private arrangements. The question of discrimination and the effective denial of political equality disappeared in a debate over where the boundary should be located between governmental intervention and private rights.

There can be no doubt about the intentions behind the introduction of literacy tests and the white primary, just as there can be no doubt that the principles used to justify these practices were a subterfuge to conceal the intent. Furthermore, it was self-evidently the case that the vast majority of Americans and their political representatives welcomed these particular strategies and the many others that were deployed to conceal the substantive issues. They were only too willing to ignore the plight of the blacks, and so they readily accepted the terms of the debate constructed by the southerners. Therefore, in the short term, the South was successful: the denial of legal and political equality continued. However, the problem simply could not be wished away. The position of blacks in American society has been, since the creation of the Republic, the primary domestic political issue, which can be ignored temporarily but never permanently. Blacks and their political allies from the early decades of the twentieth century constantly strove to place the issue of civil rights at the top of the political agenda. They had great difficulty in doing so and felt compelled to resort to civil disobedience to achieve their objective. But when they succeeded by the end of the 1940s and early 1950s, a series of reforms emerged. These legislative and judicial reforms came about, to a large extent, because the electorate, confronted by the unconcealed reality of southern behaviour, could not accept it as legitimate. The denial of political and legal equality violated a central tenet of the political culture.

What can be deduced from this brief account of how blacks were prevented from voting? First, the importance of equality did not prevent blacks from being treated unequally. Nor does it prevent racial discrimination that takes place currently against blacks and other racial minorities, particularly Hispanics. However, and secondly, the belief in equality did, and does, affect the politics of civil rights. Southerners who wanted to disfranchise blacks had to recognize the nature of the political nature. They could only achieve their objective by protecting their intentions with camouflage and parading their objectives in different clothes, activities which proved, in the long run, to be untenable. Similarly today, discriminatory practices are deliberately shielded by the construction of elaborate arguments which are intended to divert attention. Discrimination cannot be advocated openly; the political culture will not permit it. So, like other characteristics of the political culture, the belief in equality does permit a range of practices, though it also establishes perimeters which cannot be transgressed.

Private property

Property plays a pivotal role in the political writing of John Locke. According to Locke, the principal reason why men left the state of nature and joined together in a civil society was the inadequate protection of private property in the state of nature. Thereafter the institutions of these newly formed societies had 'no other end but the preservation of property'. Without entering the long and intricate debate over which British philosophers had the greatest influence over the American colonists, it is incontestably true that Locke's views on property were endorsed and further developed by Americans. 'Property must be secured', wrote John Adams, who was to succeed George Washington as President, 'or liberty cannot exist' (Freund, 1961, p. 35). This view that property itself is the matrix, the seedbed that must be cherished if other values, such as equality or civil liberties, are to flourish, has always found expression in America. John Adams's great antagonist, John Taylor of Virginia, the radical philosopher of agrarian democracy, was no less attached to property than Adams: 'The rights of man include life, liberty and property, according to the prevalent fashion of thinking in the United States. The last right is the chief hinge upon which social happiness depends' (Freund, 1961, p. 35). Again in the 1820s, Daniel Webster, a powerful and influential public figure, echoed these same sentiments: 'Life and personal liberty, are no doubt to be protected by law; but property is also to be protected by law, and is the fount out of which the means of protecting life and liberty are usually furnished. We have no experience that teaches us that any other rights are safe, where property is not safe' (Freund, 1961, p. 36). Adams, Taylor and Webster are but three of a long line of public figures from all points of the political spectrum who elevated property to the first rank of American values. There was a national view on private property, and while today it is perhaps less prominent in the national consciousness, it is still discernible. What were and are the consequences of this consensus?

The first consequence was that the American Constitution protected private property through the Fifth Amendment and subsequently through the Fourteenth Amendment. Second, American politicians have been far more wary than their European counterparts of interfering with the disposition and use of private property. They knew that it was likely to make a number, possibly a large number, of their constituents unhappy, and even if their constituents were appeased, politicians were aware that courts and judges were going to scrutinize their actions carefully. The third and most interesting consequence is that despite the agreement over the importance of private property, economic policy in the United States was never governed, as is frequently alleged, by the requirements of *laissez faire*. It is often asserted that *laissez faire* was the guiding economic doctrine throughout the eighteenth and nineteenth centuries and continued to dominate economic policy-making well into the twentieth century. Even today, it is argued, the effect of governmental reluctance to intervene in the economy is evident; the result of two centuries of minimalist government is discernible.

There is an element of truth in this observation. It is true that the current level of governmental intervention in the American economy is less than in other Western democracies. For instance, expenditure by the federal government, as measured by a percentage of the gross national product, currently hovers at the 25 per cent level, whereas in most Western European countries the figure is appreciably higher. As a result of this lower level of governmental expenditure, the non-defence services provided by government, whether federal or state, are less elaborate than those found in Europe. There is, for example, no nationally funded or sponsored medical insurance scheme available to all citizens. Indeed, there was no governmental medical insurance available even for elderly citizens until 1964, and medical provision for the poor can vary considerably between the individual states. So the profile of governmental intervention in the United States is, and to some extent always has been, less prominent than in those societies where governmental intervention has been more acceptable and where private property and private economic arrangements are less valued. Nevertheless, it would be entirely inappropriate to suggest that economic policy, from the colonial period onwards, was characterized by the absence of governmental intervention. Nothing could be further from the truth. Government, both state and federal, consistently intervened in a variety of ways for a multitude of reasons. Politicians did not bow to the mandates of *laissez faire* and impose a self-denying ordinance against intervention in the economy. Quite to the contrary, they ignored doctrinal consistency in favour of political reality. If their constituents did not want intervention they did not get it, but if they did the politicians were only too willing to provide it. As William Letwin has pointed out:

> Economic doctrines have never as much influenced the making of American economic policy as have political and constitutional considerations. The reason why the whole of American economic policy looks so incoherent – with mercantilist, socialist liberal or autocratic elements all living happily side by side – is that political balance rather than economic consistency has been the more powerful drive.
>
> (Letwin, 1961, pp. xxix-xxx)

So laws were passed setting the prices that could be charged for a range of goods and services, establishing minimum wage levels, particularly for women and children, and setting the level of fares on railways, among a host of economic regulations. The consensus over private property thus did not establish the primacy of one economic theory. Instead, it permitted, like other aspects of the political culture, a variety of practices and approaches. Of course, the political culture imposed limits on the acceptability of intervention. Private property, for example, could not be confiscated. Nor could it be used without compensation. Above all, laws affecting private property could not be arbitrary; they had to be reasonable and satisfy the courts that they were reasonable. But within these limits a wide array of options were permissible, and in the course of the last two centuries several of them were put into operation.

Government and politics

A further characteristic of the political culture is the considerable suspicion that Americans have of the institution of government and the activity of politics. This attitude was formed early in the American historical experience. By the time of the Revolution, most Americans shared the belief that government was a profoundly dangerous, albeit necessary, institution. They formed this belief because of the colonial experience, an experience they found exceedingly unhappy, or at least they believed they did in the 1770s, and which they attributed to George III. The king, they claimed, was a tyrant, and the acts of his tyranny were documented by Thomas Jefferson in the Declaration of Independence. But why did George III behave like a tyrant? A part of their answer was that all men had the propensity to misbehave, and George III was no different to any other man. The only, and crucial, difference between George III and any other man was his ability to impose his rule on the American colonists. Their property and their civil liberties were at the mercy of the whim of the king or his representatives, who disrupted their private lives by arbitrary decisions.

This view of their colonial experience convinced Americans that the principal threat to the 'pursuit of happiness' emanated from government. Government was potentially too powerful, and if it was uncontrolled, as the colonists claimed the British system was in the 1770s, then its authority would be abused by those who were in control of the machinery of government, regardless of whether they were monarchs or politicians in a republic. The political process, instead of protecting the interests of the citizenry, was often used as a vehicle by those who wished to promote their special interests to the detriment of the general welfare. Therefore it was hardly surprising that when the ex-colonists convened in Philadelphia in 1787 to decide how they should govern themselves, the constitutional structure that emerged was driven by the overriding fear of tyranny – governmental tyranny. The primary objective of the Constitutional Convention was to protect Americans from the activities of their politicians. Whether those who met in Philadelphia were successful is still unclear, but it *is* clear that the Convention both reflected the attitudes of contemporaneous Americans and helped to inculcate these beliefs into subsequent generations.

Over the following two hundred years the suspicion and worries of government have been a consistent element of the political culture. Occasionally its prominence may have receded, only to surface rapidly when events have appeared to confirm its validity. It is the continuing existence of these attitudes, for instance, that in part explains the response to the abuses of governmental power that are collectively labelled Watergate. The events of Watergate, the precise details of which are discussed in Chapter 4, culminated in the resignation of President Nixon in 1974. Why did Nixon become the first President to resign his office? The answer to this question lies in a political culture that is extraordinarily sensitive to the abuse of power, and the electorate consequently took an extremely grave view of Nixon's behaviour. In other political cultures Nixon's actions would not have proved to have been politically fatal. It is well known that several foreign governments, those of China and Egypt for example, were entirely bemused by Watergate, and could not begin to comprehend why the revelations were causing Nixon political difficulty. In the United States, however, Watergate re-awakened the fears that may have been temporarily dormant in the national consciousness, but which, when they were restored to the earlier primacy in the American mind, helped to destroy the Nixon presidency.

American attitudes towards government and politics have not remained static for two hundred years, however. It would be most unusual if they did not reflect the developments that were taking place in the economy and society. The colonists' hostility towards government was formed in an agrarian society, where the ownership of land was widespread, without any great concentration of wealth and concomitant political and economic power. In such a landscape, the institutions of government could, and did, loom large and appear threatening. However, the landscape was transformed by the end of the nineteenth century. The yeoman farmers and the small rural towns were being replaced by the burgeoning industrial connurbations with their blue-collar workers in the developing mass-production industries. Even in the agricultural sector, the multitude of family farms were starting to succumb to the imperatives of the economies of scale. While the drive for industrial efficiency led inexorably to larger but fewer units, the ownership of industry was being concentrated in fewer hands, raising the fear of monopoly. The formation of unions merely increased the anxiety of those Americans who resented the growing power of both capital and labour. No longer did government pose the only worry. There were many other powerful organizations that threatened the liberty and property of Americans. Indeed, by the early decades of the twentieth century, government, far from posing a threat, appeared to be the only institution capable of curtailing these concentrations of private power. The political process became the principal avenue for representing the interests of the individual citizen. Accordingly, attitudes towards government became far more positive, a development which was accentuated by the increasing expectation on the part of Americans for government to solve social and economic problems.

Certainly, by the 1930s there had been a clear change in attitudes towards government. The election of Franklin D. Roosevelt in 1932, during the most severe economic depression in US history, inaugurated a new relationship between governments, particularly the federal government, and the electorate. Roosevelt's New Deal (see Chapter 3) did not only fund an array of new programmes in areas where federal government activity had been non-existent, but fostered the belief that the federal government had both the responsibility and the capacity to deal with the nation's social and economic ailments. The New Deal was enthusiastically welcomed. Roosevelt was elected to the presidency on an unprecedented four occasions.

However, with hindsight, the New Deal was most probably the high-water mark of American confidence in government. By the end of the 1960s, the faith in government to resolve problems was gravely eroded, and the election of Richard Nixon in 1968 and 1972, Ronald Reagan in 1980 and 1984, and George Bush in 1988 provided the electoral confirmation of it.

So have current American attitudes completed a full circle and returned to those of the late eighteenth century? The answer is no, because while the optimism of the New Deal years has been replaced by a more jaundiced view, no one can deny that 'big' government is here to stay. There is acceptance, possibly a resigned acceptance, that a large federal government is a permanent feature of the political landscape. Of course, the fear of government continues to strike a chord of concern in the American mind, but it has to share its place in the hierarchy of American worries with the considerable power of private organizations. American attitudes towards government and politics are just like other elements of the political culture: they contain tensions and instincts that pull in different directions.

The characteristics of the political cultural outlined above are not intended to be a comprehensive list. They are, however, among the most salient characteristics. There are, of course, others which have been implicit or mentioned fleetingly or not at all. The importance of individualism is woven into the fabric of the political culture. The stress that Americans place on legality, enshrined in the view that the United States has a government of laws not men, has also helped to constitute the political culture. It is a broadly based and complex culture. Indeed, it is so complex and diverse that it cannot be described fully but can only be represented in a drastically simplified outline. It cannot be easily pinned down or briefly summarized. As a result, the political culture seems to be inchoate, offering no clearly marked signposts. It appears to offer no coherent and consistent advice. The American political culture is diffuse and difficult to grasp because the nation is so extraordinarily heterogeneous. It is a nation which required room to accommodate its multiplicity of traditions and required and obtained a political culture that was and is permissive. Consequently, American politicians do not receive specific guidance. They can choose from a wide array of public policy options, all of which will be acceptable to the political culture. Of course, this does not mean that the culture does not establish boundaries. It simply means that boundaries are generously drawn and that politicians and the political institutions have considerable room for manoeuvre.

1.3 Reflections on the political culture

There is a series of questions about the American political culture that must be asked, even if they cannot be conclusively answered. How did the culture evolve? To whom does it belong? Whose interests does it serve? Clearly these are very substantial questions with which numerous scholars have struggled over a considerable period of time; unsurprisingly, no single agreed view has emerged, but a variety of positions. At the risk of oversimplifying a complex subject, these positions can be placed in two broad categories of competing explanations. The first view argues that the political culture is a 'dominant ideology' which has been constructed and imposed by those who control the levers of economic and political power in the United States. This elite created and used this ideology to justify above all their own dominance and control and the maintenance of capitalism:

> The dominant ideology is more powerful in the United States than in any other capitalist democracy. Most political debates take place within the framework of this ideology, a situation related to the absence of a broadly based working class movement pressing for fundamental change. So powerful is the dominant ideology in this country that existing economic and political arrangements frequently appear not merely as the best possible arrangements but as the only possible ones.
>
> *(Katznelson and Kesselman, 1979, p. 29)*

If those who believe in a dominant ideology have no doubts about how the political culture has emerged and to whom it belongs, neither have those who conceive of the American political culture as the sum of a host of individual experiences. According to this pluralist view, the political culture emerged out of a complex interplay of individuals' responses to their environment, their personal circumstances and private relationships. In one important sense this view of a national political culture is paradoxically a private one; it has been formed almost independently of political authority. It places individual Americans at the centre of the political culture and was created by them out of a distillation of their own experience.

Clearly, the two competing categories of explanations are not compatible, although interestingly, in the literature on the subject, they do not diverge widely over the characteristics of the culture. They do, however, interpret these characteristics in a very different manner. For instance, there is no debate over the importance placed on equality, but equality is viewed by those who lean towards the dominant ideology explanation as advice by the elite to pacify the poor and dispossessed with the promise of a better tomorrow. To pluralists, equality has been rooted in the American history, experienced by millions of Americans; even those who are disadvantaged have seen the force of the egalitarian impulse. So these explanations of the political culture cannot be reconciled, and it is not the purpose of this book to do so. Nor is it the intention here to suggest which of these views is the more convincing, although there are important weaknesses in both. The extent and mechanics of elite control which are central to the theory of a dominant ideology are difficult to sustain in such a heterogeneous and diverse society with a fragmented political system, while those who argue on behalf of a political culture created by mass participation must recognize that some very large categories of Americans – blacks, native Americans and women – were either excluded at some stage from public life or were less influential participants than other Americans. The political culture must to some extent reflect this configuration of participation. But although these explanations have weaknesses, they nevertheless raise questions about the political culture and indeed about the entire American political process that cannot be left aside. This book will return to them in subsequent chapters, even if it cannot provide definitive answers.

Notes

1. The foreign policy of isolationism, which was not finally abandoned until 1941, was in large part derived from the American sense of being a nation apart as well as from a sense of moral superiority.
2. The states of Alaska and Hawaii joined the Union in 1955.
3. Several states, however, did grant women the vote before 1920.

References

BAILYN, B. (1968) *The Origins of American Politics*, New York, Vintage.

CREVECŒUR, J. H. ST JOHN DE (1963) *Letters from an American Farmer*, New York, Signet.

FREUND, P. (1961) *The Supreme Court of the United States*, Cleveland and New York, Meridian Books.

GOLDMAN, E. (1952) *Rendezvous with Destiny: a History of Modern American Reform*, New York, Alfred Knopf.

HARTZ, L. (1955) *The Liberal Tradition in America*, New York, Harcourt, Brace and Co.

KATZNELSON, I. and KESSELMAN, M. (1979) *The Politics of Power*, 2nd edition, New York, Harcourt, Brace, Jovanovich.

LETWIN, W. (1961) *A Documentary History of American Economic Policy*, Garden City, New York, Anchor Books.

POTTER, D. (1954) *People of Plenty: Economic Abundance and the American Character*, Chicago, University of Chicago Press.

TOCQUEVILLE, A. DE (1966) *Democracy in America*, 2 vols, London, Fontana. (First published 1835-40.)

WILLIAMSON, C. (1960) *American Suffrage from Property to Democracy*, Princeton, Princeton University Press.

Further reading

HEALE, M. J. (1977) *The Making of American Politics*, London, Longman.

KANMEN, M. (1972) *People of Paradox: An Inquiry Concerning the Origins of American Civilisation*, New York, Vintage Books.

POLE, J. R. (1978) *The Pursuit of Equality in American History*, Berkeley and Los Angeles, University of California Press.

2   The Constitution

On 25 May 1787 the delegates to the Federal Convention assembled in Philadelphia to commence work on the somewhat daunting task of considering 'the situation of the United States to devise such further Provisions as shall appear to them necessary to render the Constitution of the Federal Government adequate to the emergencies of the Union' (Hunt and Scott, 1920, p.xlix). The fifty-five delegates drawn from all of the original thirteen states met at a time when the mood of Americans can best be described as an uneasy bitter-sweet blend of hope and apprehension: 'No moon ever dawned more favourably than ours did', wrote George Washington to James Madison in 1776, 'and no day was ever more clouded than the present' (Rossiter, 1963, p.41). While Americans continued to bask in the achievement of the Revolution and the astonishing military success over the British, their feelings of accomplishment were now accompanied by a growing sense of disquiet that all was not well with their nation. The years after the British surrender in 1781 had seen a gradual but progressive erosion of the confidence and assuredness that was so apparent in the Declaration of Independence. In 1776 Americans appeared to know both the cause of their problems and the solutions to them. However, a decade later they were far more unsure and hesitant. So what had brought about the uncertainty and why did the perceptions of 1776 no longer look quite so persuasive a decade later?

2.1   The causes of the Revolution

The intricate web of political and economic tensions, ideas and beliefs that account for the breakdown in the relationship between the American colonies and Britain cannot be described in this book. The relationship was far too complex to be dealt with briefly. Nevertheless, there are several observations worth noting and considering; among them is the fact that American disenchantment with Britain was very slow in emerging. Although there was a growing awareness that the interests of the colonies, both political and economic, and those of Britain were not identical, America's attitudes towards Britain were nevertheless positive. Indeed, until the 1760s there was a widespread and general satisfaction with Britain. The British political system and the British Constitution, in particular, was an object of American admiration. It was seen as the 'best possible pattern of government, and in 1752 William Livingston described the British Constitution as 'infinitely the best' (Vile, 1967, p. 125). So American disillusionment with Britain and its system of government came relatively late in the day, but when it did come, it spread rapidly and deeply.

The trigger for the disenchantment, ironically, was the British victory over the French and Indians in the Seven Years' War in 1763, a victory which was greeted enthusiastically by the colonists. Unfortunately, the war had been a substantial drain on British resources and, moreover, the fruits of victory – vast tracts of land ceded by France to Britain – were going to be very expensive to maintain and defend. It was, of course, the British government's attempt to raise part of its revenue requirements from the colonies that profoundly upset the colonists. The Stamp Tax of 1765, the Townshend Duties of 1767 and the Tea Act of 1773 were greeted in America with anger and disbelief, and began the process of convincing the colonists that a break with Britain was essential.

Why did successive British governments introduce these measures and persist with their attempts to levy taxes on the colonies in the teeth of intense American opposition? There are several explanations, but perhaps the most convincing is that British politicians did not pay a great deal of attention to the colonies. As Barbara Tuchman says, they 'were not interested in Americans because they considered them rabble or, at best, children whom it was inconceivable to treat...as equals'. The British 'attitude was a sense of superiority so dense as to be inpenetrable'. Consequently, according to Tuchman, 'The American Problem...was never...a primary concern of British politics until the actual outbreak of hostilities' (Tuchman, 1981, pp. 159, 286). But if the British felt a combination of contempt and indifference and suffered from a profound lack of knowledge about the colonies, the Americans, by contrast, spent a great deal of time and energy in the 1760s and 1770s considering and debating their relationship with Britain. How was it that the constitution described as 'infinitely the best' had allowed the outrages, at least in American eyes, of the Stamp Tax and the Townshend Duties? Why had the 'best possible pattern of government' tried, in the words of the Declaration of Independence, to establish an 'absolute tyranny' in America? Should America be independent and, if so, how could it justify the break with Britain? The response to these and other questions absorbed Americans, but by 1776 they appeared to be confident of the answers.

2.2 The view from 1776

By 1776, the vast majority of colonists accepted the case for independence. The grievances against Britain and George III, on whom they focused so much of their anger, were numerous and substantial, and were documented by Jefferson in the Declaration of Independence. Most Americans approved of Jefferson's portrait of George as 'a prince, whose character is thus marked by every act which may define a tyrant, unfit to be ruler of a free people'. Consequently, they were convinced of the need to break with Britain. Moreover, they felt able to justify the decision. The Declaration of Independence, issued by the Continental Congress on 4 July 1776, eloquently stated the American case, a case which was heavily in debt to the social contract theorists. The impact of Hobbes, Rousseau and, above all, John Locke, is detectable in the Declaration. The view of government articulated by Jefferson is clearly influenced by Locke. This is not intended as an endorsement of the claim that Locke was the dominant influence on Jefferson, nor as a contradiction of the view that Jefferson owed a greater debt to David Hume and others of the Scottish Enlightenment than to Locke (Wills, 1978). However, it is an indication of the degree to which social contract theory informed the intellectual climate of late eighteenth-century America.

The theory of the social contract

Interestingly, Locke's major work, *Two Treatises of Government,* was written shortly before the Glorious Revolution of 1688. The events of 1688 themselves were to become for Americans 'a theoretical precedent for their own self-determination' (Sutherland, 1965, p. 100). The exchange of James Stuart for the more acceptable William and Mary was a transaction that was agreeable to Locke and congenial with his view that in a political society, the legitimacy of government is dependent on the consent of the governed. Locke arrived at this position as a consequence of his belief that men, prior to the formation of a political society, lived in a state of Nature. In Nature, men are 'all free, equal and independent'. The only way men could divest themselves of this freedom and independence, or in Locke's words 'natural liberty', was by agreeing with other men to 'join and unite into a community'. Why did men wish to revoke their 'natural liberty'? 'They did so...for their comfortable, safe, and peaceable living one amongst another, in secure enjoyment of their properties and a greater security against any, that are not of it' (Laslett, 1965, pp. 374–5). The social contract was thus an agreement freely entered into. Those who made the contract ceded their freedom and independence, their sovereignty, to the newly formed political society. The authority of the political society was consequently based on a prior act of volition. The rulers of this society derived their authority solely from the consent of the governed. Furthermore, the consent was conditional. The social contract, in this respect, was like any other contract. If the rulers and institutions of the political society did not succeed in achieving the original purpose of the agreement, then the contract was null and void. Thus, if the government acted in such a manner as to lessen the safety of its subjects, threaten the peace and diminish the security of their property, then the contract was broken. Both the authority of the government to rule and the obligation on the part of its subjects to obey it were no longer operable.

Even from this brief sketch, it is evident why the Lockean version of the social contract had such powerful attractions for Americans in 1776. For if the British and George III were guilty as charged of a series of tyrannical acts, then the colonists no longer bore any obligation to obey the edicts of the Crown or its representatives. British rule ceased to have legitimacy. The case for revolution and independence was self-evident. As Jefferson wrote in the Declaration of Independence,

> Men...are endowed by their Creator, with certain unalienable rights; that among these are life, liberty and the pursuit of happiness. That, to secure these rights, governments are instituted among men, deriving their just powers from the consent of the governed; that whenever any form of government becomes destructive of these ends, it is the right of the people to alter or to abolish it, and to institute a new government.

The theory of the separation of powers

Americans were in no doubt that George III, his ministers and his representatives in the colonies were guilty of abusing their authority. The actions of the British were both the cause and the justification of American independence. But why had the British acted in such a manner? The colonists had an explanation which drew heavily on the theory of the 'separation of powers'. The separation of powers, by the late eighteenth century, was not a new doctrine but one with a long and established history. The sources for the central ideas of the doctrine can be detected in Aristotle and are currently present in the work of several medieval philosophers. However, the theory first emerged in a recognizable form at the time of the English Civil War. Interestingly, it was also used in that turbulent period to provide an analysis that encouraged the overthrow of the established order. The prominence of the doctrine receded temporarily with the restoration of the English monarchy, but its importance was restored by Locke, who incorporated and developed the theory in the *Two Treatises of Government*. Moreover, Locke's version of the separation of powers had a profound impact on Charles Louis de Secondat, Baron Montesquieu, the person most identified with the doctrine of the separation of powers and the man most influential, in this respect, with Americans of that revolutionary generation.

Montesquieu's most important work, *De l'Esprit des Lois*, was published in 1748, and the discussion of the separation of powers is only a part of a more ambitious and 'scientific' examination of the nature of government. Nevertheless, the separation of powers is central to *De l'Esprit des Lois* because Montesquieu believed that political liberty for the ordinary citizen can only be ensured if government is organized on the principle of the separation of powers. What precisely does Montesquieu mean by this? 'In every government', he wrote, 'there are three sorts of power: the legislative; the executive in respect to things dependent on the law of nations; and the executive in regard to matters that depend on the civil law' (Montesquieu, 1949, Vol. 1, p. 16). In modern parlance, Montesquieu is referring to the legislative, executive and judicial powers, and it is his firm conviction that these three powers should be exercised by three separate branches of government: legislative, executive and judicial. Each branch should be confined to the implementation of its own power, and the personnel who operate these powers should be different. What would happen if this separation of powers, institutions and people were transgressed? Montesquieu had no doubt about the consequences:

> When the legislative and executive powers are united in the same person, or in the same body of magistrates, *there can be no liberty,* because apprehension may arise lest the same monarch or senate should erect tyrannical laws, to execute them in a tyrannical manner. Again, there is no liberty if the judiciary power be not separated from the legislative and executive. Were it joined with the legislative, *the life and liberty of the subject would be exposed to arbitrary control;* for the judge would be then the legislator. Were it joined to the executive power, the judge might behave with violence and oppression.
>
> *(Montesquieu, 1949, Vol. 1, p. 16).*

Jefferson, who copied extracts of *De L'Esprit des Lois* in his notebooks, and others of this generation found Montesquieu extremely persuasive. Nor was Montesquieu's reputation in America affected by his admiration for the British system of government, which he believed, rather eccentrically, utilized the principle of the separation of powers. Whether Montesquieu's admiration was misplaced, as most commentators have suggested, is not germane here, but certainly by the 1770s, while Americans accepted his analysis that liberty could only be guaranteed through the use of the separation of powers, they rejected his view that Britain operated the doctrine. For, by the middle of the eighteenth century, the British Constitution was famed for being 'balanced', where powers and function were, in part, deliberately fused. Indeed, the 'balanced Constitution' was a source of British pride, rather than an object of shame, and its virtues were proclaimed widely. Furthermore, the colonists could point to a series of practices – rotten boroughs, placement – which blurred the demarcation lines even further, and allowed the executive, the Crown, to encroach on the powers of the legislature. Some would have gone further and argued that the Crown now controlled Parliament and that, as a result, a tyranny had emerged – an executive which abused its power and which had to be renewed and replaced by a new political order based on the theory of the separation of powers. By 1776, this doctrine provided the only acceptable basis for government in America.

The democratic character of 1776

There has been a continuing debate in American historiography over whether it is accurate to contrast the democratic tenor of the Revolution with the counter-revolutionary atmosphere of 1787 and the Constitution. Without entering this debate, it is inescapable that the decade of the Revolution exudes a democratic flavour. Of course, there are difficulties with using the word 'democratic': the existence of slavery and the restrictions in the franchise are but two. Nevertheless, the fears and hopes of Americans in 1776 were essentially those of democrats. They were concerned about ensuring rights and political liberty and, above all, establishing consent. They wished to create a political system that had, if not universal, at least broadly based support. Their greatest fear was the re-emergence of tyranny in the form of an autocracy. The theories that were dominant at the time reinforced these democratic instincts, which then were articulated confidently. However, over the next ten years, the confidence began to abate and the instincts, while still alive, were mediated by the experience of government at both state and national level.

2.3   The states' constitutions and the Articles of Confederation

The first experiences that Americans had of self-government came at state level. Several state constitutions were conceived at the height of revolutionary fervour in 1776, the first of which was the Constitution of Virginia, written in June of that year; other states soon followed. In 1781 the Articles of Confederation and Perpetual Union, which had been drawn up in 1776, were ratified by all thirteen states and came into operation at national level.

How successful were these first attempts at government? The success, or lack of it, varied from state to state, and opinion is still divided over the Confederation, but what is clear is that the activity of government proved far more complex and difficult than Americans had anticipated.

The state constitutions

The separation of powers provided the organizational basis for government in the state constitutions. With ranging degrees of rigour or purity, the powers and the personnel were separated, but some of the consequences of this separation were unexpected. Of course, one of the principal objectives of these constitutions was to control the power of the executive, and in that the authors of these documents were successful. But what also emerged, somewhat surprisingly, were very powerful legislatures, which became the dominant institution in these systems of government. In their collective hostility to executive power, state governors were normally given the sole function of administration, with no independent base of authority as a result, they became 'no more than an errand boy' for legislatures (Vile, 1967, p. 142).

The experience of several states was that all power gravitated towards the legislature. Did the legislatures use their dominant position wisely? There is no easy overall answer to this question, but unfortunately there were numerous abuses in several states. There were instances of retrospective legislation, of governmental intervention in private contracts, and interference with private property rights, all of which gave rise to concern. Furthermore, the legislatures meddled in every category of government activity, including that normally reserved for the judiciary. By 1787, a disenchantment had set in and legislative tyranny had joined executive tyranny as an object of disapproval. The separation of powers was no longer as persuasive a theory.

The Articles of Confederation

The period of Confederation in many ways mirrored unease over the state constitutions. Although there is a view that the Articles of Confederation were a success, the vast majority of historians believe that they were a failure. They were a failure because the Congress, the principal institution of the Confederation, lacked the power to fulfil its duties. In the Articles, the Congress was charged with 'the management of the general interest of the United States', but its authority to fulfil its task was woefully inadequate.

The essential difficulty was the Congress's dependence on the thirteen states. It had no powers of compliance, no right to enforce its view on the states. It was unable, for instance, to levy taxes. Instead, it had to rely on the states' willingness to impose taxes and hand over the revenue to the Congress. The states also retained the right to impose duties on imported goods, thereby preventing the formulation of a national policy on trade and commerce. Most worrying of all was the inability of the Congress to conduct a satisfactory foreign policy. Agreements between the Confederation and other nations foundered on the reluctance or the inability of the states to enforce them. Consequently, the Confederation and its emissaries abroad were treated with barely concealed contempt. These inadequacies brought about a growing realization that the states had to relinquish control in certain areas and that the United States required a national government with greater powers over commerce and foreign relations in particular. Thus, the period of Confederation, as well as the experience of the state constitutions, had increased awareness of the requirements and complexity of governing. It had given Americans a more acute appreciation of power and had shaken both the diagnosis and prescriptions that were commonly offered at the time of the Revolution.

2.4   The Federal Convention

The delegates

The fifty-five delegates to the Federal Convention thus met in Philadelphia at a moment, if not of intellectual confusion, then of uncertainty. Nevertheless, they retained a unity of purpose. They continued to believe in the values of the Declaration of Independence. They shared the same objectives but were somewhat perplexed about how to achieve them or, to put it more precisely, about how to achieve collective agreement on a course of action. For it must not be forgotten that the delegates, who are known as the Founding Fathers and whose place is secure in the pantheon of American heroes, were also politicians operating in the highly charged atmosphere of a political convention, representing the very different interests of the thirteen states. The divergence of interests between the slave and non-slave states is well known, but there were other differences, in particular the conflict between the small and the populous states. So it was incumbent on the delegates not only to grapple with the intellectual problems of writing a constitution, but also to reconcile these disparate interests. The end result, the American Constitution, was both a product of the intellectual climate and the multiplicity of compromises and deals that were made to guarantee a majority within the Convention. The detail of the Constitution, as opposed to its overall shape, owes as much to these political manoeuvres as it does to the persuasiveness of any particular theory. Thus the Constitution lost a degree of intellectual coherence in exchange for political viability. The delegates, of course, were not only politicians; they tended to be men of substance in their own right. They were, as a group, better educated and wealthier than the population at large. Over 60 per cent, for instance, were lawyers. This fact, that they were men of property and status, led some historians to conclude that the Constitution, in the words of Charles Beard, the historian most identified with this school, was 'essentially an economic document' intended to protect the 'economic advantage' of the delegates and the propertied classes in general (Beard, 1965, p. 324). Unsurprisingly, Beard's interpretation was contentious and aroused an enormous controversy, although it would be true to say that Beard and those who shared his beliefs emerged somewhat the worse from the extended debate that followed the publication of his book.

The difficulty with Beard's work is that it viewed the delegates in only one dimension. It saw them only as owners of property, in a society where the main division was between those with and without property, and attempted to place far too great a weight on this one attribute, a weakness which other scholars were able to expose. But despite the flaws, Beard and his school did raise some important questions which, at the very least, bear consideration. If the Constitution cannot be categorized as an 'economic document', does it nevertheless seek to protect particular interests? Similarly, did the delegates represent any particular interests, and what were their attitudes towards property and the unpropertied?

Of course, with all such questions there is no clear-cut answer, although it is unlikely that the attitudes of the delegates were very far removed from the other owners of property, at least on the subject of property. It was noted in Chapter 1 that private property was highly valued in eighteenth-century America. Even those whose opinions diverged on numerous matters agreed that the right to own property was a key and crucial liberty inextricably linked to the maintenance of other civil liberties. Moreover, there were fears over the threat posed by the unpropertied, expressed by Madison and several others, and worry over what they would do if they controlled institutions of government. To some extent this sustains the Beard view of a clear split between those with and without property, but of course this division over property took place in a society where property ownership was reasonably widespread, where land was available, and where there was no legal disability to owning property – at least for white males. Consequently the division between the propertied and the unpropertied was not fixed. There was no necessarily permanent class of the unpropertied. So while delegates did indeed represent the interests of property, that interest was served by the extension of property ownership and not by the subordination of the propertyless. While this process of acquisition was taking place, there may well have been attempts to abuse property rights, although such abuses were not limited to those without property, but could well emanate from one set of property owners towards others, as was the case during the period of Confederation. The delegates therefore protected property in the Constitution. So those who view the Constitution as an 'economic document' and see the members of the Convention as representatives of property have a point, but it is a point which must be placed within the social context of 1787.

Despite the weaknesses of Beard and his school, they made one further valuable contribution. They helped to demystify the Founding Fathers. They helped to restore the Founding Fathers from being philosopher-statesmen, or in Jefferson's even more emotive phrase about the Convention 'an assembly of demi-Gods', to mere mortals. They were no longer seen as distant from the hurly-burly activity of everyday life but were firmly rooted in a social milieu. The fact that they were intimately aware of the political and economic realities of the colonies does not diminish them or disparage their achievements. Quite to the contrary, it enhances both their abilities and what they wrought in Philadelphia. But most importantly, it establishes a perspective on the Constitution that must not be lost sight of.

The American Constitution

There can be little doubt about the common purpose of the Founding Fathers. They wished to create a political system for the United States based on consent, which permitted the representation of diverse opinions and interests, guaranteed political liberty, and protected the most important civil liberties and property rights. They were also aware that by 1787 they needed an effective national government, the absence of which might threaten the very survival of the United States. Their immediate political experience, both colonial and post-colonial, had convinced them of the dangers that emanated from government, but neither could they ignore what Alexander Hamilton referred to as the damaging 'inefficiency' of the Confederation. The problem, however, was that government, and in particular effective government, could threaten all the other objectives. This was the central paradox that faced the Founding Fathers. How did they resolve it? Indeed, did they resolve it?

It is perhaps appropriate to say that the Founding Fathers attempted to strike a balance between the competing values, but it is clear where their preferences lay in the balance they struck. For, in the final analysis, the American Constitution is driven by its fear of government – not only the institutions of government but those who could gain control of the levers of power and misuse it. Above everything else, Americans had to be protected from this possibility. Civil liberties, property rights and political liberty could only be assured if government was controlled. This is a view that is most cogently expressed by James Madison in the *Federalist Papers* (see Chapter 1).

In *Federalist No. 10*, Madison declares his belief that the underlying problem that faces all societies is the existence of factions. What is a faction? A faction occurs where 'a number of citizens whether amounting to a majority or minority or the whole...are united and activated by some common impulse of passion or of interest, adverse to the rights of other citizens' (Rossiter, 1961, p. 78). Must factions exist? Madison is in no doubt that factions are endemic to society, indeed to human nature: 'The latent causes of faction are...sown in the nature of man'. They emerge from 'a zeal for different opinions...passions...and the diversity in the faculties of men' (Rossiter, p. 79). Are there different kinds of factions? As many as there are different opinions and passions, but Madison believes that 'the most common and durable source of factions has been the various and unequal distribution of property. Those who hold and those who are without property have ever formed distinct interests in society' (Rossiter, p. 79). Are factions harmful? Factions, according to Madison, were by definition dangerous. The interests they pursued were always contrary 'to the permanent and aggregate interests of the community'. As evidence for this proposition, Madison points to the state constitutions: 'Complaints are everywhere heard...that our governments are too unstable; that the public good is disregarded in the conflicts of social parties; and that measures are too often decided not according to the rules of justice and the rights of the minor party, but by the superior force of an interested and overbearing majority'. He is in no doubt about the cause of the behaviour: 'These must be chiefly, if not wholly, the effects of the unsteadiness and injustice with which a factious spirit has tainted our public administration' (Rossiter, p. 78). Is there a faction that is especially dangerous? The answer, according to Madison, is yes. The majority faction is the source of the greatest danger and poses the most considerable problems. It is this fear, the fear of majority faction, that is at the centre of the Madisonian view of government:

> If a faction consists of less than a majority...the majority [is able] to deflect its sinister views by regular vote. It may clog the administration, it may convulse society; but it will be unable to execute and mask violence...When a majority is included in a faction, the form of government, on the other hand, enables it to sacrifice to its ruling passion of interest both the public good and the rights of citizens. *To secure the public good and private rights against the danger of such a faction, and, at the same time, to preserve the spirit and form of popular government, is then the great object to which our enquiries are directed.*
> *(Rossiter, 1961, p. 80)*

What can be done about the majority faction? It cannot be wished away and it cannot be abolished; or perhaps it can be abolished, but the cost to personal liberty would be too great: 'the remedy would be worse than the disease'. Consequently, it has to be controlled, but how? The American Constitution provides the answer, or at least one answer.

The Constitution's strategy to control the majority faction is constructed essentially around three elements. The first is that certain crucial matters are removed from the arena of everyday politics. A good example of this is the first ten amendments to the Constitution, also known as the Bill of Rights, where particularly important civil liberties are specifically guaranteed by the Constitution. This guarantee can only be modified or rescinded by the process of constitutional amendment, and cannot be tampered with by either the executive or by legislation of a traditional kind. Furthermore, the process of constitutional amendment is long and elaborate. Article V provides two alternative procedures for amending the Constitution, but the procedure that has been primarily used requires an amendment to be passed by a two-thirds majority in both Houses of the Congress and ratified by three-fourths of the state legislatures. Apart from the Bill of Rights this process has been used successfully on only sixteen occasions.

Secondly, a federal structure was adopted which created two distinct levels of government, one at state level, the other nationally. Moreover, the national, or federal, government would be given specific and limited responsibilities and powers, and those powers not designated to the federal government were reserved for the states.

The third element of the strategy was to subdivide the powers allocated to the federal government on the broad lines indicated by the doctrine of the separation of powers, but on this occasion the doctrine was modified by the notion of checks and balances which is, perhaps, the Founding Fathers' wholly original contribution to the art of constitution-making.

The Bill of Rights

The Bill of Rights guarantees the freedom of speech, press and religion (the First Amendment); prohibits unreasonable searches and seizures of persons and their effects by government (the Fourth Amendment); and protects a person's right not to incriminate him- or herself in criminal proceedings (the Fifth Amendment). It protects these rights and others (see Appendix 1), and its constitutional importance, some would say pre-eminence, is taken for granted currently, although its origins might give the appearance that it was an afterthought. It was not a part of the original Constitution, and it had to wait until 1791 to become a part of the Constitution. Consequently it might not seem to be an integral element of the Founding Fathers' strategy. It is certainly true that several participants in the Convention did not believe that a statement guaranteeing civil liberties warranted inclusion in the Constitution – a view that is endorsed by Alexander Hamilton in *Federalist No. 84*.

It is important to note that the opposition to the inclusion of a Bill of Rights was almost exclusively based on the belief that it was redundant, and that the Constitution emerging in Philadelphia would provide adequate protection. There was no lack of enthusiasm for protecting civil liberties. However, the confidence of Hamilton and the majority of the Convention in the original Constitution was not shared in the states. A recurrent theme in the debates over ratification of the Constitution which took place in the state legislatures after 1787 was the concern over the absence of a Bill of Rights. Indeed, the doubts expressed were of such gravity that the process of drafting and ratifying the first ten amendments commenced as soon as the American Constitution came into operation in 1789. James Madison was the principal author of these amendments, and his close involvement is an indication of the importance of the Bill of Rights and its intimate relationship to the constitutional structure. The Bill of Rights vividly illustrates the Madisonian view that there are some matters that are far too important to be entrusted to the hurly-burly of politics. The arena of political activity must be constructed carefully, its perimeters precisely drawn, and that which is most precious to men be removed to the other side of the boundary. If, however, civil liberties could not be removed entirely, then a series of obstacles – in this case, specific constitutional guarantees – needed to be placed between them and those politicians, who, inevitably, will wish at some juncture to interfere with them.

Federalism

The attraction of a federal structure was that it diffused power. It allocated responsibility and power to two separate levels of government and accordingly dispersed power between the federal government and the thirteen states, thereby rendering impossible, in the first instance, the accumulation of authority in one set of hands. Furthermore, the Founding Fathers were confident that both the federal and state governments would zealously guard their constitutionally designated roles and functions, and so there would be little danger over time that the federal government would be dominant or that it would be excessively weakened by the states.

A further reason why federalism was attractive to the framers of the Constitution was its suitability as an instrument of compromise. One of the central conflicts at the Convention was between the more populous states and the smaller ones. The hostility emerged in various forms and shaped several of the debates at the Convention, including those over the powers of the federal government. While the overwhelming majority of the delegates were persuaded that the new federal authority would have to be substantially more powerful than the Confederation, they were aware that any increment in power would be at the expense of the states. Accordingly, the enthusiasm for this was dependent on the size of the states. Delegates from Virginia, Massachusetts and Pennsylvania, the three most populous states, were sanguine about this development because they were confident of their ability to control the federal government, a confidence which was shared by the delegates from Delaware, Rhode Island, Georgia and the others, but without any of the enthusiasm. Therefore, while they were prepared to acquiesce in the creation of a more powerful national government, they also wanted to safeguard the interests of the states, particularly the smaller ones. A federal structure was thus able to provide such assurances, and because it was also able to satisfy the desire to limit and control the powers of government, its attractiveness to the delegates was enhanced. The American version of federalism, with its separate but overlapping jurisdiction, satisfied both political theory and reality.

Checks and balances

The Founding Fathers' most ingenious creation was the institutions of the federal government. They certainly needed their ingenuity because here they had to confront directly their desire for a government that was effective but controllable. Their solution was to create an elaborate and intricate structure that aroused and continues to arouse admiration for its intellectual virtuosity, but which from its inception has also raised doubts over its unnecessary complexity.

What were the causes of the complexity? Although the framers of the Constitution relied on the concept of the separation of powers to provide the essential structure of the federal government, they were aware of its inadequacy and that it needed to be modified. This they did by attaching to it what appears to be two contradictory devices. First, they gave the three branches a degree of independence from each other. They designated specific and limited powers to each branch of government, powers which could not be modified by the other branches. They established a constitutionally independent base of authority for the executive, legislature and judiciary. The clear objective was to ensure that the executive, the presidency, would not replicate the experience of the state constitution and become subservient to the legislature, the Congress. But at the same time the Founding Fathers used a second device which was to create a degree of interdependence and, in violation of the principle of separation, a fusion of powers. The presidency, for instance, was not designed solely as an executive institution; it was also allocated a legislative function through its power of veto over Bills passed by the Congress. Similarly, the Congress was permitted to intervene in matters traditionally within the domain of the exec-utive. The intention behind the points of fusion was to ensure that legislation, or other forms of policy-making, could only emerge from the federal government with the co-operation of President and Congress. How-ever, the Founding Fathers did not wish to create a political system which co-operated smoothly. Instead it was their hope that these points of inter-dependence would not encourage agreement but foster hostility and ten-sion. The presidency and Congress would carefully guard their roles, functions and powers, and rather than working in harmony would check and balance each other. Madison, in a speech to the Federal Convention, provides the rationale for the notion of checks and balances:

> A people deliberating in a temperate moment...on the plan of Government most likely to secure their happiness, would first be aware, that those charged with the public happiness, might betray their trust. An obvious precaution against this danger would be to divide the trust between *different bodies of men, who might watch and check each other.*
> *(Farrand, 1911, Vol. 1, p. 423)*

But if the intention of Madison was to make sure that the branches of government check and balance each other, were these points of fusion and interdependence sufficient to bring this about? After all, why could not the President and the Congress strike a partnership for their mutual advantage? Why should not the ambitions of the President and those of the Congress be realized through co-operation? It was certainly the intention of the fram-ers to set ambition against ambition, and in order to fulfil it they added a further ingredient to the constitutional mixture. They established each of the political institutions of the federal government – the presidency, the Senate and the House of Representatives – with both different constituen-cies and different modes of elections. This combination, they believed, would provide the President, Senators and Representatives with different ambitions, goals and routes to success. As a result they would co-operate only on those occasions when all of their varied constituencies were in agreement. Otherwise the Founding Fathers hoped conflict would be endemic. Was their hope fulfilled? Before an answer to that difficult ques-tion can be attempted, it would be useful to examine the institutions of the federal government in further detail.

The presidency

The office of the presidency, in one sense, posed the greatest difficulties for the Convention, because there were not appropriate contemporary models of executive institutions from which the delegates could draw instruction, let alone inspiration. The 'normal' executive of the late eighteenth century was the hereditary monarch which, of course, was an unthinkable option to the Convention. Accordingly, they had to design a new institution with-out any real guidance. They knew what they did not want – the executives of the state constitutions, or another tyrant on the lines of George III – and were determined to avoid those earlier mistakes, but because of the absence of other examples, they had to ask and answer some basic questions. Should there be a plural or unitary executive? How long should a term of office be? Should the officer or officers be re-electable? What powers and limits should be delegated and placed on the executive? These and other questions weighed heavily on the Convention, and the answers that emerged were, in truth, the product of a series of compromises. This should not be read to indicate that the presidency is a less coherent institution as a result of compromise, but perhaps that the delegates were less confident about this institution than the others.

The presidential office that the delegates created had a unitary executive with independent powers. The most important of these powers were that the President was Commander-in-Chief of the armed forces and head of the executive branch (Article II, Section 2). He (and there is no doubt that the delegates only ever envisaged a male President) was given the authority to make treaties and to appoint ambassadors, federal judges and Cabinet officers among others (Article II, Section 2). He was also, as mentioned above, given the power of veto over Bills passed by the Congress (Article I, Section 7), and the entitlement to make recommendations to the Congress on legislative matters (Article II, Section 3). While all of these powers are independent of any other branch, and cannot be diminished or removed other than by an amendment to the Constitution, they cannot be fully exercised without the co-operation of Congress. The President's power as Commander-in-Chief is mediated by Congress's right to declare war and to raise money to pay for the armed forces (Article I, Section 8). Similarly, his authority over treaties and appointments is limited by the requirement that the Senate must give its approval (Article II, Section 2). Finally, his power of veto can be overturned by a two-thirds majority in the House of Representatives and the Senate. These were the checks and balances on the presidency, the sources of friction between President and Congress to which were added the elaborate electoral arrangements for the presidency.

The Convention found it particularly difficult to decide the length of the term of office. Proposals varied from fifteen or twenty years, with the incumbent President ineligible to run for re-election, to the plan that was finally adopted of four years and no restriction on eligibility, which was subsequently changed by the Twenty-second Amendment in 1951 to a maximum of two terms in office. Clearly the Convention was torn by its fears of tyranny and desire for stability and efficiency. But having resolved this matter, the Convention then made a series of decisions which had a profound effect on the institution and its relationship with the the rest of the federal government. The presidency was the only national institution: it was the only one to have a nationwide constituency, but it was a national constituency of a particular kind. The delegates decided just before the end of the Convention to adopt the device of an electoral college for the election of a President. The college is composed of representatives from each state, and each state is allocated the number of votes in the college equal to the state's representation in the Congress. The state's representative in the electoral college was, in 1787, to be chosen by the state legislatures. As a result of these decisions, the Founding Fathers had distanced the President from mass opinion. They had deliberately created two layers of insulation, the electoral college and the state legislatures, between the presidency and what they saw as the whims and the temporary and dangerous passions of factions. The President, they hoped, would be able to take a long-term perspective over the nation's problems and avoid being swayed by the ebb and flow of popular opinion. The presidency was conceived of as the brake, the restraining hand of the federal government; it would provide the balance for the Congress, and the House of Representatives in particular.

The Congress

The legislative power of the federal government resides in the Congress. The delegates were familiar with the concept of legislative power, and the powers that are set out in Article I are recognizably legislative in character, apart from the variations mentioned above, such as the Senate's power of advice and consent. Despite the delegates' familiarity with the subject, the debates over the Congress were nevertheless long and difficult, and the final outcome was, once again, the result of a sequence of compromises. One such compromise, between the Virginia plan for a bicameral legislature with representation based on 'the number of free inhabitants', supported by the larger states, and the New Jersey proposal of a unicameral legislature with all states having precisely equal votes, which drew the approval of the smaller states, has been described many times before. The result was the Connecticut plan, which the Convention finally adopted; this proposed a bicameral Congress, with one house, the Senate, where each state had two votes, and a House of Representatives, where representation would vary according to population. Although each state would have at least one representative in the House, the total number of districts or constituencies in each state would depend on the size of the state's population. Once more the Convention created political institutions with different geographical constituencies, and yet again it attempted to accentuate this distinction by providing them with differing electoral procedures. The Founding Fathers wanted to create two institutions which shared the legislative power, but which did not share the same views and instincts because they did not want them to represent the same interests.

The House of Representatives, the delegates decided, should be elected directly, with each Representative elected for a term of two years. A Senator, by contrast, was to be elected for six years, but the elections were to be staggered so that one-third of the Senate was to be elected every two years. In the Constitution of 1787, Senators were appointed by the state legislatures, although this was changed to direct election by the Seventeenth Amendment in 1913. But in the grand design of the Founding Fathers, there was an attempt to devise a mechanical balance between the House of Representatives and the Senate. On the one hand, the House of Representatives, with its frequent elections and intimate knowledge of the electorate, would know and represent the views of its constituents, however transient and even if they were inimical to what Madison called 'the permanent and aggregate interests of the community'. As a result, the House would be the most restless, dynamic and perhaps erratic institution of the federal government. On the other hand, the Senate's role in the Founding

Fathers' design was to restrain and moderate the instincts of the House. Because Senators were isolated, to some extent, from the populace, by their term of office and by the state legislatures, they could be more dispassionate. Since they were less dependent on the electorate, they could resist the temptation of immediate political popularity and serve the permanent interests of the nation. The Senate, like the presidency, was intended to dampen and curtail the enthusiasms of the House. This is not to suggest that the House was seen as a wholly dangerous body; it was not. Its anticipated energy and drive were just as important to the federal government as any attribute of the two other 'political' institutions. The framers valued the House's representation of mass opinion and consequent dynamism as essential, but also as politically dangerous if its dynamism was entirely uncontrolled and its energy was not partly diverted into, if not constructive, then at least harmless avenues.

The federal courts

If, in the event, the electoral arrangements and the checks and balances between presidency, Senate and the House of Representatives did not succeed and did not prevent these institutions from threatening the political freedom and civil liberties of Americans, the framers relied on the federal courts, as the final element in this elaborate constitutional structure, to protect the citizenry. However, the precise intentions of the Founding Fathers with regard to the federal judiciary remain unclear. The source of the judiciary's authority from the start of the nineteenth century until today is their power of judicial review.

Judicial review enables the federal courts to decide whether actions of the President, Congress, state governments or those of any other political actor or institution violate the American Constitution. The federal judiciary, over this period, have been the guardians of the Constitution. They have had the power to decide whether the President and Congress have exceeded their constitutionally designated powers, and they have exercised it frequently. Unfortunately, Article III of the Constitution, which established the judicial branch, did not explicitly give the federal courts this power (see Chapter 3). Despite this lack of clarity, the United States Supreme Court asserted the power of judicial review in 1803, and ever since it has been an established fact of political life and a very significant limitation on the power of the Congress and the presidency. Every Act of Congress, each presidential executive order, is potentially available for scrutiny by a federal judiciary appointed for life, apart from the somewhat unlikely sanction of impeachment. Consequently judges could ignore those immediate political pressures that the House of Representatives found so persuasive and which even the Senate and the President would not be able to dismiss entirely. The federal courts were deliberately isolated from the body politic, and the Founding Fathers found comfort from the isolation, for in the final analysis the Constitution of the United States relies on an unelected body to safeguard its integrity.

The Constitution in retrospect

'The American Constitution', wrote William Gladstone in 1878, 'is...the most wonderful work ever struck off at a given time by the brain and purpose of man'. The admiration was understandable. The Constitution was a remarkable achievement, which is perhaps all the more striking a century after Gladstone's judgement.

The Constitution has provided the political framework for a society that has been in constant flux over the past two hundred years, and yet only twenty-six amendments have been attached, and ten of those were adopted in 1791. The Constitution has endured, and that in itself is a testament to the acumen, wisdom and foresight of the Founding Fathers. Of course, they would have been surprised and disconcerted at some of the developments. Several of their predictions have gone awry. The House of Representatives did not become the radical and slightly dangerous body they feared. The presidency, far from being removed and distant from the political fray, became by the early nineteenth century the 'people's institution'. Perhaps the development they would have found most disconcerting was that the 'democratic' principle which they recognized had to be incorporated in the Constitution but which also had to be controlled, had become, in one important sense, the dominant principle of American politics by the middle of the nineteenth century. The Madisonian fear of the majority faction had greatly diminished within a few decades of 1787. Even if there were residual worries about majoritarianism, they were articulated only with considerable hesitation. The United States, within a relatively short period of time, had become aggressively democratic and assertively populist. Politicians were only too anxious to pay homage to the people; the wishes of the electorate became paramount. But despite this substantial change in the intellectual climate, the Constitution essentially remained intact. The most important legacy of the Founding Fathers was unchanged. They intended to create a Constitution which made it difficult for the institutions to act in concert, and they succeeded. They hoped that a simmering antagonism, breaking out into open hostility, would characterize the relationships between the states and the federal government and between the institutions of the federal government, and their hopes were fulfilled.

The American system of government, more than any other Western democracy, finds it difficult to act with dispatch. Numerous American Presidents have envied the relative ease with which a British Prime Minister and Cabinet has sought and received the approval of Parliament. But, of course, the Founding Fathers did not value speed; quite to the contrary, they believed in extended debate and a slow and cumbersome decision-making process. They wanted all interests, however small, not only be able to make their views known but also to affect the decisions taken; and once again they succeeded. The American political system they created has an unparalleled number of points of access. The vast array of interests that exist in the United States can, and do, use this access to the political process in both Washington and the state capitals to great effect. They have been able, throughout the history of the United States, to block and hinder proposals, either legislative or administrative, which they believed were invidious or unhelpful to themselves. This ability, in turn, has continually frustrated those Americans who have wished to use the political system for the purposes of reform. The Founding Fathers, of course, would find considerable cause for satisfaction with this state of affairs. Nevertheless, it must be remembered that they inhabited the political and economic landscape of an agrarian society with no concentration of economic and political power. Whether they would have been confident that their late eighteenth-century prescriptions were appropriate for the conditions that exist today is another matter.

References

BEARD, C. (1965) *An Economic Interpretation of the Constitution of the United States*, New York, The Free Press.

FARRAND, M. (1911) *Records of the Federal Convention of 1787*, Vol. 1, New Haven, Yale University Press.

HUNT, G and SCOTT, J. B. (1920) *Debates in the Federal Convention of 1787*, New York, Oxford University Press.

LASLETT, P. (ed.) (1965) *John Locke: Two Treatises of Government*, New York, Mentor.

MONTESQUIEU (1949) *De L'Esprit des Lois*, translated by Nugent, T. and Pritchard F., New York, Appleton. (First published 1748.)

ROSSITER, C. (1963) *1787: The Grand Convention*, London, MacGibbon and Kee.

ROSSITER, C. (ed.) (1961) *The Federalist Papers*, New York, Mentor.

SUTHERLAND, A. (1965) *Constitutionalism in America*, New York, Blaisdell.

TUCHMAN, B. (1981) *The March of Folly*, London, Abacus.

VILE, M. J. C. (1967) *Constitutionalism and the Separation of Powers*, Oxford, Clarendon Press.

WILLS, G. (1978) *Inventing America: Jefferson's Declaration of Independence*, Garden City, New York, Doubleday.

Further reading

MAIN, J. T. (1969) *The Anti-Federalists: Critics of the Constitution 1781–1788*, Chapel Hill, University of North Carolina Press.

WILLS, G. (1981) *Explaining America: The Federalist*, Garden City, New York, Doubleday.

WOOD, G. S. (1981) *The Creation of the American Republic, 1766-1787*, Chapel Hill, University of North Carolina Press.

3 The Federal Judiciary

'The judiciary', wrote Alexander Hamilton in *Federalist No. 78,* 'has no influence over either the sword or the purse; no direction either of the strength
or of the wealth of the society; and can take no active resolution whatever.
It may be truly said to have neither FORCE nor WILL, but merely judgement' (Rossiter, 1961, p.465). Hamilton's analysis of judicial power reads
curiously two centuries later. His portrait of a rather powerless branch, less
influential than the other institutions of the federal government, is not
borne out by two hundred years of American history. Indeed, the power of
the courts, and that of the United States Supreme Court in particular, has
always struck observers of American politics as one of the distinctive features of the American political process. The authority of the judiciary, and
especially the nine justices of the Supreme Court, to decide issues which in
other Western democracies would be decided by politicians in the legislative and executive branches of government, is not only a distinctive characteristic of the American political system, but is today perhaps rather
incongruous in a society that is prone to asserting its democratic virility
and its faith in majoritarianism. But, of course, while it may be difficult
today to gain support for a constitution that places so much power in the
hands of nine unelected judges, the Founding Fathers had no such problem. They had no faith in majoritarianism, and the non-elected status of
the federal judiciary increased the attractiveness of the courts. Nevertheless,
and despite the general enthusiasm for the judiciary and the Federal Convention, the Constitution does not give the federal courts the power of
judicial review – that is, the power to review the actions of the other
branches of government, either federal or state. The Founding Fathers did
not say that the United States Supreme Court should be what it has
become: the final arbiter of the American Constitution. Judicial review is
the source of the great authority of the federal courts. How, then, did the
courts acquire the power of judicial review, and what were the intentions of
the Founding Fathers in the matter?

3.1 Judicial review

The doctrine of judicial review aroused strong passions in the first half of
the nineteenth century. It was one of the issues that established the political divide between those who embraced the growing populism of American
society and those who were dismayed by it. Inevitably, a central question
in this highly charged debate was whether the Founding Fathers intended
the federal courts to possess the right of review – a question which has
never been resolved with any semblance of finality. Even when the emo-
tion dissipated after judicial review had become a settled and uncontrover-
sial fact of American political life, there was no noticeable benefit to the
clarity of the answers. Nor has the academic world been able to provide a
conclusive answer. However, there is a view which commands the support
of a substantial number of scholars that the Constitution implicitly incorporates the notion of judicial review.

There is certainly no doubt that by the late eighteenth century Americans were familiar with the doctrine of judicial review, a doctrine with an established history even in Britain. The sovereignty of the British Parliament and its supremacy over the courts is now well established, but this was not always the case. In 1610, the Chief Justice, Lord Coke, refused to enforce an Act of Parliament because he believed that legislation was subordinate to a higher law. Coke's decision in Dr Bonham's case was rapidly overtaken by events in Britain, and is now relegated to the status of an eccentric aberration in British constitutional history, but in America, Coke's view took root. His belief in a fundamental law to which legislation is inferior was sustained and encouraged by William Blackstone, whose *Commentaries on the Laws of England* had an enormous influence on American jurisprudence. Americans were also familiar with the practice of judicial review. During the colonial period the Privy Council exercised a form of judicial review over the colonial assemblies, and after the Revolution several state courts held invalid those laws which the judiciary believed had violated the state constitutions. Furthermore, there is evidence of considerable support for judicial review at the Federal Convention and thereafter. One indication of this support is to be found in *Federalist No.78* by Alexander Hamilton.

Of course, there were voices, some influential, raised against judicial review; above all, the Constitution does not explicitly authorize it. Accordingly, those who believe that the Constitution implicitly incorporates judicial review have turned away from historical documentation to a slightly different kind of argument, namely that while judicial review may or may not have been 'consciously intended by the Founders [it was] nonetheless fully consistent with their intentions' (Eidelberg, 1968, p.215). This is a persuasive argument because judicial review is in perfect harmony with the framers' hopes and fears. The federal courts' guardianship of the Constitution complements their distrust of politics and politicians. The judicial guarantee calms their concern over governmental interference with civil liberties. Judicial review thus sits easily in the Founding Fathers' view of the world, but whether it was intended will never be conclusively resolved and, in one important sense, does not need to be, for in 1803 the United States Supreme Court made the entire debate irrelevant.

Marbury v. Madison

The case of *Marbury* v. *Madison* developed out of the confused circumstances of a presidential transition. The election of 1800 had been contested by the incumbent President, John Adams, and Thomas Jefferson. Jefferson won the election, which took place in November of that year, but was not due to take office until 4 March 1801. However, in the interval between the election and the inauguration of Jefferson, Adams' party, the Federalists, who controlled the Congress, passed an Act which authorized the President to appoint as many Justices of the Peace in the District of Columbia as he believed were necessary. President Adams nominated forty-two men, the Senate confirmed the nominations, and the President signed their commissions. However, in the haste to beat the 4 March deadline, four of these so-called 'midnight' judges did not receive their letters of commission; one of the four was William Marbury. On taking office, President Jefferson and his Secretary of State, James Madison, who was responsible for the delivery of the letters, refused to give the commissions to Marbury and the other three appointees. Thereupon, Marbury turned to the United States Supreme Court for a ruling to require Madison to show cause why the Supreme Court should not issue a write of *mandamus* under the Judiciary Act of 1789, which would compel him to deliver the commissions. The Supreme Court and its Chief Justice, John Marshall, were in a quandary; they appeared to have two equally unattractive options. The Court could comply with Marbury's wishes and require the Jefferson administration to deliver the commissions. However, there was a strong possibility that Madison would refuse to obey the Court's order, and as there was no practical method of enforcing the Court's judgement, the Supreme Court would suffer a devastating blow to its credibility and prestige. On the other hand, if the Court merely refused to grant Marbury his write of *mandamus*, then it faced another kind of political humiliation. Its decision could be interpreted, and would be by the Court's opponents, as a sign of political cowardice, an unwillingness to confront the presidency. Both options threatened to damage the Court's standing, and in those early days of the Republic the damage would have been fatal. Chief Justice Marshall, however, chose neither of these alternatives. Instead, he wrote an opinion that is one of the landmarks of American constitutional history. First, he declared that Marbury did have a right to the commission and that, furthermore, a writ of *mandamus* issued under the Judiciary Act of 1789 was indeed the proper remedy in this case, *if* the Judiciary Act of 1789 itself was constitutional. But did the Court have the power to decide the constitutionality of an Act of Congress? 'Certainly, all those who have framed constitutions', wrote Marshall, 'contemplate them as forming the fundamental and paramount law of the nation, and consequently the theory of every such government must be that an act of the legislature, repugnant to the constitution, is void'. But who or what institution should decide, in the event of an apparent conflict between the Constitution and legislation? Marshall was in no doubt about the answer: 'It is emphatically the province and duty of the judicial department to say what the law is...the courts are to regard the Constitution [as] superior to any ordinary act of the legislature, the Constitution and not [the] ordinary act must govern'. Considering the significance of the decision, the Chief Justice was remarkably brief. He did not present an extended and intricate argument in favour of judicial review; he asserted it. But if his opinion, in a sense, was deficient intellectually, it was a deficiency that was more than compensated for by Marshall's political astuteness. Having asserted the general principle of judicial review, the Chief Justice proceeded to utilize his newly established authority. The Judiciary Act of 1789 was unconstitutional, Marshall argued, because it violated Article III of the Constitution. As a consequence, no writ of *mandamus* could be issued and Secretary of State Madison could not be instructed to deliver the commissions. Marshall had disarmed the Jefferson administration. They had 'won' the case and so they accepted the decision and implicitly the reasons that lay behind it. Judicial review had been established by stealth.

3.2   The courts and the development of the Constitution

The subject of judicial review returned to the Supreme Court in two further cases, *Fletcher* v. *Peck* (1810) and *Cohens* v. *Virginia* (1821), when the Courts reaffirmed the authority of the federal courts to exercise it. Within a relatively short span of time the right of the federal judiciary to be the final arbiter of the Constitution was widely accepted and has remained unchallenged since. It is an authority that the courts have not been reluctant to exercise. Precise estimates vary, but approximately eighty federal statutes and over 700 pieces of state legislation have been held unconstitutional by the Supreme Court.

Why has the Court found it necessary to declare legislation unconstitutional so frequently? Was it because both the federal and the state governments have deliberately attempted to invalidate provisions of the Constitution? Or has the Court been overbearing, wielding its power of judicial review somewhat indiscriminately? To a certain extent both these elements have played a part, but there are two more significant reasons which account for the substantial number of unconstitutional statutes. The first is that the Constitution has not proved to be an easy document to interpret. The confusion over judicial review has been repeated many times over. To take a further example, the First Amendment to the Constitution contains the provision that 'Congress shall make no law ... abridging the freedom of speech, or of the press'. Did those who wrote and passed the Amendment intend that the Congress should pass literally no law? If that was the intent, then there could be no law against libel, slander or pornography. There could be no sanction against a person who knowingly and misleadingly shouted 'Fire!' in a crowded theatre. More serious, there could be no limit on what is said or published, even when the United States is engaged in a war. Did the framers really want to have no law at all, or was the Amendment primarily concerned with preventing the Congress from passing legislation that threatened the freedom to express ideas and beliefs on political, social and economic issues? In other words, the framers did not wish to protect pornography and sedition, but they were worried about the federal government using its power to threaten political liberty. The Supreme Court, unsurprisingly, endorsed this view of the First Amendment, but in doing so the Court created for itself equally substantial problems of interpretation. After all, what is pornography? When is speech seditious and when is it the legitimate expression of opinion? The list of questions can be extended with no difficulty, but the answers, unfortunately, are not as easy to come by. The Court has grappled with these problems for the best part of two centuries, and, to date, has not resolved them definitively. Inevitably, in this climate of uncertainty legislation has been found unconstitutional, not only because politicians were anxious to tamper with the liberties of their constituents but also because the constitutional position has always been uncertain.

A second cause for the large number of statutes found unconstitutional is that because of judicial review the courts have had to undertake the task of constitutional adaptation. The Founding Fathers were clearly aware of the conditions that prevailed in American society in 1787, and the Constitution, they believed, was appropriate for these conditions. While they undoubtedly hoped that they had created, in the words of Chief Justice Marshall 'a constitution intended to endure the ages to come', the Founding Fathers could not have foreseen the speed of change that was about to occur in the United States and which threatened to make the Constitution irrelevant to a polity, society and economy in a process of constant and rapid development. It was incumbent on the courts to ensure that the Constitution was flexible enough to accommodate these developments and yet remain faithful to the spirit of the Founding Fathers – a task that has proved to be profoundly difficult.

The 'commerce clause' (Article I, Section 8) of the Constitution provides an illustration of the problem. The commerce clause gives the Congress the power 'To regulate Commerce with foreign Nations, and among the several States and with the Indian Tribes'. The intention behind the clause, unlike some other sections of the Constitution, is clear. The Founding Fathers believed that one of the central problems of the Articles of Confederation was the absence of national authority to regulate commerce, and accordingly they included the commerce clause in the Constitution. However, in their desire to disperse power, they did not wish the Congress to interfere with those economic arrangements that lay exclusively within the states. Inter-state commerce was within the power of congressional regulation, while intra-state commerce was under the jurisdiction of the states. In 1787, the Founding Fathers found it easy to distinguish between these two categories. If production and trade crossed state boundaries, then it ceased to be intra-state commerce and was subject to congressional control. The categorization of economic activity was a relatively simple matter in an agrarian economy. However, the character of the American economy began to change: industrialization transformed the Founding Fathers' simple equation. The economy, by the second half of the nineteenth century, was sophisticated and increasingly interdependent and national in outlook. Large, complex organizations emerged that owned manufacturing plants and administrative offices in numerous states, while the financial control of these institutions was increasingly located in those cities of the East and Mid West that had developed sophisticated capital markets. Indeed, it was possible to argue, by the early twentieth century, that all commercial activities impinged, however minimally, on intra-state commerce. However, if the judiciary accepted this proposition, they would have had to put aside the Founding Fathers' wishes to limit congressional power over commerce. Instead, they attempted to develop new criteria, which took into account the current economic realities but which still attempted to preserve an essential distinction between inter- and intra-state commerce. These criteria were in a continual state of development as judges sought to accommodate the shifting structure of the American economy. But this process of development by definition, meant constitutional uncertainty: what was intra-state commerce one day was no longer the following day, and, as a result, legislation foundered in this process of constitutional adaptation.

The significance of the federal courts' role in adapting and interpreting the Constitution cannot be underestimated. The impact of these activities on the American political process has been enormous. The federal judiciary, as a consequence of their position as arbiters of the Constitution, have had a crucial effect on the making of public policy. Ever since *Marbury* v. *Madison* they have attempted to establish the constitutional perimeters within which public policy can be made. Legislation or other instruments of policy-making, which have not accepted these limitations, have been declared unconstitutional. In the United States, courts and judges have constructed the constitutional arena within which Presidents, Senators, Governors, Parties, etc. operate. The judiciary, and particularly those who have sat on the United States Supreme Court, have had a profound influence on the development of American society, a fact which is readily apparent from a brief examination of some of the more fateful decisions made by the Supreme Court.

The Supreme Court until 1865

The judicial history of this period is dominated by the personalities of two Chief Justices, John Marshall (1801–35) and Roger B. Taney (1836–64). Through the force of their personalities and intellects, they gave the Supreme Court a style of leadership that perhaps has not been repeated. While it would be oversimple to suggest that there was an underlying unity to all their decisions, their judgements, collectively, did have a sense of direction. The issues that absorbed the Court during this time, apart from judicial review, were federal/state relations and, towards the middle of the nineteenth century, slavery. The relationship between the states and the federal government throughout this period was problematic. This was a time of rapid national development. Between 1820 and 1860 some five million immigrants arrived in a country which had expanded from being a nation located on the Atlantic seaboard to one which stretched to the Pacific and incorporated most of the land between the present Canadian and Mexican borders. In order to cope with these and other developments, there was a necessary outpouring of federal legislation; but, paradoxically, this nation-building was taking place at a time when people's paramount loyalty was still offered to the individual states. The prerogatives of the states were guarded zealously, and state governments were only too anxious to assert their autonomy. Consequently, federal and state power frequently came into conflict, which only the Supreme Court could resolve. Throughout this period, the decisions of the Court consistently sustained national power. The judgements emphasized the power of the federal government. The states' view, which stressed their own authority and advocated restricting the scope of the federal government, was received unsympathetically. Marshall's reading of the Constitution always uncovered support for upholding the authority of the federal government at the political cost of intense hostility from the states. In *Fletcher* v. *Peck* (1810) and *Dartmouth College* v. *Woodward* (1819), also known as the *Dartmouth College Case*, the Court dealt a blow to state autonomy; and in a series of cases, of which *McCulloch* v *Maryland* (1819) and *Gibbons* v. *Ogden* (1824) are the most notable, the Marshall Court sustained the primacy of the federal government in certain areas of governmental activity. By the time of Marshall's death in

1835, the Court had established the constitutional context within which the federal/state relationship would evolve.

When Roger B. Taney was appointed Chief Justice in 1836, there were fears that under his influence the Court would, if not reverse, then dramatically change direction. These fears, and in some cases hopes, did not materialize. The Taney Court continued to interpret the Constitution on broadly similar lines and, perhaps because familiarity induces acquiescence, the opposition to the Court's judgements gradually diminished, so that the 1840s were, in many ways, an era of judicial good feeling.

Unfortunately, this aura rapidly eroded as the profoundly contentious issue of slavery took the centre of the political and, subsequently, judicial stage. Since the formation of the Republic, slavery, 'the peculiar institution' of the southern states, contained the seeds for destroying the Union. Its existence aroused intense passions which were increasingly difficult to control. Politicians, from the Founding Fathers onwards, were aware that they had to achieve a *modus vivendi* between the slave and the non-slave states, otherwise the Union was in jeopardy. The Missouri Acts of 1820 were an attempt to achieve such an accommodation. These Acts, known as the 'Missouri Compromise', permitted the states of Missouri and Maine to join the Union as slave and free states respectively, but also went on to declare that in all areas north of a specified degree of latitude, slavery was abolished.

The Missouri Compromise defused the conflict temporarily, but slavery could not be ignored for long. The increasing agitation over the issue made the Congress re-examine the Missouri Compromise and modify it in response to the pro- and anti-slavery forces. Furthermore, in 1857, the Supreme Court delivered its verdict on the Missouri Compromise. The case of *Dred Scott* v. *Sandford* (1857) arose when Scott, a slave, had been taken by his owner to a free state, Illinois. Scott then began his course of litigation, arguing that his residence in a non-slave state automatically made him free. It was some eleven years before the case reached the Supreme Court. When Taney announced the decision on 6 March 1857, it was greeted by a storm of abuse and derision. The Court's verdict, which was not unanimous, first declared the Missouri Compromise unconstitutional on the grounds that the Court could discover no constitutional authority which granted Congress the power to abolish slavery. Second, and controversially, Taney claimed that Scott's legal standing in the case was problematic: only a citizen could bring a suit in court, and negroes could not be citizens; thus Scott had no right to bring an action. The *Dred Scott* case engulfed the Court in criticism. Those who wished to abolish slavery found the Court's opinion gratuitously insulting. It is not, however, the purpose here to discuss the merits of Taney's opinion but to point out the enormous impact of a judicial decision on the political process. The Court killed the Missouri Compromise and, as it did, the skirmishing between the North and South increased in tempo. The Civil War was that much nearer.

The Supreme Court and the economy 1865–1945

From the end of the Civil War, the workload of the United States Supreme Court was dominated by one issue, the regulation of the economy by government, either state or federal. Of course, governmental regulation of the economy was not a post-Civil War phenomenon; it had existed since the foundation of the Republic and, indeed, was accepted practice during the colonial period. However, the rapid industrialization of the American economy changed the position substantially because industrialization brought in its train a variety of social and economic problems. The federal and state governments, responding to pressures from their electorates, passed legislation which attempted to ameliorate the more damaging effects of this new industrial order. For instance, Bills imposing minimum wages and maximum hours of employment were passed by several state legislatures, as were statutes which set the prices that could be charged for a variety of goods and services. The federal government imposed a tax on incomes above $400 and attempted to eliminate child labour from factories. The response to this flood of legislation from manufacturers, railroad companies and, in general, from all those who believed their property rights were adversely affected, was to turn to the courts and challenge the constitutionality of the legislation. So how did the Supreme Court deal with these conflicting claims? 'With difficulty' would be a flippant but accurate answer.

Since the vast majority of regulatory legislation, until the 1930s, was passed by the states, most of the appeals were based on the Fourteenth Amendment, ironically one of the post-Civil War amendments which was intended to deal with slavery and its aftermath. The Fourteenth Amendment did contain, however, a clause which read that, 'No state shall...deprive any person of life, liberty or property, without the due process of law'. The interpretation of this clause, known as the 'due process' clause, was central to the outcome of the litigation before the Court. To what extent did the due process clause of the Fourteenth Amendment permit the state government to intervene in private economic arrangements? The Supreme Court's answer is still a subject of considerable controversy. There is a view, most probably held by a majority of scholars, that the justices of the Court, along with the rest of the legal profession, were hostile to this kind of legislation and were determined to have it declared unconstitutional. There are other explanations of the Supreme Court's behaviour which do not detect any consistent hostility or indeed consistency of any sort because the judiciary found the issue enormously difficult to come to terms with. But neither explanation can conceal the fact that, once again, the Supreme Court played a crucial part, if not in deciding, then in constructing the reference of the pre-eminent issue on the nation's political agenda.

The 'New Deal' Court

The financial collapse of 1929 and the severe economic depression that followed in its wake, dramatically increased the involvement of the federal government in the American economy. In the presidential election of 1932, Herbert Hoover, the incumbent, undoubtedly lost because he was identified with the Depression and an inability to solve it. By contrast his opponent Franklin D. Roosevelt had promised the electorate 'a New Deal'. On taking office in March 1933, President Roosevelt and a Congress controlled by the Democratic Party enacted, within a hundred days, fifteen major Bills. This was an unprecedented achievement and, regardless of the merits of the legislation, it was a testament to presidential leadership and congressional energy. The events of those 'hundred days' have been recounted many times and from very different perspectives, but most accounts agree that in the spring of 1933, Washington was alive with a sense of expectancy that had been absent from the capital for a long time. The 'New Dealers', while fully aware of the perilous state of the economy, were also exhilarated by the enormity of their task. In this heady atmosphere President Roosevelt and his advisers were understandably preoccupied with economic recovery and were not concerned with what they saw as constitutional niceties. But if the Roosevelt administration was blasé about constitutional consider- ations in 1933, it was decidedly less so by 1935. For as time passed the constitutionality of the New Deal was being frequently challenged in the lower courts, and the administration grew increasingly fearful over the United States Supreme Court's response to the New Deal – fears which proved to be well founded.

The Supreme Court found several Acts unconstitutional, in fairly rapid succession. The centrepiece of the New Deal's industrial strategy, the National Industrial Recovery Act, was declared invalid in the 'sick chicken' case, *A. L. A. Schechter Poultry Corporation* v. *United States* (1935). The Agri- cultural Adjustment Act, which was intended to restore the health of the agricultural sector, was also held unconstitutional in *United States* v. *Butler* (1936). Several other pieces of legislation were struck from the statute books. The reasons offered by the Court varied from case to case, but the objection that was raised most frequently was that federal government did not possess the authority under the commerce clause to regulate all the activities that the Roosevelt administration wished. Furthermore, the Court found several of the administrative procedures written into the National Industrial Recovery Act and other statutes constitutionally dubious.

Was the Supreme Court's response to the New Deal justified? There are, unsurprisingly, a number of different answers to this question. One ex- planation of the Court's record is that the Roosevelt administration suffered the consequences of its lack of thought about constitutional proprieties. A large number of the constitutional difficulties mentioned in the judicial decisions could have been avoided if legislation had been drafted with greater care and precision. Another view, and a majority view, is that four of the nine justices of the Court were unremittingly hostile to the New Deal; with the occasional support of two other justices, they were able to command a majority. The New Deal, in this analysis, was undermined by political malice rather than constitutional argument.

There are problems with this explanation but, significantly, it was believed by President Roosevelt, who while maintaining his normally genial public persona, was privately furious with the Court. In an administration that was renowned for its accessibility, Roosevelt and his closest advisers secretly devised a counter-attack on the Court. Their strategy was unveiled in March 1937 after Roosevelt had won a striking victory in the presidential election of 1936. Roosevelt's proposal, which was almost immediately chris- tened the 'Court packing plan', was nominally an efficiency measure, aris- ing from the administration's fear that there were too many federal judges over the age of 70 and that their age impaired their effectiveness. Under the administration's proposals, if any judge over the age of 70 failed to resign or retire, then the President would have the right to appoint an additional judge. If all of the justices on the Supreme Court who were over 70 failed to resign, then President Roosevelt, under the Court packing plan, could make six further appointments. Although there were perfunctory attempts to structure the debate in terms of judicial efficiency, the real conflict rapidly came to the fore: it was a contest over the authority of the United States Supreme Court and the federal judiciary in general. Was the Supreme Court still the final arbiter of the Constitution? Did its rulings still have to be accepted, however politically unpalatable?

At the start of the congressional campaign to pass the Court packing plan, the advantage lay with the Roosevelt administration. The New Deal was a considerable political success, Roosevelt was enormously popular, and the Democratic Party commanded majorities of over two to one in both the Senate and the House of Representatives. The Court's treatment of the New Deal, by contrast, had been greeted with dismay and disapproval. It was not a popular institution in 1937. Nevertheless, the Court packing plan was defeated, the first major defeat for the Roosevelt administration and one which was to have a profound impact on the Democratic Party.

Why was the plan defeated? Paradoxically, one of the reasons was without doubt Roosevelt's popularity and success. His opponents painted a picture of a President drunk on his own success, and then they raised the spectre of dictatorship. The President was too powerful for his and everybody else's own good. The Constitution, they suggested, was being unbalanced by the President's quite extraordinary persuasive powers over Congress. Over the previous four years Congress had passed virtually the entire legislative programme proposed by the President. The Congress was no longer an effective check on the presidency; the Supreme Court still was, they argued, and therein lay the reason behind the opposition to the Court packing plan. This charge of aggrandizement and dictatorship, which in retrospect may look somewhat far-fetched, nevertheless was and continues to be a potent one in America. Roosevelt's secretive and devious handling of the plan fuelled these fears, and consequently his initial political advantage disappeared in a storm of criticism.

What also emerged from this episode was the fundamental political strength of the Court. Despite its transient unpopularity, the Court's position as guarantor of the Constitution was not questioned seriously by the electorate or their representatives in Congress. Even a popular and powerful President could not threaten the Court's authority. Interestingly, in the aftermath of the Court packing plan, the Supreme Court appeared to change its mind over the New Deal. Certainly after 1937 the New Deal had no further problems with the judiciary. Some scholars have viewed this change as a tacit recognition by the Court that it had to acquiesce to the New Deal, while others have interpreted the events as the consequence of new legislation that was constitutionally sensitive, in addition to the traditional process of judicial adaptation to new economic realities. But whatever the explanation, the New Deal experience re-emphasized the authority of the Supreme Court and its powerful support from the electorate.

The modern Court

The striking characteristic of constitutional history since the Second World War has been that the judiciary are no longer concerned with governmental intervention in the economy. The great constitutional debates over the regulation of the economy were either resolved by the end of the 1930s or, if particular problems proved to be too intractable, the Supreme Court simply washed its hands of them. Instead, the Court found itself absorbed with the equally problematic concerns of civil liberties and civil rights. As early as 1938 the Court announced its intentions in *United States* v. *Carolene Products Co.* to scrutinize, with particular care, any governmental restriction on those freedoms guaranteed by the Bill of Rights, and the Court has been, over these past four decades, unsympathetic to any attempts by either the federal or state governments to interfere with the civil liberties of Americans. Indeed, it would be true to say that the Supreme Court has interpreted the first ten amendments to the Constitution in such a way as to impose substantially new restrictions on the power of government. Similarly, in the field of civil rights, the Court has altered radically the constitutional context within which government can make policy. The most dramatic of these judicial developments in both civil rights and liberties occurred under the Warren Court.

The Warren Court (1953–69)

When President Dwight D. Eisenhower appointed as Chief Justice of the United States a fellow Republican, Earl Warren, no one, least of all President Eisenhower, foresaw that the Supreme Court with its new Chief Justice to the fore was about to embark on a remarkable period of constitutional development. Warren had been a moderately conservative Republican Governor of California and was expected by Eisenhower and most observers to conduct himself in a broadly similar manner as Chief Justice. It was anticipated that the Court under Warren's leadership would be a consolidating rather than an innovative body. To the chagrin of President Eisenhower, these expectations were not fulfilled: the Warren Court turned out to be one of the great reforming Courts in judicial history. By the time of Warren's resignation in 1969 the Supreme Court had, in some senses, wrought a constitutional revolution – a revolution that was most apparent in the field of civil rights.

Until 1954 all of the eleven southern states, plus some of those on the borders of the South, racially segregated their citizens. Black and white children, for instance, were enrolled in separate schools. Services, other than education, were also provided on a racially separate basis. This policy of *de jure* racial segregation – legally enforced racial segregation – was constitutional. In 1896, the United States Supreme Court in *Plessy* v. *Ferguson* had interpreted the equal protection clause of the Fourteenth Amendment as allowing segregation. The South could segregate, ruled the Court, as long as each race was offered equal facilities: 'separate but equal' was the governing doctrine. However, in 1954, in one of the Supreme Court's most historic decisions, *Brown* v. *Board of Education*, the Court reversed itself. In an opinion written by Warren, a unanimous Court declared that segregation was inherently unequal and therefore unconstitutional. Although the judgement in *Brown* applied only to schools, the court soon made it clear in a series of decisions that no service provided or regulated by the states could any longer be offered on a segregated basis. *Brown* was greeted with dismay and anger in the South, and although several states immediately refused to implement the necessary changes, the impetus towards de-segregation proved irresistible in the medium term. The importance of *Brown* cannot be underestimated. Although the entire South may not have complied instantly with *Brown*, *de jure* segregation was ended by the judgement. A deeply rooted social practice was terminated by a judicial decision. Furthermore, *Brown* had a profound impact on the American polity. It heartened the black community, invigorated the civil rights movement, and reinforced the drive for legislative reforms, which culminated in the passage of the Civil Rights Act of 1964 and the Voting Rights Act of 1965.

Civil liberties also provided the Warren Court with a fertile ground for judicial creativity. The Court's attitude to the entire range of civil liberty issues was governed by a profound suspicion of the power of government; consequently the Court was very reluctant to permit any new limitations on the Bill of Rights and moreover showed a positive enthusiasm to review any existing restrictions. For instance, in *New York Times Co.* v. *Sullivan* (1964) the Supreme Court reduced the press's vulnerability to the liberal laws. The decision made it extremely difficult for public officials to sue a newspaper for libel with any hope of success. Again, in *Engel* v. *Vitale* (1962) the Court refused to permit the state of New York to allow a prayer to be recited in schools because it violated the First Amendment to the Constitution.

However, the Court's greatest suspicions were focused on those agencies of government that were involved in the process of criminal justice. The Court indicated its belief that the balance had swung too greatly in favour of those in charge of criminal prosecutions. As a result the Court, in a series of decisions, proceeded to redress this balance. In *Gideon* v. *Wainwright* (1963) the Warren Court found in the Sixth Amendment a constitutional right that all defendants in a criminal trial had an entitlement to legal representation, regardless of their ability to pay for it. *Mapp* v. *Ohio* (1961) re-examined the Fourth Amendment's prohibition against unreasonable searches and imposed new guidelines on the police. Most controversially, the Court reinterpreted the Fifth Amendment's protection against self-incrimination in *Escobedo* v. *Illinois* (1964) and *Miranda* v. *Arizona* (1966) and imposed a new code of conduct on the police when they interrogated a criminal suspect. The cumulative effect on these and other decisions was that by 1969 the Court had substantially diminished governmental discretion in the area of civil liberties; both state and federal government had far less freedom to manoeuvre.

The decisions of the Warren Court had the most extraordinary impact on American society. Long-established practices and customs were transformed, and they were changed by judicial decisions, not by legislative statute, nor by executive orders of the President. Inevitably these judgements aroused antagonism, particularly on the part of those who did not wish to change their existing behaviour. Warren and other justices were not popular in the South or with those who felt that the Court had damaged 'law and order'. There were others who, while sympathetic to the effect of the judgements, were unhappy about the manner in which the Court was arriving at its decisions. Many students of judicial behaviour felt that the Warren Court was not interpreting the Constitution, but creating a new one that it found congenial. Were the justices behaving like politicians and was the Warren Court acting like a legislature? Regardless of how desirable it was to abolish segregation and to redress the balance between the criminal suspect and the police, was the Supreme Court the appropriate institution to do so?

This growing sense of disquiet, allied to the political opposition, made the Court vulnerable, and a major issue in the presidential election campaign of 1968. The victorious Republican candidate, Richard Nixon, pledged that as President he would only appoint those who were 'strict constructionists', judges who would interpret the Constitution rather than impose their own beliefs. Nixon soon got the opportunity to fulfil his campaign promises. In 1969 Earl Warren resigned, and Nixon nominated Warren E. Burger to replace him as Chief Justice. Nixon also nominated a further three justices, Harry Blackmun in 1970, and Lewis Powell and William Rehnquist in 1972. Nixon's Republican successors as President, Gerald Ford and Ronald Reagan, each made one appointment to the Court under Chief Justice Burger, John Paul Stevens in 1975 and Sandra Day O'Connor, the first woman to sit in the Court, in 1981. So did these six Republican appointees produce the counter-revolution that President Nixon desired?

The Burger Court (1969–86)

When Chief Justice Burger resigned in 1986, there were few observers who argued that the counter-revolution, promised by President Nixon, had taken place. The Burger Court had disappointed its more conservative political supporters but pleasantly surprised those who expected the decisions of the Warren Court to be overturned on a fairly substantial scale. It did not roll back the jurisprudence of its predecessors. On the whole it was a consolidating Court, although it made some decisions that can only be described as remarkably radical. So the Burger Court is not easy to classify. It was both cautious and innovative, but nevertheless interpreted the Constitution in a hitherto unprecedented manner.

Perhaps the greatest retreat from the positions established by the Warren Court occurred over the process of criminal justice. Here the Burger Court restored to the police some of the powers that were removed by its predecessors. In *Oregon* v. *Hass* (1975) and *Jenkins* v. *Anderson* (1980), the majority of the justices on the Burger Court made clear their view that the pendulum had swung too heavily in favour of the criminal suspect. Nevertheless, although the Court modified the interpretations of the the Warren Court, it did not do so very substantially, and certainly did not restore the the pre-Warren position on police interrogation or on trial procedures. The fears of many who had welcomed the Warren Court's judgements on the process of criminal justice, and who believed they were about to be overruled by the Burger Court, were not fulfilled. The decisions were cautious and deliberate and this instinct is to be found in several other areas of constitutional interpretation. For instance, the Burger Court was expected to be less protective over the freedom of the press. To some extent this fear was borne out. The justices were not as instinctively opposed to government interference with the media as was the Warren Court. Nevertheless, in one of the most dramatic cases of this period, *New York Times Co.* v. *United States* (1971), the Court rejected the attempt by the Nixon administration to prevent the New York Times from publishing a series of articles based on the Pentagon Papers, which at the time were a secret and highly classified history of the Vietnam War. The Court dismissed the administration's request for an injunction on the ground that publication would cause grave and unacceptable damage to the United States. The Court held that under all but the most extraordinary circumstances the President does not have the inherent power to prevent newspapers, or other organizations, from publishing classified information. Yet again the Burger Court demonstrated that although it was a different judicial animal from its predecessor, it was not about to alter substantially the direction of the Warren Court's decisions. Caution and consolidation are the hallmarks of the decisions concerning the freedom the press. Interestingly these characteristics were strikingly absent when the Court turned to the the issues of civil rights and abortion.

Civil rights is one of the areas where the Burger Court was at its most adventurous. The Court had to grapple with the problems of *de facto* segregation and positive discrimination or affirmative action. In the aftermath of the *Brown* decision, the Court became aware that declaring *de jure* racial segregation unconstitutional was only part of a solution to integrating American life. While *de jure* segregation was the normal practice in the South, it was uncommon in the North. However, despite the absence of *de jure* racial separation, the black experience in the northern states was nevertheless a segregated one. For instance, most blacks attended schools that were almost exclusively black, because they registered at those schools which were in their neighbourhood. As blacks had been the victims of discrimination over housing – discrimination that was often illegal as several states had laws prohibiting such behaviour – residential patterns were often racially exclusive. Consequently racial segregation in schools emerged in the North without it being legally enforced. But according to the Court, *de facto* segregation was as unconstitutional as the *de jure* variety. In a series of cases which included *Swan* v. *Charlotte Mecklenburg Board of Education* (1971) and *Keyes* v. *Denver School District* (1973), the Court held that *de facto* segregation also violated the equal protection clause of the Fourteenth Amendment. But what was the Court's remedy? Their solution was 'busing': to transport black and white children across one or more school districts in order to achieve a racial balance in each school that approximated the racial composition of the entire area. Busing proved to be very controversial and managed to antagonize both the black and white communities, but as with other decisions the Court's authority prevailed.

The policy of positive discrimination or affirmative action was not devised by the judiciary; it arose out of administrative interpretation of the Civil Rights Act of 1964. However, it fell to the courts to decide whether the Act, or the relevant section of it, was unconstitutional. The overriding objective of the Civil Rights Act was to achieve equality of treatment for all Americans including the racial minorities. But how could this equality be achieved? Could it be attained by a policy of non-discrimination?

There were difficulties with such a policy. First, it placed the burden of proof on the government. The government would have to show, for example, that an employer was guilty of discrimination, which could only be done on an individual case-by-case basis, a process that was time-consuming and not notably successful. Secondly, even if an employer did not discriminate, blacks and other minorities were still likely to be adversely affected because of past discrimination. Their historic disadvantages of poor housing, poor education and inadequate training made it difficult for them to succeed in an open competition. As a result of these considerations the federal government began to develop affirmative action guidelines which placed the onus of proof on organizations to show that they were not guilty of discrimination. They could demonstrate the absence of discriminatory practices if they employed or, in the case of a university, admitted a percentage of minorities roughly equivalent to the percentage of the population in their area. Of course, to achieve this target universities and companies had to discriminate in favour of minorities. Universities could not admit students solely on academic merit, for if they did so the target would not be achieved. Instead, blacks who had significantly weaker qualifications had to be accepted in preference to white applicants with stronger academic credentials, if universities were going to obtain the desired racial balance.

The problem for the Burger Court was whether these acts of reverse discrimination were constitutional. The Court's answer was to give a qualified yes. The Court endorsed the principle of affirmative action in *Regents of the University of California* v. *Bakke* (1978), *Steelworkers' Union* v. *Weber* (1979) and *Fullilove* v. *Klutznick* (1980). However, the Court took issue with particular affirmative action programmes, and in *Firefighters* v. *Stotts* (1984) showed a reluctance to elevate the principle of affirmative action over all other considerations. The Supreme Court under Chief Justice Rehnquist is still in the process of examining the issue and all its ramifications, but the fact that the Court has endorsed the principle of positive discrimination cannot be underestimated.

In the arena of civil liberties the Burger Court's most innovative and unexpected decision concerned abortion. Abortion is as contentious an issue in the United States as it is in most Western democracies, but whereas in other nations it has been a matter for legislative decision – whether to permit abortion and if so under what conditions – in the United States the Supreme Court has provided the decisions. In *Roe* v. *Wade* (1973) and *Doe* v. *Bolton* (1973) the Court struck down state anti-abortion laws as an unconstitutional intrusion into the decision of a woman to terminate her pregnancy. The Supreme Court uncovered a constitutional right for a woman to have an abortion. Of course, these decisions have not ended the controversy over abortion, but unless the Court reverses itself, the only avenue that the anti-abortion movement has available is to support the passage of a constitutional amendment to overturn the *Roe* judgement.

Perhaps the most dramatic illustration of judicial power since *Marbury* v. *Madison* arose out of *United States* v. *Nixon* (1974). In 1974 the United States was in the throes of a major political scandal that threatened to develop into a constitutional crisis. The 'Watergate affair' (see Chapter 4) was nearing its *dénouement*. President Nixon and several of his close associates were under investigation by a Special Prosecutor for an alleged criminal conspiracy to obstruct justice. In the course of his investigation, the Special Prosecutor wanted to examine tape recordings of conversations held in the Oval Office of the White House – recordings which had been made on the instructions of President Nixon. However, when the Special Prosecutor requested to see the tapes, the President refused to hand them over. Consequently the Special Prosecutor turned to the courts, who ordered Nixon to present the tapes to the Court. The President appealed the decision to the Circuit Court of Appeals, but the Special Prosecutor successfully sought an immediate hearing before the Supreme Court. The argument presented on behalf of the President was that the tapes were protected by the doctrine of executive privilege, a doctrine that was not well established constitutionally, but which several Presidents since the end of the Second World War had claimed with increasing frequency. Nixon insisted that the tapes were entirely within the control of the executive branch, because the concept of the separation of powers suggested that neither the Congress nor the judicial branch had any jurisdiction over them. Unfortunately, for President Nixon that is, a unanimous Supreme Court rejected this argument. Chief Justice Burger's opinion dismissed the claim of executive privilege, at least in the circumstances of this particular case. The Court at a stroke resolved the crisis, for within two weeks of the judgement President Nixon resigned. There are few decisions which have had such an immediate and momentous political consequence.

The Burger Court did not fulfil the hopes and fears of those who expected to witness a severe judicial reaction to the Warren Court. The Court did not take a distinct and consistent view over the entire range of constitutional issues, and in that sense it, rather than the Warren Court, has been in harmony with traditional judicial practice. But, of course, that does not mean that the Burger Court judgements have had less impact than those of its predecessors: the cases mentioned above are a testament to the societal influence of its judgements.

The Rehnquist Court (1986–)

The Burger Court, as noted above, was a disappointment to many of its more conservative supporters. Not only did it fail to overturn the Warren Court decisions over a broad range of issues, but its own judgements on civil rights and abortion profoundly upset conservatives. Consequently, when Chief Justice Burger resigned in 1986, President Ronald Reagan took the opportunity to continue the process of attempting to refashion the Supreme Court in a more congenial, i.e. conservative, direction. He appointed Associate Justice William Rehnquist to fill the vacancy. Rehnquist was believed to be the most conservative of the Justices on the Burger Court, but was deemed, by those who sympathised with his views as well as those who did not, to possess both a powerful intellect and the necessary diplomatic skills to be an effective Chief Justice. Rehnquist's place was filled in turn by Antonin Scalia, who also conformed to the criteria laid down by President Reagan's Attorney General, Edwin Meese. But perhaps the clearest indication of the administration's intentions occurred during the unsuccessful nomination of Robert Bork in 1987. Bork was a distinguished judge and had been an equally distinguished law professor, although throughout his career as judge and professor he had never disguised his 'conservative preferences'. He had also been, even more controversially, an important participant in the dismissal of the Special Watergate Prosecutor, Archibald Cox, during the prolonged and painful death of the Nixon presidency (see Chapter 4). In short, Bork was a very controversial figure, yet he was nominated by President Reagan because both the President and Edwin Meese believed that he and the other Reagan appointees would lead the Supreme Court in the direction that the administration wanted. However, the Senate refused to confirm the Bork nomination after one of the most intense and bitter confirmation battles.

The Reagan administration, having lost the battle for Bork, may not have lost the war. The President subsequently nominated Charles Kennedy, who was confirmed relatively easily by the Senate in 1988, in spite of the fact that Kennedy supported the same broad positions taken by Bork, although with greater diplomacy and discretion. Moreover, the election of George Bush has given the Republicans four more years in which to make further judicial appointments. It is more than probable that Bush will have the opportunity to nominate several justices. Justices Blackmun, Brennan and Marshall are over eighty and are likely to resign in the near future. If President Bush and his Attorney General, Richard Thornburgh, take the same view of appointments as their predecessors, then the impact on the Court may well be substantial, while it must always be remembered that appointments do not invariably work out in the manner that Presidents intend. But returning to the present, in what way have the Reagan appointees begun to influence the direction of the Rehnquist Court?

It is far too early to offer a definitive answer to this question. The Rehnquist Court has not established a distinctive style or adopted a set of characteristics that are distinctively its own. However, the early indications are that the Rehnquist Court will be cautious as the Burger Court was in most respects, but without the radical and spectacular innovative judgements that the Burger Court made on occasion. If these early indications prove to be an accurate predictor of the future, then there will be no sudden shifts in direction or any dramatic new departures. The Court is unlikely to stake out new territory as the Warren Court did so frequently and the Burger Court did somewhat less frequently. Of course, this caution will also mean that the Rehnquist Court is unlikely to overturn, at least directly, the most contentious decisions of recent years, on abortion and affirmative action. The Court, if it is going to do anything in these areas, is far more likely to chip away at the existing judgements. One indication of this approach was evident in the 1989 case on abortion, *Webster* v. *Reproductive Services*. The Court had the opportunity in *Webster* to reconsider the *Roe* decision and to overrule it if a majority of the Court so wished.

Although some members of the Court, notably Justice Scalia, wished to do precisely that, the majority chose not to go down that road. Instead they decided to limit, in effect, the impact of *Roe* and constrain the right of a woman to have an abortion by ceding a degree of control to the individual state governments. The Court permitted the individual states, if they so wished, to impose certain limitations or restrictions on abortions but without giving the states the authority to ban abortions generally. The states after *Webster* have the opportunity to formulate some of the rules governing abortion, which *Roe* had almost entirely removed from their jurisdiction. *Webster* is seen by most observers as a retreat from *Roe*, but a retreat that does not fundamentally damage the notion of a woman's right to an abortion. The major question that arises from *Webster* is whether the case was a stage to the eventual goal of overruling of *Roe* or whether it was an end in itself. Did *Webster* reflect the Court's wish to return to the states and the political process some capacity to design the rules governing abortion, or was it just an initial decision in the process of removing the constitutional right to an abortion? The answer to this question is not known at this stage. There is a range of views over how the Court will treat the issue of abortion in particular, as there is over the general direction of the Rehnquist Court. What is certain, however, is that the Rehnquist Court will be very closely observed over the next few years, not only to evaluate its response to the issue of abortion but to decide whether the long promised judicial counter-revolution has finally arrived.

Although the future direction and thrust of the Rehnquist Court cannot be predicted with any confidence, there can be no doubt that the judgements issued by the Court will have a very substantial impact on American society. Whether the long-promised counter-revolution occurs or not, the Rehnquist Court will leave an important mark on the society and polity. Indeed, ever since *Marbury* v. *Madison*, the federal courts, and above all the Supreme Court, have been making public policy. The courts, as much as the President, Congress and the states, have determined the fate of the economy, slavery, civil rights and civil liberties, issues which had been placed at the top of the nation's political agenda. The Supreme Court cannot avoid the inescapable reality of the political system of the United States that its judgements have a profound impact on the American polity. As long ago as 1835, Alexis de Tocqueville noted: 'Americans have given their courts immense political power...the peace, prosperity and very existence of the Union rest continually in the hands of these...judges' (de Tocqueville, 1966, pp. 124, 185). But if the Supreme Court has such a profound political impact, is it a legal body? Can it best be understood as a judicial or a political institution? Are its members judges or politicians? These are questions that have been asked continually over the past two hundred years; one of the reasons why they have been posed repeatedly is that they are not easy questions to answer.

3.3 The Supreme Court: law and politics

The Supreme Court and all the federal courts clearly inhabit an intensely political environment – a fact which is reinforced by the process of judicial appointment. From the very foundation of the Republic the appointment of Supreme Court justices has been controlled not by the requirements of the judicial and legal process, but by the imperatives of presidential and congressional politics. Presidents and Senators have not been interested in the judicial ability and legal competence of their nominees, other than to avoid embarrassment; they have usually been too busy ensuring their candidate's political acceptability. Indeed, if there is a continuous strand which links all judicial appointments, it is that Presidents have sought to use the appointments in order to reinforce their own political position. The precise nature of the advantage varies from case to case, but there are certain common themes that can be identified.

The first, and perhaps the most standard, motive is the politics of presidential recognition. If the President wishes to inform a social or religious minority, or even a particular region, that it is held in especially high esteem, then an appointment to the Supreme Court of a member of that group has been a traditional form of presidential patronage. Thus in the early nineteenth century regional considerations loomed large in appointments, but by the latter half of the century religious factors had become increasingly important. The absence of a Catholic and Jewish seat on the current Court is only a recent development. But in keeping with the tradition, President Lyndon B. Johnson appointed the first black to the Court in 1965, and President Reagan's nomination of Justice O'Connor was perceived correctly as a gesture to the growing importance of women in the political process. The rationale behind all of these considerations is either to secure or improve the President's political standing with the specific group.

A second motive is to influence directly the Court's decision. On the face of it this appears to suggest that Presidents do take an interest in legal matters and do consider the judicial and legal abilities of their appointees. In fact, presidential attempts to alter the Court's direction have usually arisen because the Supreme Court is suffering a temporary bout of unpopularity. Presidents have seized on this fact and have attempted to translate the Court's unpopularity into support for themselves. President Nixon and President Roosevelt provide examples. This is a route, however, that is fraught with political danger, as both Presidents discovered. Roosevelt's 'Court packing plan' came to nought, and Nixon's intention to 'pack' the Court with 'strict constructionists' ran into difficulty with the Senate, which refused to confirm two of his nominees, Harold Carswell and Clement Haynsworth – the first time the Senate had refused to confirm a Supreme Court nomination for half a century.

A third reason for presidential appointments is a trade of political favours. The trade can take various forms. There were, for instance, the alleged arrangements between candidate Eisenhower and Warren at the Republican convention of 1952: Warren's support was to be rewarded with a seat on the Court. More commonly, a judicial appointment is a reward for past services; but the fact that appointment to the Court is only within the President's gift does focus the mind and loyalty of the potential recipient.

All three of these factors operate within the context of presidential politics. The central question that the President asks is, 'whose appointment will maximize my political advantage?' Consequently the composition of the Supreme Court is mostly dependent on the imperatives of presidential politics. So if the membership of the Court is highly politicized and its rulings have an enormous political impact, then the Supreme Court must be a political institution. Unfortunately the position is not quite so straightforward.

There is a recurrent theme in presidential observations about their judicial appointments. Eisenhower's disenchantment with Warren is well documented. Not so well known is Eisenhower's disappointment with Justice Brennan, another of the leading figures on the Warren Court; and his unhappiness is matched by that of other Presidents. Nixon was not overdelighted by the performance of his appointees, notably Justices Blackmun and Powell, and President Harry Truman said that his biggest mistake was 'Putting Tom Clark on the Supreme Court of the Unites States. That damn fool from Texas' (Miller, 1974, p.242). Almost every President has expressed regrets, perhaps not as emphatically as Truman, over some of their appointees. Part of the explanation for this collective disillusionment is that the process of appointment is dominated by immediate political factors, and that Presidents and their advisers rarely think about medium- and longer-term considerations. A more substantial reason, however, is that Presidents have never really appreciated the unusual character of the Supreme Court. They have thought of it as just another, albeit very important, political body. But if, indeed, it is a political institution, then it is a political institution of a very distinctive kind.

On 27 May 1935, the New Deal suffered its worst ever day in the Supreme Court. On this 'Black Monday' President Roosevelt turned to his aides and asked bitterly: 'Well, where was Ben Cardozo? And what about old Isaiah?' (Gerhart, 1958, p.130). Justices Benjamin Cardozo and Louis D. Brandeis were seen by the Roosevelt administration as friends and yet, on that day, the two judges had joined with the other seven in finding two Acts and one executive order unconstitutional. To Roosevelt, such behaviour was hard to understand. Even though Roosevelt had not appointed Brandeis and Cardozo, he saw them as friends; consequently their judgements smacked of disloyalty. Roosevelt's reaction of surprise and irritation was identical to that of all Presidents in similar circumstances. But to Brandeis and Cardozo, loyalty to the Roosevelt administration did not enter their calculations. Their decisions in the three cases were not determined by their support, or the lack of it, for the New Deal, but the fact that the Supreme Court is also a legal institution. Constitutional and legal considerations far outweighed any others. Indeed, the legal process provides the structure, the context within which the Court operates. The Supreme Court, like any other Anglo-American court, is not in control of which cases it hears. It is dependent on the vagaries of litigation. The Supreme Court does not have the power to commence proceedings; it is in that sense, like other courts, a reactive institution. Furthermore, the Supreme Court is almost exclusively an appellate court. Although in a few but rarely used categories it is a court of original jurisdiction, the overwhelming majority of its case-load is composed of appeals from the lower federal courts and the state court system. The Supreme Court, in fact, does exercise discretion over which appeals it will hear, as it receives far more cases than it can possibly cope with, but its discretion is not unfettered, and moreover an appeal must be made in the first place. So while its discretionary powers over appeals allow it to shape its workload to a certain extent, fundamentally it is controlled by the numerous individual decisions of litigants and their lawyers.

The fact that Supreme Court judges are not just another variant of *homo politicus* is also evident in the process of judicial decision-making. A politician may cast a vote in any way that he or she pleases, subject, of course, to the knowledge that he or she will have to justify the decision to the electorate in the near future. A judge, on the other hand, in cases involving constitutional interpretation, is constrained by several factors. First, he or she must weigh the intentions of the Founding Fathers. Second, the judge must take into account two hundred subsequent years of judicial interpretation of the Constitution. Third, and despite some examples to the contrary, stability, continuity and the evolutionary development of the law, rather than any dramatic change in direction, are important determinants of a judicial decision. These are the characteristics of a legal decision, and they distinguish it from a political decision. But of course, judges can, if they wish, ignore the characteristics which make a legal decision unique; they do not have an electorate looking over their shoulder who can dismiss them. They can, indeed, make their decisions on the basis of liking the New Deal, preferring affirmative action and supporting the Bush administration. But the vast majority of the federal judiciary over the past two centuries have believed that it is their judicial duty to interpret the Constitution and not to impose their personal political preferences. Judges have constantly noted the difference between their own personal predilections and what the Constitution requires or permits; they have had no difficulty in distinguishing between their public duty and their private beliefs. However, this must not be read to suggest that the judicial task is only reliant on recognizing the difference between private beliefs and public duty. For even when that recognition takes place, the task of a judge is fraught with difficulties. Judges, like anyone else, can unconsciously come to believe that their public duty and personal views are one and the same, although there is no shortage of critics on and off the bench to tell them what they are doing. But, more significantly, even when judges do set out just to interpret the Constitution, they can arrive at very different conclusions. They do so because constitutional interpretation is an art, not a science. It is imprecise and inexact; it permits considerable room for disagreement and it is enormously difficult. The Founding Fathers' intentions are often unclear, as is the collective voice of the Supreme Court over two centuries. Nor is the process of constitutional adaptation any easier to achieve. But it is important to establish that the Supreme Court does attempt to read the minds of the Founding Fathers and its predecessors, because it informs us of a unique characteristic of the American political system.

The Supreme Court is at the heart of the American political process. The nine justices on the Court resolve the great political issues of the day, but they are justices and not politicians. The process by which they make their judgements is different from that of members of Congress or Senators. They are not interested in public opinion. Indeed, they have been deliberately isolated from the electorate. They have no contact, no real intimacy with the wider public. Supreme Court justices do not have a structured mechanism for divining public opinion. Thus they do not know and cannot know what people want. Yet in a nation that prides itself on the quality of its democracy, nine unelected judges can decide the fate of a society. It is, perhaps, the central paradox of twentieth-century American democracy.

References

EIDELBERG, P. (1968) *The Philosophy of the Constitution,* New York, Free Press.

GERHART, E. (1958) *American's Advocate: Robert H. Jackson,* Indianapolis and New York, Bobbs-Merrill.

MILLER, M. (1974) *Plain Speaking,* New York and Berkeley, Medallion Books.

ROSSITER, C. (ed.) (1961) *The Federalist Papers,* New York, Mentor.

TOCQUEVILLE, A. DE (1966) *Democracy in America,* 2 vols, London, Fontana.

Further reading

BLASI, V. (ed.) (1983) *The Burger Court: The Revolution that Wasn't,* New Haven, Yale University Press.

HODDER-WILLIAMS, R. (1980) *The Politics of the US Supreme Court,* London, Allen and Unwin.

McCLOSKEY, R. G. (1960) *The American Supreme Court,* Chicago, University of Chicago Press.

4   The Presidency

The American political culture is and always has been ambivalent about political power. It is a culture that is fascinated by power and its attributes. The accumulation of it, whether it is political or economic, is an indicator of success, and those who possess it exude a certain kind of glamour. But Americans have also been inculcated with the belief that power can seduce and corrupt. The institutions of government may require it and government officials may need to exercise it, but power is also profoundly dangerous. The institution that is perhaps most affected by this ambivalence is the presidency.

The Founding Fathers, conscious of the colonial experience, created an institution which reflected their fears of executive tyranny, but they would almost certainly be dismayed by the development of the presidency. It is not, nor has it been for most of the past two centuries, the institution which restrains the wayward desires of the Congress, and more particularly the House of Representatives. The President has not been the aloof figure, distant from the political fray, that was originally envisaged. Indeed, American history sometimes appears to be composed, almost exclusively, of a series of images – images of Presidents leading the nation through periods of crisis and travail. There is George Washington, the father of the nation, guiding the country though its turbulent early years, and Abraham Lincoln, the great emancipator, freeing the slaves and saving the Union. In the twentieth century, there is a vivid picture of Franklin D. Roosevelt preventing the collapse of the economy during the Great Depression. In between the scenes of these three 'great' Presidents, there are the portraits of the lesser, but only slightly lesser, figures of Thomas Jefferson, Andrew Jackson, Woodrow Wilson and Harry S. Truman, also rescuing the country from crises of only marginally slighter magnitude.

The President as hero is located prominently in the collective American consciousness. However, this notion has had to coexist uneasily with the fear that Presidents can become too powerful. Roosevelt may have saved the nation in the 1930s, but he was also the cause of the Twenty-second Amendment, which states that 'no person shall be elected to the office of the President more than twice'. The traumas produced by the Vietnam War and the Watergate affair reinforced these deep-seated fears. So Presidents, particularly those in the twentieth century, have sought political success without making themselves vulnerable to the charge of dictator. It is not an easy task, but if a President is indecisive or not assertive enough, then he is in danger of being classified as weak and of not fitting the heroic mould. Hero or weakling, dictator or incompetent, are charges that have been hurled at numerous Presidents. These accusations reflect America's profound ambivalence over power. Presidential power both repels and attracts – an awkward fact with which Presidents have had to live.

4.1   The growth of the presidency

The Founding Fathers, as was noted in Chapter 2, had less guidance over the presidency than with any of the other institutions; as a result, it is unsurprising that their intentions went awry. From 1789 onwards, Presidents have been more influential participants in the political process than the framers of the Constitution anticipated. The Founding Fathers envisaged a patrician figure controlling the populist instincts of the House of Representatives. In fact, by the 1830s the presidency had succumbed to the democratic impulses that were abroad in the nation. From Andrew Jackson onwards, the presidency became the people's institution, the political focus of their hopes and aspirations. This irrevocably altered the relationship between the presidency and the other institutions of both state and federal government. After Jackson, only the President spoke with an authentic national voice. He represented a mass national constituency, while Congress and the state legislatures reflected local and special interests. Jackson claimed to speak for the entire nation, and the reality of that claim modified the constitutional balance of 1787.

Of course, Jackson's achievement was not universally welcomed. 'I look upon Jackson as a detestable, ignorant, reckless, vain and malignant tyrant', wrote Chancellor Kent, 'This American elective monarchy frightens me'. Henry Clay, another figure of considerable political weight, also found Jackson's presidency unhappy: 'We are in the midst of a revolution, hitherto bloodless, but tending rapidly towards...the concentration of all power in the hands of one man' (Corwin, 1948, p.24). However, Kent, Clay and others of a similar political persuasion soon realized that the Jacksonian 'revolution' was permanent. Jackson had not created an elective monarchy, but he had democratized the presidency and there was no political advantage – indeed there was considerable disadvantage – in resisting the fact.

A further reason why the Founding Fathers' intentions were not fulfilled was that the presidency soon proved to be the only institution capable of acting with dispatch. An early indication of this ability was Thomas Jefferson's purchase of the vast territory of French Louisiana in 1803, without consulting the Congress. Presidents were able to act swiftly, particularly in a crisis, and the Civil War provided President Lincoln with the occasion for a dramatic exercise in executive power. In some senses, Lincoln did become a 'dictator' for the duration of the conflict.

> Unquestionably the high-water mark of the exercise of executive power is found in the administration of Abraham Lincoln. No President before or since has pushed the boundaries of executive power so far into the legislative sphere. No-one can ever know just what Lincoln conceived to be the limits of his powers. Even a political review of them presents an imposing list of daring adventures. Under the war power, he proclaimed the slaves of those in rebellion emancipated. He devised and put into execution his peculiar plan of reconstruction. In disregard of law, he increased the army and navy beyond the limits set by statute. The privilege of the writ of *habeus corpus* was suspended wholesale and martial law declared. Public money in the sum of millions was deliberately spent without congressional appropriation.
>
> (Binkley, 1947, p.127)

In the next major crisis that confronted the United States, the First World War, Woodrow Wilson, like Lincoln, took the reins of decision-making into his hands. The Congress was relegated into a subordinate and much diminished role. This presidential dominance was also evident in crises of less grave proportions. George Washington called out troops to put down an insurrection by farmers in Pennsylvania because they were unhappy over a tax on the manufacture of whisky. Similarly, in events that foreshadowed the Civil War, Andrew Jackson dealt with the problem that arose from South Carolina's claim in 1832 that it could nullify an Act of Congress. Jackson issued a proclamation to the people of South Carolina dismissing nullification as an 'absurdity'. In these and other emergencies, the presidency was the only institution capable of coping with the circumstances. The Congress was an inchoate body, incapable of making decisions quickly. Senators and Representatives required leadership, and Presidents were not unwilling to seize the opportunity.

However, the history of the presidency through the nineteenth and early twentieth centuries did not see a consistent expansion of presidential authority. There was an ebb and flow of presidential power because the presidency flourished during emergencies which are, by definition, a temporary condition, a period of extraordinary events; but when normality was restored, presidential domination also came to an end. The fear of dictatorship re-emerged, and Congress reasserted itself. Indeed, throughout this time there was almost a cycle of presidential domination followed by a sequence of congressional reassertion. Lincoln's successors, Andrew Johnson and Ulysses S. Grant, had to deal with a Congress determined to reassert itself. Similarly, the Presidents who followed Wilson into office, Warren Harding and Calvin Coolidge, were forced to take a back seat to the Congress.

If, by the 1920s, the presidency had established its primacy in the political process during crisis, it had to accept an equal relationship with the Congress at other times. Indeed, in some ways during these periods of normality the Congress was frequently the more influential policy-maker. Legislation, for instance, was almost exclusively devised within the Congress; the presidential role only encompassed the decision on whether to exercise the veto. The tempo of politics in the nineteenth and twentieth centuries was such that there was time for the rather ponderous machinery of the Congress to deal with the political demands that were being made. Moreover, the scale of demands was limited. Until the 1930s, the federal government's arena of politics, by contrast to that which exists today, was narrowly defined. The extent of governmental activity in both the economy and society was slight. Although the federal government did not ignore demands to ameliorate the impact of industrialization, the profile of governmental intervention in comparison with the current array of programmes was minimal. Furthermore, United States foreign policy, apart from the First World War, was based on the doctrine of isolationism, which meant that American relations with the rest of the world, apart from the Western hemisphere, were not extensive. The United States did not play a full role in the world community until the nation entered the Second World War in 1941. The complex web of alliances, treaties and military commitments which led to the stationing of American troops abroad has only been a feature of the post-1945 world. Consequently, Congress, until the 1920s, was able to process the demands that entered the political arena, but that political arena was about to be transformed.

4.2 The modern presidency (1933–)

The Great Depression, if it did not start, certainly accelerated a fundamental change in political behaviour in the United States. Until the 1930s, economic and social reform, when sought, was usually channelled through the political system of the states. This must not be read to mean that federal legislation in this area was non-existent, but that the overwhelming majority of such legislation was passed by the states. There were numerous reasons for this position, the most important being the legitimacy of federal intervention in the economy and society. The courts, throughout the nineteenth and early twentieth centuries, were cautious but inexact over the precise constitutional reach of the federal government. This uncertainty undoubtedly affected the numerous participants in the political process, who, on the whole, did not turn to the federal government to solve their problems. Voters and other actors in the political process, if they required political solutions, looked to state legislatures and governors. The presidency and the Congress were not seen as the appropriate bodies to deal with a range of social and economic issues; they did not possess the legitimacy to do so.

The Great Depression transformed this notion of legitimacy. The sheer scale of economic dislocation and hardship overwhelmed the states. Their inadequacy was revealed, and both the general public and the special interests turned to the federal government for recovery and reform. The administration of Franklin D. Roosevelt was not reluctant to respond, and from the New Deal onwards the federal government has become the principal recipient of demands for governmental interventions, demands which, over the succeeding half-century, have been made with increasing frequency and have been of a much more elaborate nature. As a result, in the 1980s the range of federal government activities is nearly as extensive as those of other Western democracies. The American welfare state is not as complete as its Western European counterparts, but it is, nonetheless, in place. The federal government does not provide quite as many services as the governments of Britain and France, but what it does provide currently is incomparably greater than the range of services offered before 1933.

The impact of these developments on the political process has been dramatic. The Congress has been unable to cope with the scale and pace of these claims on the general government. It has lacked the expertise and the time to process these demands; only the presidency, through an enormously expanded federal bureaucracy, has been able to undertake this task. In this sense the United States has been little different from other Western democracies, which have also experienced a rapid increase in the size of their bureaucracies because of the growing responsibility of their central governments for social and economic problems.

Just as significant as the growth of the federal civil service has been Congress's willingness to accept that it is not only the responsibility of the executive branch to administer these new laws, but that it is also incumbent on the presidency to devise new programmes and to suggest a list of priorities over which proposals and policies should be enacted into law. From the New Deal onwards the President has presented annually to the Congress a comprehensive legislative programme. While the Congress has never endorsed a presidential programme in its entirety, the legislative outcome each year reveals the dependence of the Congress on the President's proposals. Although the Congress usually amends or rejects a substantial percentage of the legislative programme, the President's programme nevertheless establishes the context and reference of congressional debate. In the United States, as in other Western political systems, the growth of governmental services has caused the balance of power to swing decisively away from the legislature towards the executive. In the United States, however, this presidential ascendancy has been reinforced by the end of American isolationism.

The conduct of foreign policy has always been a source of difficulty for the Congress. Diplomacy requires secrecy and speed, and the Congress is not noted for either. Hence the presidency has always been pre-eminent over the making of foreign policy – a pre-eminence that has been a matter of some concern. The concern was muted until 1941 because foreign policy, apart from a few temporary episodes, did not loom large on the nation's political agenda. However, since 1941 it could be argued persuasively that the involvement of the United States in the world community has dominated the politics of the past half-century. The nation turned its attention away from domestic matters and towards the cold war, the intricacies of American–Soviet relations and the concomitant strategic and military issues.

This movement of foreign policy from the periphery of the American political stage immeasurably enhanced the presidency. The presidency now 'controlled' the dominant issue of American politics. The modern presidency has thus emerged in response to the growth of the state at home and the exercise of American power abroad, developments which have substantially altered the American constitutional balance. However, it should not be assumed that because the modern presidency is a more influential participant in the making of public policy, the President is able to impose his personal will more easily than his predecessors. Indeed, in some senses the reverse is true, for paradoxically the very developments that have enhanced the presidency have also created new and formidable difficulties for the President.

4.3   The institutions of the modern presidency

The presidency's expanded role within the political process has had a substantial impact on its internal organization. The presidency has had to adjust to and accommodate its growing responsibilities, and perhaps the most striking and visible change has occurred in the federal bureaucracy.

Table 4.1

Departments	Date of establishment
State	1789
Treasury	1789
Interior	1849
Justice	1870
Agriculture	1889
Commerce	1913
Labor	1913
Defense	1949
Housing and Urban Development	1965
Transportation	1966
Health and Human Services	1977
Energy	1979
Education	1979

The bureaucracy is not a creation of the modern presidency. It came into existence along with the Constitution in 1789 in order to enable the President to fulfil his constitutional responsibility of administration. Initially, three departments were created, those of the Treasury, State and War, and over the next two centuries, new departments were formed while others were closed or merged, so that by 1985 there were thirteen executive departments (see Table 4.1). Given the extraordinary changes in the nature of government, this has been a modest rise in the number of executive departments, but it is an increase that disguises the spectacular growth in the number of civilian employees, which has risen from a few hundred in 1789 to a current figure of approximately three million. Moreover, two and a half million of that figure have been added since 1933. The dramatic expansion and sheer size of the federal civil service has created a series of problems for the President, although the roots of these problems have been of a rather longer standing.

The duty of the federal bureaucracy is clear, and its lines of control are explicit. It is there to assist the President and to follow his orders. However, Presidents have discovered that the real world is rarely that simple. All Presidents have found it difficult to enforce their instructions and to ensure that their directives are carried out in the way they were intended, a fact to which Franklin D. Roosevelt has attested:

> The Treasury is so large and far-flung and ingrained in its practices that I find it almost impossible to get the action and results I want...But the Treasury is not to be compared with the State Department. You should go through the experience of trying to get any changes in the thinking, policy and action of the career diplomats and then you'd know what a real problem was. But the Treasury and the State Department put together are nothing compared with the Na-a-vy. The admirals are really something to cope with...To change anything in the Na-a-vy is like punching a feather bed. You punch it with your right and you punch it with your left until you are finally

exhausted and then you find the damn bed just as it was before you started punching.

(Rossiter, 1960, pp.60, 61)

Roosevelt's wry observation has been replaced by a harder edge of hostility, for Presidents, since then, have been under far greater pressures. Their growing responsibilities have reduced the time to monitor their instructions through an increasingly complex bureaucratic hierarchy. As a result, presidential directives disappear within the bureaucratic maze in Washington, and so presidential frustration and antagonism have grown. All modern Presidents, regardless of party and their location on the ideological spectrum, have seen the civil service, their nominal subordinate, as a political enemy, and in some cases as their principal opponent. The Washington bureaucracy is now perceived by Presidents as a serious competitor for power, limiting and reducing their range of options. So why have Presidents developed this view? There are numerous reasons, but the various reasons have a common strand: that the President and the bureaucracy have divergent interests.

The presidential attitude towards the federal bureaucracy is governed by this central perception, that the members of the civil service no longer serve the interests of the President. They do not serve the President for two separate but closely linked reasons. The first, and most commonly mentioned, reason is that of 'clientelism'. The bureaucracy, according to a frequently recited presidential complaint, identify themselves not with the President but with those groups and institutions – clients – with whom they have forged a close and intimate relationship. The civil servants no longer see themselves as ambassadors of the President but rather as representatives of their clients. Presidents do not believe, for example, that the Department of Agriculture will be an effective advocate for their policies and programmes to those who work in and service the agricultural sector, because the primary loyalty of the Department is not to the President but to those agricultural interests. In any conflict between those interests and the President, the Department will not side with the President, and indeed will, if necessary, hinder and sabotage presidential policy. Nor is the Department of Agriculture unique; all the other executive departments are equally culpable in presidential estimation. The Department of Defense is in thrall to the large corporations who manufacture military equipment, and the Department of Labor is beholden to the labour unions. The list can be extended easily.

Unsurprisingly, Presidents are dissatisfied with this position, and over the past few decades several Presidents have used their powers of appointment to restore their control over the bureaucracy, powers which are considerably more substantial than they are in Britain, for instance. Political appointments extend far beyond the top echelon of the civil service, reaching well into the middle ranks. Nevertheless, the confidence of successive Presidents, at the outset of their administration, that they could deal with the bureaucracy has evaporated gradually. Their appointees not only fail to control the bureaucrats but usually succumb to the blandishments of the civil service. 'Going native' was how John Ehrlichman, Special Assistant to

President Nixon, described the phenomenon of political appointees, including members of the Cabinet, being 'captured by the bureaucracy' (Hess, 1976, p.199).

The net result of 'clientelism' and the inability of Presidents to counteract it is that the President profoundly distrusts the federal bureaucracy. Presidents have no faith in its ability to administer impartially and, more importantly, distrust its advice. The advice, they feel, is tainted because the bureaucracy owes its allegiance elsewhere. Consequently, they do not want to hear the advice and they wish to keep the civil service at a distance – a desire that is reinforced by the divergent political perspectives of the President and the federal bureaucracy.

Even when the President has no reason to be suspicious of the bureaucracy's motives, he often finds their advice unhelpful, and on occasion worse than unhelpful. The presidential agenda is rarely static. New problems arise and old ones depart from the agenda with startling rapidity. As a result, Presidents have to be briefed on a wide array of issues, and although their individual capacity to absorb material varies, all Presidents have made known their distaste for long memoranda and over-elaborate analyses. They prefer their information easily digestible, with policy options clearly labelled and explicitly stated. They want clarity and above all decisiveness, which not only helps them to deal with the problem but also assists them when they have to explain their actions to a wider electorate. Complexity, by contrast, blurs the presidential vision, but, unfortunately, complexity is a hallmark of bureaucratic advice, not out of a desire to be unhelpful but because civil servants are specialists. Unlike Presidents, they do not divide their time between a large number of issues, but concentrate their attention on a narrowly defined area which they get to know extremely well. Their knowledge fosters complexity, it encourages the search for problems, and makes them aware of the inadequacies in all the alternative courses of action. So they frequently counsel caution, emphasizing difficulties, which Presidents rarely wish to hear. Presidents want their world neatly divided and painted in sharply contrasting colours. Instead, they receive from the bureaucracy a portrait where the lines are blurred and confused and coloured in varying shades of grey. The presidential and bureaucratic perspectives are simply very different. So, once again, Presidents do not want to listen and wish to insulate themselves from the federal bureaucracy, and they have succeeded to a large extent. The ramifications, however, have been considerable.

The Cabinet

The Cabinet, which contains the heads of all the executive departments, plus those whom the President chooses to invite, has suffered from the modern President's disregard for the bureaucracy, although it has never ranked high in presidential estimation. It was Abraham Lincoln who was reported to have rejected the unanimous vote of his Cabinet: 'Seven noes, one aye – the ayes have it' (Fenno, 1959, p.29). Lincoln's remark, apocryphal or not, does illustrate the fact that 'No situation is more a body of one man's men than the American President's Cabinet' (Daniels, 1946, p.29).

Therefore the influence of the Cabinet has varied according to presidential taste, although it would be broadly accurate to say that until the 1930s, Presidents did rely on their Cabinets for counsel. However, from Franklin D. Roosevelt onwards, the Cabinet as an instrument of government has waned in influence. The decline has not been uninterrupted, because some Presidents, particularly Dwight D. Eisenhower, used their Cabinets more than others. Eisenhower, however, did not arrest the Cabinet's decline, which resumed under subsequent Presidents. Interestingly, most subsequent Presidents, including Jimmy Carter and Ronald Reagan, noted the Cabinet's decline and promised to restore its prominence; equally interestingly, these promises have not been fulfilled. So why has the power of the Cabinet waned?

The Cabinet as an instrument of collective decision-making has never been that influential. Whatever influence it did possess received a fatal blow from Roosevelt's dislike of Cabinet discussion and his preference for dealing with Cabinet members on an individual basis. Cabinet discussions were perfunctory and no real business was transacted. Since Roosevelt, no President, bar Eisenhower, has used the Cabinet as a forum for the making of public policy. However, the power of individual members of the Cabinet has not declined quite so precipitately. The Secretary of State was, and still is, a powerful political actor, and that is still true for the Secretaries of Defense and the Treasury; even so, their individual influence has diminished. Presidents have seen them increasingly as spokesmen for their Departments and consequently they have suffered a similar fall from presidential grace as the bureaucracy. Presidents do not trust their Cabinets, they are wary of their advice. A member of President Nixon's Cabinet, Walter Hickel, the Secretary of the Interior, was even unable to arrange a meeting with the President. Nixon's distaste for his Cabinet may have been unusually vehement, but it does indicate the suspicion and low regard that Presidents have for the members of the Cabinet. It also indicates the importance and influence of the Executive Office of the President, which has in part replaced the bureaucracy and the Cabinet in presidential affection.

The Executive Office

'The President needs help', declared the President's Committee on Administrative Management in 1937. The pressures on him had multiplied to the point, the Committee believed, where the President could not be expected to fulfil his constantly growing responsibilities without an enlarged presidential office. Accordingly, two years later in 1939, President Roosevelt established by executive order the Executive Office of the President. It was a decision that was seen as significant at the time, but even so no one foresaw how profound an impact the creation of the Executive Office was to have on the American governmental process. The increase in its size from barely 1,000 employees in 1940 to over 5,000 in 1985 is one indication of its rise in governmental importance. But the increase in numbers, dramatic though it is, understates the far greater rise in its influence, for the Executive Office has become the principal instrument of presidential government. The President now relies on it to provide him with the information, the analysis and the policy recommendations, activities that were previously controlled by the federal bureaucracy and the Cabinet. The resources of the Executive Office are such that it can fulfil these presidential demands, a conclusion that emerges from even a brief examination of its structure.

The Executive Office is composed of a number of organizations, of which only one, the White House Office, was also created in 1939. The others, apart from the Office of Management and the Budget, which was already in existence, have been added to the structure at different times and reflect the growing responsibilities of the presidency. The principal organizations are the National Security Council, the White House Office, the Office of Management and the Budget, the Council of Economic Advisers, and the Office of Policy Development.

The National Security Council (NSC) was formed in 1947 to advise the President on 'domestic, foreign and military policies relating to the national security'. From its creation it has been a serious and successful competitor for power with both the Department of Defense and the State Department, but particularly the latter. Presidents, regardless of party, have relied on it and its principal officer, the National Security Adviser, to a far greater extent than the State Department and the Secretary of State. In every administration since Eisenhower, the National Security Adviser has been a far more significant policy-maker than the Secretary of State. McGeorge Bundy overshadowed Dean Rusk in the administration of John F. Kennedy, as did W.W. Rostow when he became National Security Adviser in the Johnson administration. Zbigniew Brzezinski emerged as the principal foreign policy adviser in the Carter administration. Carter's Secretary of State, Cyrus Vance, resigned when his advice was ignored over the attempt to rescue the American hostages being held in Iran. President Reagan's second National Security Adviser, William Clark, had far greater access to the President, a fact which undoubtedly contributed to the frustration and eventual resignation of Reagan's first Secretary of State, Alexander Haig. However, the most striking instance of presidential preference for the NSC occurred in the first Nixon administration, when Nixon's Secretary of State, William Rogers, was barely informed, let alone consulted, over certain key areas of foreign policy. One of the most substantial foreign policy achievements of the Nixon administration, the *rapprochement* with China, was planned by the President and his National Security Adviser, Henry Kissinger, in the confines of the White House. Nixon and Kissinger were the architects of the policy, while the Secretary of State and the entire apparatus of the State Department were excluded from the decision-making process. President Nixon's disdain for the State Department was unusual in its intensity, but his preference for the NSC has been shared by most Presidents.

The White House Office was created in 1939 and is staffed by those aides who are closest politically to the President. They are drawn from those who have had a long association with the President and have assisted him in the nomination and general election campaigns. These aides see the President far more frequently than anyone else and they are given the tasks of managing the White House and controlling access to the President, tasks which have high visibility. Consequently the White House staff have a significant impact on moulding the public perception of the administration. The success of President Reagan's first administration, indicated in the opinion polls and subsequently in his overwhelming election victory, was due in no small part to the triumvirate that organized the Reagan White House: Chief of Staff James Baker, Deputy Chief of Staff Michael Deaver, and Counsel to the President Edwin Meese. They managed the White House smoothly, diverting the controversial and potentially damaging issues away from the President and thereby preserving Reagan's genial and non-partisan public persona. By contrast, Nixon's aides Bob Haldeman and John Ehrlichman exacerbated the difficulties of the Nixon administration. They presented a public face that was, in turn, taciturn and aggressive. Undoubtedly, they ran the White House according to their perception of President Nixon's wishes, but, in doing so, they reinforced those characteristics of the President that were to prove so damaging. In order to protect the President's privacy, they made Nixon inaccessible to those who were not part of the President's inner circle. In this claustrophobic and inbred atmosphere, Nixon's instinct that the world outside the White House was populated with his enemies conspiring against the administration, flourished with disastrous consequences. The experience of the Nixon and Reagan administrations is not unique, for the White House staff have emerged as key political figures in every administration of the modern presidency and to a considerable extent the political success of an administration is dependent on them.

The Office of Management and the Budget (OMB), in its earlier manifestation as the Bureau of the Budget, was established in 1921 and was incorporated into the Executive Office in 1939, where it has been and continues to be one of the most important weapons in the President's armoury. Each year the OMB constructs the budget and produces the President's legislative programme. Both of these tasks require the OMB to ask for and receive the financial and legislative requirements of the entire federal government. This comprehensive annual survey of the federal government gives the President a substantial advantage, because it results in the only full picture of all the activities of the federal government and it is a presidential picture. The Congress and the bureaucracy rely on it. The Congress may modify individual elements, but it cannot provide an alternative portrait, although the Congress has attempted to establish its own source of economic and financial information through the creation of the Congressional Budget Office (CBO) in 1974. However, the formation of the CBO is an indication of Congress's sense of disadvantage over its reliance on the OMB, a sense that has abated but not disappeared.

The Council of Economic Advisers (CEA) was established in 1946 to advise the President on economic policy. Its formation ended the President's reliance on the Treasury Department, a development welcomed by most Presidents who have trusted the CEA to a greater extent than the Treasury bureaucracy, although the influence of the CEA has fluctuated more widely than most of the other institutions of the Executive Office.

The Office of Policy Development (OPD) was created in 1981 by President Reagan to advise him on domestic policy. Its formation was, in some senses, an attempt to reconstitute the Domestic Council, an Executive

Office agency established by President Nixon in 1970. Nixon wished to create a domestic equivalent to the National Security Council. He wanted the Domestic Council to formulate and co-ordinate domestic policy recommendations, and under John Ehrlichman the Domestic Council was one of the more influential institutions of the Executive Office. However, its star waned in the reaction to the Watergate affair, leading to its abolition in 1977 by President Carter. Interestingly, Carter found it necessary to replace the Domestic Council with a policy staff under aide Stuart Eizenstat, to advise him on domestic policies. The Office of Policy Development has, in turn, replaced the Carter structure and reflects the need that successive Presidents have felt for systematic and coherent advice on domestic policy from within the Executive Office.

The Executive Office: an overview. The Executive Office is a crucially important instrument of presidential power. It has within it the resources to construct the President's political strategies in both the domestic and foreign policy arenas. It provides him with significant advantages in his relationship with the Congress and, perhaps more significantly, it restructured the relationship between the President and the bureaucracy. The Executive Office provides the President with an alternative to bureaucratic advice, an alternative that successive Presidents have preferred for one reason more than any other: the staff of the Executive Office owe their principal allegiance to him. Their appointments are the result of either a long-term association with the President or of an intellectual and political commitment to his administration. Consequently, they take his instructions without interminable bureaucratic wrangling; their success is dependent on his success. Therefore the President trusts them. He has confidence in the staff of the Executive Office that they will safeguard his political interests. There are few discordant voices. There is less presidential suspicion and frustration. The Executive Office offers a more comfortable environment.

It is therefore unsurprising that Presidents have become reliant on the Executive Office. It enhances his power, improves his control over the process of government, and is politically congenial. The combination is irresistible. It is so irresistible that Presidents have ignored the potential dangers of their dependence on the Executive Office. Their sense of ease has concealed a degree of political isolation. Their preference for harmony has excluded voices, both congressional and bureaucratic, that disrupted the harmony. But Senators, Representatives and bureaucrats offer information, expertise and a perspective that Presidents can only ignore at their peril. Unfortunately, the modern presidency has a penchant for listening only to those who have an agreeable message. Of course, Presidents do vary: Reagan and Bush have been more accessible than most of the recent occupants of the Oval Office. However, three out of four of Reagan's immediate predecessors, Carter, Nixon and Johnson, found the national political climate increasingly unattractive and took solace in the comfort of the White House. Their presidencies suffered from their isolation. The isolation of Presidents is a problem, but it is a problem that is not always recognized at the time. Moreover, although isolation is a difficulty, it will always be subordinate to the immense advantages that Presidents derive from the Executive Office.

The Vice-Presidency

'The Vice-Presidency', said John Nance Garner, 'is not worth a pitcher of warm spit.' Garner, who was Franklin D. Roosevelt's first Vice-President, was reflecting on his own unhappy experience as Vice-President. The unhappiness of the Vice-President is almost a permanent state of affairs and results from the fact that the vice-presidential nomination at both major parties' conventions is in the gift of the candidate who has just secured the presidential nomination. The process by which presidential candidates select the vice-presidential nominee is governed by the answer to one question. Which of the available candidates will increase the chances of electoral victory? The answer, since the earliest conventions, has been a candidate who is already a substantial political figure and an erstwhile rival of the presidential nominee. While the rivalry is normally put aside, or at least concealed from public view for the duration of the election campaign, it regularly re-emerges thereafter and sours the relationship between President and Vice-President. Richard Nixon did not enjoy his eight years as Vice-President with President Eisenhower, nor did Lyndon B. Johnson find any fulfilment in his three years as Vice-President to John F. Kennedy. Interestingly, when both Johnson and Nixon became President, they had uneasy and difficult relationships with their respective Vice-Presidents, Hubert H. Humphrey and Spiro T. Agnew. The only recent relationship that has given the appearance of being satisfactory was between President Carter and his Vice-President, Walter Mondale, although even here the political problems of the Carter administration led Mondale to distance himself as discreetly as possible from the Carter White House. By contrast, the public relationship between President Reagan and George Bush existed in the context of a successful administration, but even so it was undoubtedly affected by the memory that Bush was Reagan's principal opponent for the Republican nomination in 1980, when Bush made several unkind remarks about Reagan. Furthermore, until 1980 Bush was identified with that strand of the Republican tradition that was markedly less conservative than that of Reagan and his followers, and Bush did not conceal his ambitions to succeed Reagan as President. Bush's relationship with his Vice-President, Dan Quayle, has been forced and correct rather than intimate. Quayle, who became an electoral liability because of his youth and inexperience, has been kept at a distance by the Bush White House, who are anxious not to be too closely identified with Quayle.

All these factors, at the very minimum, do not smooth the relationship between the two figures. In much the same sense that Presidents distrust the federal bureaucracy, they have distrusted their Vice-Presidents. Presidents can never be sure of their Vice-Presidents; their interests diverge. In the insecurity of the White House staff and the Executive Office, Vice-Presidents often appear as potential opponents rather than allies.

4.4 Presidential power and its limits

The social, economic and political conditions of the last fifty years have altered the balance of the American constitutional system. The changing character of the American economy and society and its relationship with the rest of the world have enhanced the power of the presidency. In a very important sense, the American political system has become a presidential system of government. The political process now requires a continued sequence of presidential initiatives in foreign policy and in the domestic political arena to function satisfactorily. Modern Presidents impose themselves with far greater effect on the political environment than their counterparts in the nineteenth century, other than those who were in office at a time of national crisis.

But while all of this is undoubtedly true, the history of the modern presidency is not a record of unparalleled success. Indeed, over the last twenty years several Presidents – Johnson, Ford, Carter and above all Nixon – have not left the White House in triumph. So why is it that if the power of the presidency has been expanded so substantially, several recent Presidents have fared so poorly? Why have Presidents, given the resources they command, not been able to impose their will on the political process? The answer lies in a delicate and intricate relationship between a political culture, political institutions, political actors and the constantly changing climate of politics. The answer must be pieced together with care.

In 1962, a poll on presidential greatness was conducted among seventy-five experts on the presidency. Most of these experts were academics, either historians or political scientists, and their collective judgements were revealing. According to the poll, five men could be considered great Presidents (Bailey, 1966, p.24). They were, in order of rank, Abraham Lincoln, George Washington, Franklin D. Roosevelt, Woodrow Wilson and Thomas Jefferson. Interestingly, they had all been men who exercised the power of the presidency to its fullest extent. They were also 'activist' Presidents who had tried to impose themselves on the political process, and clearly the combination of these characteristics was valued by those who participated in the poll. So, in one important sense, the poll informs us more about those who voted and their collective understanding of the presidency in 1962 than about the order in which they ranked the Presidents, for the early 1960s saw the apogee of enthusiasm for presidential power. The Founding Fathers' cautionary words on executive tyranny were dismissed, and a broad spectrum of opinion, extending far outside the academic community, welcomed the expansion of presidential power. Why was this so? The answer is that the United States was governed by a consensus that existed from the end of the Second World War. It was a consensus that extended to both domestic and foreign policy and which encouraged the delegation of power to the President. So what were the characteristics of this consensus? Before the consensus is outlined it is important to consider what is meant by the notion of consensus in the context of post-war American politics.

In some senses it is easier perhaps to note what consensus does not mean. It does not mean that the United States, in those years, was a nation without conflict, or that there was an absence of division. It should not be taken to suggest that the country was without problems, or that these years were an era of good feeling, where the relations between the multitude of groups and interests that constitute the US polity were characterized by sweetness and light. Nor does it mean that there was a comprehensive agreement about all aspects of domestic and foreign policy to which every sector of American society gave its approval. But if consensus does not suggest any of the above, what does it mean and what is its use in describing and analysing the post-war American political process?

The notion of consensus is used in this book to depict those periods when there was a greater degree of agreement over the fundamental construction of policy-making, and when the level and extent of debate over public policy was less intense and robust than at other times. Consensus does not mean that there was no debate and division, but it indicates something about the level and character of the debate. Perhaps this point is best illustrated by an example. The legitimacy of the welfare state was questioned less in the twenty-five years after the Second World War than either before the war or since 1975. Why was this the case? The reasons are complex and not easy to identify, but certainly the legacy of the New Deal, the great post-war economic expansion, the growing confidence over the management of the economy, the belief in the solubility of problems, and the increasing claims on the federal government, combined to create a political climate supportive of the American welfare state. Nevertheless this climate, or consensus, did not mean that all proposals to extend the government provision of welfare were welcomed. On the contrary, each proposal, whether it was for medical care for the aged or to establish new levels of minimum wages, aroused considerable debate and political activity, which resulted in some proposals being passed and others not. Thus to suggest that there was a consensus over the existence of a welfare state does not mean that there was a fixed and precise societal agreement over the exact shape and dimension of the welfare state. However, it does mean that debate over social welfare issues during those years was of a demonstrably different quality than in the periods that both preceded and succeeded those two and a half decades.

The use of consensus in this book does not conceal any hidden belief about the process through which consensus comes into existence. It should not be read as implicitly endorsing any particular analysis of policy formulation. Consensus, as deployed here, can accommodate both pluralist and elitist explanations of the political process. It is not definitionally hostile to elitist explanations, and indeed it is accepted here that certain key foreign policy issues are more amenable to elitist formulation. Surveys of the American electorate make it evident that most American voters are not very knowledgeable, let alone sophisticated, over foreign policy matters. Consequently those who make foreign policy have a greater degree of latitude, as far as the American electorate is concerned, compared with those involved in domestic policy-making. Of course, the latitude is not absolute. Foreign policy does have to be explained and justified to the electorate. Moreover, as international and internal issues have become increasingly interrelated, the differences between domestic foreign policy-making have narrowed and will continue to do so. Nevertheless, the making of foreign policy on certain issues still retains a distinctive character, with fewer participants and an electorate more willing to endorse the views of those in authority than on domestic matters. Consensus can embrace such a process of policy-making as well as those where elite views are less salient.

So consensus as used here does not imply that America was a harmonious society, nor does it impose one view of the policy-making process. Its principal role is an instrumental one, in that it allows the post-war years to be subdivided and categorized and it provides an explanation for the demonstrably different style of politics in two and a half decades after the end of the Second World War.

The post-war consensus

By the end of the Second World War, the controversy over the New Deal had abated. There was broad agreement across the party divide that the federal government had a significant role in the nation's economy and in the creation and maintenance of a welfare system. There were still those in the Republican Party, unreconstructed conservatives, who wanted to roll back the New Deal, but in 1940, 1944 and 1948 the Republicans chose presidential candidates who recognized that the New Deal was a permanent feature of the political landscape. In 1952 the Republican Party nominated Dwight D. Eisenhower, who shared the same view and whose administration did not diminish but expanded the level of governmental activity in the economy and society. Interestingly, the context of this consensus occurred at a time when there was a growing confidence in the American economy. The immediate post-war fears that the conditions of the 1930s would return were gradually eroded. Instead, the United States, along with other Western nations, embarked on one of the longest sustained periods of economic growth. The growth was linked to a Keynesian conviction that the federal government could maintain this expansion through the correct mixture of monetary and fiscal policies. Thus there was the prospect of unrivalled prosperity, a prosperity that would alleviate, in time, most of the nation's social ailments. Indeed, the two decades from the end of the war were characterized by an extraordinary degree of confidence. Certainly, the United States had its problems: an incidence of poverty that was all the more striking in the wealthiest nation, and there were difficulties with civil rights and the rising tide of crime. However, these problems and others coexisted with the widespread assumption that they were soluble. Economic growth, harnessed to the appropriate governmental policies, would resolve these difficulties.

President Johnson's legislative programme between 1964 and 1965, known as the Great Society, was fuelled by the belief that social ailments were amenable to the application of money and the correct techniques. This confidence in the combination of economic growth and social engineering enormously enhanced the presidency, for it was the only institution that possessed the expertise to devise the new policies. The Congress could not, and accepted that it could not; it looked to the President.

Of course, this did not mean that the Congress accepted every presidential proposal. John F. Kennedy, for instance, had substantial difficulties with the Congress, although Dwight D. Eisenhower persuaded the Senate and House of Representatives to pass a high percentage of his legislative programme. The most successful President in this respect was Lyndon B. Johnson during his first three years of office. The vast majority of his proposals were endorsed by the Congress. These included the War on Poverty in 1964, Medicare – the provision of medical care for the elderly – also in 1964, and the Model Cities legislation in 1965, which was a programme of urban redevelopment. These statutes were three among many that were passed and were in some senses the culmination of the New Deal agenda. They were also the high point of the post-war domestic consensus – a consensus that was about to crumble.

American foreign policy, in the two decades after the end of the Second World War, also commanded a consensus, which, if anything, aroused less dissent than its domestic counterpart. Apart from those who inhabited the fringes of political life, there was no important voice raised against the direction of US foreign policy after 1948. By then the administration of Harry S. Truman had arrived at certain judgements on the nature of the post-war world and the American position in it. These judgements were to be the foundation of foreign policy until the late 1960s. Truman and his principal advisers came to the conclusion by 1947 that the Soviet Union possessed the same instincts as pre-war Germany. It was intent on world domination. They further believed that the Soviet Union would fulfil its intentions unless the United States resisted Soviet expansion, either by the Soviet Union or by its allies, wherever it occurred on the globe. The administration came to these judgements because of its interpretation of Soviet behaviour in Eastern Europe in the immediate aftermath of the war, an interpretation that was inevitably coloured by the then dominant explanation of the origins of the Second World War. That war had resulted from the alleged inadequacy of diplomacy and the policy of appeasement to control Germany, and by the failure to use military force against Nazism earlier than 1939. The administration was determined not to repeat the same 'mistake'. However, it is not germane to this discussion to evaluate the accuracy of this perception; it is sufficient to note that it was a perception embraced by a wide spectrum of American opinion. Accordingly, and with little dissent, the United States adopted the policy of 'containment': containing the Soviet Union.

In order to achieve this policy the United States undertook the role of the world's policeman, or at least the Western world's policeman. It was a role that led the United States, which until 1941 had relied on a policy of isolationism other than during the First World War, to enter into a series of regional alliances. These alliances required American troops to be stationed abroad permanently. As a result, American military forces were involved, during this period, in two major wars, the first in Korea in the 1950s and the second in Vietnam a decade later, and in several more limited military operations in the Middle East, South-East Asia and Latin America. The financial consequences of a permanent large military establishment, another novel experience in American history, were severe. Defence expenditure regularly consumed one-third of the federal budget and yet the consensus on foreign policy remained unchallenged. The foreign policies of Truman, Eisenhower, Kennedy and Johnson all shared the same fundamental assumptions. The consensus embraced both liberal Democrats and conservative Republicans, and it was a consensus which once again enhanced the power of the presidency.

The Congress in these circumstances was only too anxious and willing to submit to presidential leadership. From time to time it might carp that successive Presidents were not 'tough' enough with the Soviet Union, but essentially Congress was prepared to give the President a *carte blanche* in matters of national security. The nation was united, and Senators and Representatives had no desire to create an impression of disharmony. Accordingly a bipartisan coalition acquiesced to most presidential initiatives, with the result that foreign policy became a presidential prerogative. Foreign policy was presidential policy, which received the almost automatic ratification of the Congress. It was an unsatisfactory position, pregnant with the possibility of presidential abuse of power.

Unfortunately, the abuse of power materialized. There were several instances, but the episodes over Vietnam and what came to be known as Watergate were the most significant. These events led several scholars to speak of an 'imperial presidency', an institution which was no longer controllable by the constitutional checks and balances. But whether Vietnam and Watergate were the result of an imperial President or the consequences of a domestic and foreign policy consensus is a matter for debate.

The Vietnam War

The American military intervention in Vietnam shattered the post-war foreign policy consensus. Ironically the intervention in the first place was brought about by the logic of that consensus. Each of the first four post-war Presidents had made decisions which led to increasing American involvement in the affairs of what was initially a part of French Indo-China and which after 1954 became South Vietnam. They increased American involvement because they believed that South-East Asia was another locus of Soviet expansionism that had to be resisted.

Thus from 1954 onwards the objective of American foreign policy was to secure the non-communist status of South Vietnam, initially by economic and then military aid, but from 1961 onwards by military forces originally in the guise of advisers. In 1965 ground troops were introduced, and by 1968 there were over half a million US military personnel in South Vietnam. Despite this level of commitment, the United States was unable to fulfil its objective. It was unable to impose its military will on the war in South Vietnam, and equally disturbingly disenchantment with the war was growing in the United States. The cumulative effect was that the United States confronted an unwinnable war, while the political will to conduct such a war was disintegrating rapidly. Inevitably in these circumstances there was a search to discover who was responsible, a search that ended at the door of the 'imperial President'.

In many senses the President was indeed responsible. Truman, Eisenhower, but especially Kennedy and Johnson, had taken the crucial decisions that had drawn the United States into the Vietnamese quagmire. Johnson in particular failed to disclose vital information to the Congress. He persuaded Congress in 1964 to pass the Gulf of Tonkin Resolution, which was the legal basis of American military intervention in Vietnam, having misled the Congress into believing that the United States was the victim of an unprovoked North Vietnamese attack.

Nevertheless, it is too easy to allocate the entire responsibility for the Vietnam War to an 'imperial President'. Despite the acts of presidential deception and secrecy, the broad strategic reasons for intervention in Vietnam were endorsed by the entire body politic. The Congress was undoubtedly misled on particular occasions, but Senators and Congressmen overwhelmingly supported the objective to maintain a non-communist South Vietnam. They supported the President, until the electorate began to grow disenchanted with the war. When the disenchantment was manifest, the political position of President Johnson and his successors became more difficult. For Vietnam was not simply an isolated foreign policy failure: Vietnam marked the end of America's role as the world's policeman. The United States could not impose its will everywhere, nor did the post-Vietnam electorate wish it to. So what was the new American role? In the aftermath of Vietnam the answers were unsure and unstable. No new consensus emerged, and in its absence the Congress was unwilling to give the President a free rein – a fact which was to have grave consequences for President Nixon.

Watergate

Watergate has become synonymous with the abuse of presidential power. Initially it referred to the attempt by President Nixon to conceal or 'cover up' a burglary organized by employees of the Committee to Re-elect the President in 1972 at the Democratic Party's national headquarters in the Watergate building in Washington DC. Subsequently Watergate has also come to refer to all the other abuses that took place in the Nixon administration, which included the use of very sensitive government agencies such as the Central Intelligence Agency (CIA), the Federal Bureau of Investigation (FBI) and the Internal Revenue Service for the private political benefit of the Nixon administration. Moreover, there were instances of bribery and successful attempts by private interests to buy influence in the Nixon White House.

How can Watergate be explained? The easiest and most readily available explanation is that the presidency was corrupted by its power, a process aided by Nixon's personality. There is an element of truth in this account. The Nixon White House was unusual in that it constantly felt threatened, it claimed to see hostile forces in nearly every section of American society, and it had an exaggerated sense of its own vulnerability; to compensate for this the White House was continually devising plans to deal with its 'enemies'. In this respect the White House was driven by the personality of the President, who, while determined to demonstrate his strength in some moods, was also prone to fear the worst at other times. It was also different in that the scale of the abuses was profoundly worrying. There was a criminal conspiracy in the White House to obstruct the investigation into the burglary. The CIA and the FBI had not been used in quite the same way, although interestingly they had been used improperly by previous Presidents: the FBI had provided President Johnson with information on his political opponents, and during the Kennedy and Johnson administrations the CIA had frequently broken the rules which prohibit it from conducting operations within the United States.

So why did Kennedy and Johnson escape the censure of the Congress while Nixon only avoided impeachment by his resignation in 1974? The answer is that during the post-war consensus, Congress was prepared to ignore presidential transgressions in the interests of national security. If Presidents wished to use, or rather misuse, the CIA or FBI to protect the national interest, then the Congress was willing to turn a blind eye. Kennedy and Johnson were given this latitude even when the national security implications were slight. However, by 1974 national security was not as potent a talisman. The electorate and its representatives after Vietnam were now unsure about what constituted national security. In other words, the consensus had collapsed and President Nixon suffered the consequences.

The Ford and Carter presidencies

If there are doubts that the post-war consensus provided the conditions for the dramatic exercise of presidential power, then the experience of the presidencies of Gerald Ford and Jimmy Carter should remove them. The political climate during their terms of office was characterized by the absence of continuity. Both foreign and domestic policies were volatile. Assumptions and objectives changed with breathtaking rapidity, a rapidity that posed very substantial political problems for both Presidents. Post-Vietnam foreign policy shifted from the *Realpolitik* of the Nixon years to a foreign policy based on the principle of human rights under President Carter. The political management of these changes, which were in effect reversals of direction, were profoundly difficult. President Ford found that he could not avoid the electoral consequences of the American voters' disenchantment with the *Realpolitik* foreign policy of the Nixon years. The Carter administration's rejection of a *Realpolitik* foreign policy was initially greeted with considerable popular enthusiasm. Its emphasis on human rights resulted in public American disapproval of those countries whose internal policies the administration found distasteful. But the electoral enthusiasm for human rights foundered in the aftermath of the Iranian revolution, when it was widely believed that President Carter had mishandled relations with Iran. Carter had distanced the United States from the Shah of Iran, an old and close American ally, because of his internally repressive policies, and consequently weakened the position of the Shah's government. Whether the United States, whatever policies it adopted, had the capability of maintaining the Shah in office was most unlikely. Nevertheless, the view that a foreign policy driven by the principle of human rights would not protect the interests of the United States led the Carter administration to diminish the importance of human rights.

These sharp changes in foreign policy carried over into other closely related matters. Attitudes towards defence expenditure were similarly volatile. Such expenditure, which was sacrosanct before Vietnam, became less than popular in the 1970s. In 1976 President Carter was committed to reducing an already sharply reduced defence budget. However, by 1979, after the Iranian revolution and the Soviet invasion of Afghanistan, the political imperatives changed and there was considerable pressure to increase the defence budget. The last two years of the Carter administration saw the start of a rising trend in defence expenditure that was to continue and accelerate under President Reagan. These sharp changes in foreign and defence policy were indicative of a polity that was profoundly uncertain of America's role in the post-Vietnam world. There were brief interludes when certain policy assumptions were implemented, only to be replaced by others within a short space of time. Until the latter years of the Reagan presidency there was no settled direction to American foreign policy, a characteristic that also affected the making of domestic policy in the 1970s.

The post-war domestic consensus ended in the urban riots of the middle to late 1960s, the inflation of the 1970s and the recession that engulfed the entire non-communist world after the rise in oil prices in 1973 and 1978. Moreover, the social problems had not disappeared, despite the allocation of increased resources in the 1960s. Illiteracy was on the increase, slums were widespread despite the urban renewal programmes, and crime continued to rise. The Great Society was not about to materialize.

But if Keynesianism was discredited and social engineering no longer commanded support, what alternatives were available? The 'neo-conservatives' provided one set of alternatives which struck a responsive chord. They emphasized the efficiency of the market, the discipline of fiscal and monetary policy, a dislike of social engineering and a general instinct for 'rolling back' the federal and state governments. The impact of the 'neo-conservatism' is evident from the absence of voices, by the end of the 1970s, prepared to support high levels of government spending, relatively high levels of taxation and the formulation of new social programmes. However, the apparent dominance of neo-conservative beliefs has not been easy to translate into government policy, as the Reagan administration discovered.

The Reagan presidency

The malaise that had affected the presidency since Dwight D. Eisenhower had been in office during the 1950s, appeared to have come to an end with the presidency of Ronald Reagan. Reagan was the first American President in over a quarter of a century to have completed two terms in office, and his presidency is widely seen as having been successful. Certainly the American electorate's affection for Reagan seemed to grow during his period in office. His personal popularity, as he left Washington to return to California, was remarkably high – higher than that of any other President, at least since opinion polling began, at the end of their administration. Most commentators during those eight years gave the Reagan administration relatively high marks, but was this approval deserved? Has the praise and affection been misplaced? Certainly there were remarkable changes, both in foreign and domestic policy, that occurred while he was in office. Nevertheless President Reagan appeared to deal with these dramatic changes far more successfully than his immediate predecessors.

The Cold War. When President Reagan left office in January 1990, relations between the United States and the Soviet Union were far removed from the position when he took the oath of office in 1981. The first term of the Reagan presidency was characterized, by many commentators, as the start of the Second Cold War. It was a period of heightened tension between the superpowers, sharply increased military expenditures in both nations, and a level of hostility that was unprecedented, at least since the commencement of the Cold War in the 1940s. Reagan personally was profoundly suspicious of the Soviet Union. He had established, over a long period of time, his political credentials as a leading anti-communist, a Cold Warrior, so his characterization of the Soviet Union, during his first term, as an 'evil empire' was fully in keeping with his political persona. Equally consistent was his successful attempt to convince the Congress to increase defence spending substantially. His first term as President was driven by a determination to be unyielding towards the Soviet Union. His second term could hardly have been more different. Reagan established a close working relationship with Mikhail Gorbachev, and together they began the process of reducing the tensions between the nations. They successfully negotiated a treaty that, for the first time in post-war history, ended the deployment of a specific category of nuclear weapons. By the end of Reagan's second term the peace process appeared irreversible and the end of the Cold war in sight. It was a very real irony that this should have occurred during the Reagan presidency. The most anti-communist of recent American Presidents had apparently achieved an accommodation with the Soviet Union.

Several commentators sympathetic to the Reagan administration have claimed that the hard line of the first term brought the Soviet Union to the negotiation table. It is indeed possible that the willingness of the Reagan administration to increase defence expenditure and embark on the development of new generations of weapon systems, including the Strategic Defense Initiative (SDI), also known as 'Star Wars', did help to convince the Soviet Union that negotiations with the United States were appropriate and sensible. However, the profound difficulties that have beset the Soviet economy and polity are likely to have had a far greater impact on the Soviet leadership than the policies conducted by the United States. Gorbachev's realization that the Soviet Union could not sustain its role of global superpower as well as provide the goods and services demanded by its citizens probably was the critical factor in the introduction of *glasnost* and *perestroika* to the Soviet Union. Nevertheless, the Reagan administration's achievements in presiding over the winding down of the Cold War cannot be ignored and will be remembered.

The domestic agenda. The Reagan administration had no doubt of its primary domestic objective: namely to reduce the role of government, particularly the federal government, in the nation's economic life. Moreover, it wished to release the energy and vitality of American citizens by lowering the level of federal taxes. The Reagan administration adopted the neo-conservative political agenda. How successful was the administration in translating these goals into policy and how successful were the policies? Unsurprisingly there is a wide array of answers to both questions, although there are some points of agreement.

There is little argument that the longest period of unbroken growth in the economy since the end of the Second World War began during the Reagan years. The economic recession of the early 1980s was replaced by six years of consecutive economic growth, which also saw the rate of inflation fall while production, employment and incomes rose to unprecedented levels. The American economy was able to create several million new jobs, whereas the European experience during this period was a very substantial increase in unemployment in virtually every nation of the European Community. President Reagan certainly claimed credit for this success, which he argued was a result of the very substantial reduction of federal tax rates that the administration was able to convince the Congress to enact. However, the position of the American economy was not entirely satisfactory and in some respects had substantially deteriorated during the Reagan years.

The prosperity of the Reagan years was to a considerable extent the consequence of economic policies that also led to substantial deficits both in the federal budget and in the nation's overseas trade. The Reagan strategy of lowering taxes and increasing defence expenditures without reducing other categories of federal spending proportionately, led to a cumulative federal budget deficit over the eight years of almost $1,500 billion. In fiscal 1989 alone, the federal deficit was $160 billion, and this was after several years of attempting to reduce the deficit! The consequences of this deficit have already been significant. The increase in the national debt during the Reagan years has been greater than under all his predecessors combined. More important, though, the deficit has been funded primarily by foreigners, particularly by Japanese financial institutions. The result has been to turn the United States from the world's leading creditor nation in 1981 to the world's largest debtor by 1989.

Furthermore, the budget deficit has played its role in enlarging the balance of trade deficit by stimulating demand in the American economy to the extent that it could only be satisfied by foreign goods and services. In both 1988 and 1989 the trade deficit was running at over $100 billion per year, and in both these years the deficit had shown a substantial improvement. Most economists believe that this level of imbalance cannot be maintained without severe repercussions both for the United States and for the stability of the international economy.

The Reagan administration did not in fact achieve its goal of 'rolling back' the federal government. It was unable to reduce federal expenditures as a percentage of gross national product (GNP). Indeed, during the first four years of the administration it increased marginally from 23 to 25 per cent of GNP and remained at approximately the same levels during the second term. The composition of governmental expenditure did change, however, with defence expenditure consuming a sharply increased percentage of the federal budget, while non-defence expenditure declined. The decline in non-defence spending during the Reagan administration left very substantial problems of insufficient investment in the nation's infrastructure and in some of the principal services such as education. The final judgement on 'Reaganomics' has still to be reached.

Despite these economic problems, President Reagan and his administration retained their popularity. Perhaps his greatest achievement was in restoring the morale of Americans. The Vietnam and Watergate episodes severely eroded American confidence. The Ford and Carter presidencies failed to restore this, and in certain respects they further worsened the problem: the growth of inflation and the inability to secure the return of the Iranian hostages had increased the level of demoralization. The United States in 1981 was unsure and uncertain of its role in the world. There was a lack of belief that the United States had the capacity and ability to control its future. The contrast with 1989 could not be more striking. The country's mood, as the Reagan years came to an end, was ebullient and confident. There was a resurgence of patriotism and a restoration of national confidence, which in no small part was due to the personality of the President. He banished the introspection and self-doubt of the Jimmy Carter administration and replaced it with a sunny self-assurance that most Americans found infectious. Whether this assurance was based on substance is another matter.

The political success of the Reagan administration was due in no small part to the operating style of the President, which was in marked contrast to that of his predecessor. Carter was a 'hands on' President, anxious to be in command of all policy areas but perhaps overly interested and absorbed by detail. There is a story, possibly apocryphal, that Carter used to monitor the use of the tennis courts in the White House. Even if the story is not entirely accurate, it does illustrate the anxiety of President Carter to control all that occurred within the White House.

The operating style of the Reagan White House could not have been more different. The President was detached, to a quite striking degree, from the process of policy-making. The numerous 'kiss and tell' memoirs of Reagan White House aides are in agreement that the President gave a very broad and general indication of where he wished to see policy changes, but after having done so did not involve himself in the detail of policy-making. Donald Regan, Secretary of the Treasury during Reagan's first term, did not speak to the President alone on matters of economic policy in four years. The advantage of the Reagan style was that the President's relative aloofness from the policy-making process protected him from being overwhelmed by the day-to-day activities of politics. He was able to step back, retain his sense of perspective and his priorities and thereby give the nation an overall sense of direction. It also permitted his aides and Cabinet officers to get on with their jobs without constantly looking over their shoulders at the Oval Office. The chief disadvantage was that the President could be and was embarrassingly ill-informed, on too many occasions, about matters of considerable national and international importance. No predecessor of recent memory has 'mis-spoken', to quote the White House, quite so frequently. But an even greater disadvantage was that the President's 'hands off' style allowed certain aides and officials a freedom that they abused.

The one major scandal and indeed crisis of the Reagan administration, the Iran-Contra affair, arose out of this style of operation. Two officials within the National Security Council, John Poindexter, the National Security Adviser and Oliver North, a relatively junior official, were accused of pursuing a policy of selling arms to Iran in return for American hostages held in the Middle East. Although it is still not entirely clear who authorised the operation, the proceeds of the arms sales were channelled to the Contras, who were seeking to overthrow the left-wing government of Nicaragua. Both of these activities were illegal and were only able to take place because of the very permissive and lax procedures that President Reagan permitted within his administration.

The Bush presidency (1989–)

George Bush has to a considerable extent inherited the legacies of the Reagan administration. The foreign policy legacy has been especially positive. The Bush presidency commenced at a time when relations between the United States and the Soviet Union were better than at any time since the two nations were allies during the Second World War. In addition, developments in the international arena, particularly in Eastern Europe, have strengthened enormously the position of the United States. By contrast, the political and economic problems of the Soviet Union have worsened sharply and heightened the Soviet Union's urgency to reach an accommodation with the West. This has provided a politically congenial environment for President Bush. He has benefited politically from these developments and it has provided him with the historic opportunity to end the Cold War. The prospect is that the Bush administration will grasp this opportunity, although cautiously and carefully.

The economic front poses greater problems for President Bush. The budget deficit appears to be especially intractable. The most memorable phrase of the 1988 presidential campaign was made by George Bush and then repeated virtually every day until the election: 'Read my lips, no new taxes'. If there are to be no new taxes, will there be reductions in federal expenditures? During the campaign, Bush made it clear that he did not favour any reductions in the defence budget, while the Congress, in which the Democrats' control was strengthened by the 1988 elections, will not reduce non-defence expenditure. The result is likely to be an impasse, which will be both economically and politically difficult for the Bush administration to negotiate. It will be a major test for the political skill of the Bush administration, as the long-term political success of the administration will finally rest on the health of the American economy.

References

BAILEY, T. A. (1966) *Presidential Greatness*, New York, Appleton-Century-Crofts.

BINKLEY, W. E. (1947) *President and Congress*, New York, Alfred A. Knopf.

CORWIN, E. S. (1948) *The President, Offices and Powers,* New York, New York University Press.

DANIELS, J. (1946) *Frontier on the Potomac*, New York, Alfred A. Knopf.

FENNO, R. R. (1959) *The President's Cabinet*, New York, Vintage Books.

HESS, S. (1976) *Organizing the Presidency*, Washington, The Brookings Institution.

ROSSITER, C. (1960) *The American Presidency*, 2nd edn, London, Hart Davis.

Further reading

GREENSTEIN, E. (ed.) (1983) *The Reagan Presidency,* Baltimore, John Hopkins University Press.

HODGSON, G. (1984) *All Things to All Men,* Harmondsworth, Penguin.

LOWI, T. J. (1985) *The Personal President: Power Invested, Promise Unfulfilled,* Ithaca, Cornell University Press.

NEUSTADT, R. (1986) *Presidential Power,* New York, John Wiley.

REGAN, D. T. (1988) *For The Record,* London, Arrow.

STRUM, P. (1979) *Presidential Power and American Democracy,* Santa Monica, Goodyear.

5   The Congress

In 1985 Woodrow Wilson wrote of the Congress:

> [It] is unquestionably the predominant and controlling force, the
> center and source of all motive and of all regulative power...The
> legislature is the aggressive spirit...[it] has entered more and more
> into the details of administration, until it has virtually taken into its
> own hands all the substantial powers of government...I know not
> how better to describe our form of government in a single phrase
> than by calling it a government by the chairmen of the Standing
> Committees of Congress.
>
> *(Wilson, 1956, pp. 31, 44, 49, 52)*

A few years later, Lord Bryce, another distinguished observer of American society, also noted the great influence of Congress:

> Congress has been the branch of government with the largest facili-
> ties for usurping the powers of the other branches, and probably
> with the most disposition to do so. [It] has succeeded in occupying
> nearly all of the area which the Constitution left vacant and
> unallotted between the second authorities it established.
>
> *(Bryce, 1889, Vol. 2, pp. 711–12)*

Of course, both Bryce and Wilson were writing at the apogee of congressional power, in that half-century between the Civil War and the First
World War, but the institution they described, interestingly, would not
have surprised the delegates to the Federal Convention. The Founding
Fathers expected the Congress to attempt to dominate the federal government. In part, these expectations arose out of their experience of government in the period immediately before 1787, for when the Founding
Fathers turned their attention to the creation of a national legislature, they
found themselves on familiar terrain. They were well acquainted with
notions of legislative power and possessed considerable knowledge of the
operation of legislative assemblies. Their collective confidence is evident in
the debates, and it is no coincidence that the Constitution is far more specific about the duties and powers of the Congress than the other two
branches of the federal government. As a result, the intentions of the
Founding Fathers towards the Congress are easier to discern.

This, however, does not mean that there were no divisions and disagreements in the Convention, for there were. The debates in Philadelphia
were long and substantial – an indication of a range of positions, which
nevertheless shared similar objectives. So what were these common goals?
The Founding Fathers had three distinct, but intimately related, objectives.
The first was that the Congress should make the laws for the United States.
Secondly, it should not become too powerful, but be powerful enough to
check and balance the presidency. Finally, the Congress, and in particular
the House of Representatives, should be the 'representative' institution of
the federal government, reflecting the views and interests of the populace
at large.

To what extent have these objectives been realized?

5.1 Representation

The role and function of the Congress in the American political process has not been constant in the two hundred years since 1787. It has, along with the other institutions, been obliged to accommodate to a society and economy that has been in a perpetual state of flux. The very precise and carefully calibrated constitutional structure that the Founding Fathers devised in Philadelphia was in one sense overtaken rapidly by events.

Representation, over which the delegates agonized, is a good illustration. As was noted in Chapter 2, the three political institutions of the federal government – the presidency, the Senate and the House of Representatives – were allocated not only varying geographical constituencies, but were also given different modes of election, with the intention that each institution would represent significantly different constituents. However, within a few decades this intricate mechanism had succumbed to the 'democratization' of American life. The expansion of the electorate and the resultant political participation meant that the presidency and the Senate were no longer the 'patrician' institutions of the Founding Fathers' intentions.[1] As a consequence, the House of Representatives had ceased to be the only body that represented the mass electorate. The House could not claim, by the 1830s, to be the sole voice of the 'people'. So, in one sense, the intent of the Founding Fathers had gone awry. The House, the Senate and the President did not represent different kinds of electorates, but the same electorate, just organized on a different territorial basis. But if the intentions of the delegates were not fulfilled in this respect, they would have been confronted by the development that both the Senate and the House had become extremely effective at representing the views of their constituents.

There are several characteristics which distinguish the Congress from the legislatures of other Western democracies, but one of the most striking is the paramount place that members of the Senate and the House give to the views and interests of their constituents. Unlike Britain, for example, where members of the House of Commons temper their concern for their constituents by considerations of party, Senators and Representatives do not place a comparable emphasis on party. The reason for this is straightforward. American parties, by comparison with their European counterparts, have been weak historically and have been getting progressively weaker throughout the twentieth century. The Democratic and Republican parties have always been loose, decentralized organizations whose grip on the loyalty of voters and practising politicians has not been overwhelming. Accordingly, members of Congress, and those who wished to be members, have not been able to rely on party affiliation for electoral success. Instead, they have had to cultivate the electorate on their own behalf. They have had to develop a personal coalition. Even in those sections of the country where one of the two parties dominates, the existence of the primary election has similarly encouraged what David Mayhew (1974) has called the 'electoral connection' between members of the Congress and their constituents. Members of Congress are aware that their political survival depends on their own ability and effort. Accordingly, they devote a very high percentage of their time and energy to discovering their constituents' desires and requirements and attempting to fulfil them. In doing so, they build an exclusive link, a private connection, which they hope will be strong enough to sustain them in office. They seek to create a personal rapport which, once again, members of Congress hope will transcend party affiliation. Those who are adept at constructing a personal electoral coalition are seen as possessing, in Richard Fenno Jr's striking phrase, a successful 'home style' (Fenno, 1978). They are successful at cultivating the voters at home, an attribute that is the most valued among members of the Congress.

Almost every observer of the Congress detects the overriding concern of Senators and Representatives with the views and opinions of their constituents. Moreover, members of Congress endorse this view: 'I decided there was nothing in Washington', declared Democratic Representative Bob Bergland, 'as important as one constituent, and I dropped everything when one called' (Sundquist, 1981, p. 443). An anonymous Representative described his job as: 'Taking care of home problems. Case work, not necessarily having anything to do with legislation at all. Taking care of constituents' (Davidson, 1969, p. 80). A recently elected Representative told Richard Fenno Jr how he had spent his four years in Congress: 'The first two years, I spent all of my time getting re-elected. The last two years, I spent all of my time getting re-elected' (Fenno, 1978, p. 225). So if Senators and Representatives are to be believed they are constantly looking over their shoulders for guidance. Few, if any, are willing to ignore the interests of their constituents. In that sense, the Congress is an extraordinarily representative legislative body. It is sensitive to the slightest shift in electoral opinion.

However, it must be recognized that while legislators are desperately anxious to consult with all their constituents, their constituents' views do not carry equal weight. It is self-evidently the case that resources – money, information, status – are not equally distributed in the United States, and those who possess a disproportionate share of them, whether they are corporate bodies or individuals and are willing to use their resources in the political arena, will have a greater influence on their congressional representatives than those voters who have access to relatively few resources. Members of Congress will, of course, cultivate those who can contribute to their campaign finances and can mobilize opinion. This is not meant to suggest that Senators and Representatives are under the control of private vested interests, but that politicians whose continuance in office is dependent on their ability to create a winning coalition will be acutely aware of the configuration of political power within their constituency. They will not wish, at a minimum, to alienate those who command money and power, and indeed will hope to enlist them on their side.

Of course, there are factors that partially counterbalance the inequitable distribution of power. The most important is the franchise which is allocated equally, allied to a populist tradition hostile to the influence of special interests. Numerous political careers in the United States have prospered on attacking the concentration of power and wealth. So the crucial question is, on those issues where members of Congress face an internally divided constituency, on whose side will they fall? Who will they represent? It is broadly true that those who possess resources and are well organized are more likely to find a sympathetic ear in Washington. In a clash between the interests of the poor and dispossessed and those who are not, Senators and Representatives are more than likely, though not invariably, to side with the kind of voters who turn out on election day, contribute to campaign funds and involve themselves in campaign organizations.

Moreover, the interests of the poor are now a minority interest. In states such as New York and California there are significant areas of urban poverty which are pockets of deprivation in an affluent environment. The Senators from New York and California in such a clash of interests will almost certainly side with those who are more powerful and are in a numerical majority. Those minorities who rely heavily on the franchise rely on the vote for their political power and are unable to augment it with other resources generally; consequently they have a political problem, particularly in circumstances where there is a division along majority/minority lines. A case in point is the issue of positive discrimination or affirmative action, which was discussed in Chapter 3. Although a percentage of whites accept the case for affirmative action, most opinion polls indicate that the vast majority of white voters do not support such programmes, while the same polls also show a majority of black voters in favour. In these circumstances, apart from those constituencies where blacks are in a majority or a very substantial minority, Senators and Representatives will reflect the majority view.

So despite the 'electoral connection', or perhaps because of it, the views of a significant minority can in a sense be unrepresented. No matter how strong the desire on the part of Senators and Representatives to be sensitive to every shade of electoral opinion, some interests will be ignored. This is not to suggest that the same interests will consistently be ignored, only that some are more vulnerable, while those that have access to other resources will be better placed. In the final analysis politicians do have to judge how their own careers will be best served; they have to make their own personal calculation. Inevitably, these judgements and calculations are far from uniform. The different conditions produce a different political calculus. Moreover, individual calculations are flexible and constantly adjusting to new developments.

The answer, therefore, to the question of whom does a member of Congress represent is not quite as straightforward as it may first appear. But regardless of the precise composition of the coalition that Senators or Representatives create for themselves, the activity of creating and maintaining the coalition becomes the driving consideration, a consideration which has had a very substantial impact on how the Congress functions.

Parochialism

The most notable effect is that the Congress can be, and frequently is, parochial. It is dominated by 535 sets of individual considerations (100 Senators, 435 Representatives) which cannot necessarily be reconciled. So the Congress can appear to be, and frequently is, an inchoate body, unable to formulate policy coherently. It can also give the unfortunate impression that it places the interests of the locality above all else. National requirements, even though they are difficult to define and are subject to a variety of interpretations, are not even considered because the Congress is held in the grip of its 'electoral connection'.

It has certainly been a complaint of several Presidents that the Congress does not take a long-term national perspective, but only responds to immediate local pressures. It is a complaint that has increased in frequency over the past few decades and with good cause. The collapse of the post-war consensus on domestic and foreign policy and the continuing disintegration of the political parties has made the Congress an even more intractable body. The experiences of Presidents Ford and Carter testify to it. Both Presidents found Congress in the aftermath of Vietnam and Watergate far more assertive but not constructive in the sense of producing policy alternatives. Major problems, such as tax reform and the price and consumption of energy, were left unresolved because collectively the Senators and Representatives could not transcend their varied local interests, despite the pressing national need to simplify the tax codes and reduce energy consumption.

President Carter, the Congress and energy policy

Energy policy, an issue that straddles the domestic/international divide, provides a particularly good example of Congress's parochialism. Virtually every Western liberal democracy bar the United States responded quickly to the quadrupling of oil prices in 1973–4. Undoubtedly, the United States was in a more advantageous position than most of its European and Japanese allies. It was the world's largest oil producer, but nevertheless its position was not satisfactory. By the end of the 1960s, the United States had become a net importer of oil and the level of imports was rising sharply, so it could not isolate itself from the world oil market. Moreover, its very high consumption of oil products, in both absolute and *per capita* terms, had a considerable impact on the global demand for oil and, consequently, on its price. Therefore it was in the interests of the United States, and indeed all consumer countries, that American consumption should be reduced, a view that Japan and most of Western Europe, who were entirely dependent on oil imports and were having to accommodate to the new price levels at considerable economic cost, were pressing strongly in Washington. The Ford and Carter administrations were fully persuaded, but they could not persuade the Congress.

In 1977, the Carter administration presented the Congress with a National Energy Plan, a comprehensive measure which incorporated plans for energy conservation and included proposals for taxing energy. It was a plan which was similar to, but less drastic than, those which most countries had already adopted. But despite the evident need for and moderation of the proposals, the National Energy Plan failed to pass the Congress. It initially suffered from a jurisdictional argument, particularly in the Senate, over which committee – Finance, or Energy and National resources – had the appropriate authority to process it. But, far more important, the Energy

Plan succumbed to the plethora of interests that would have been affected by the proposals. The energy-producing states of the West and South West were ranged against the energy-consuming states of the North East and Mid-West. Energy producers who welcomed higher energy prices were reluctant for higher taxes to be imposed on profits. Nor were the producers of different types of energy – oil, gas and coal – united. Organized consumers were profoundly suspicious of the large oil companies, who, in turn, were anxious to portray themselves, somewhat unconvincingly, as innocent victims of the OPEC (Organization of Petroleum Exporting Countries) cartel. The list of players and the variety of positions in the legislative drama over the Energy Plan could be extended almost indefinitely, and they dominated the legislative process. The Energy Plan failed to pass the Congress not because of any policy inadequacy but because the Congress was driven by parochial considerations. Senators and Representatives responded to their own constituents and, as a result, did not take a national view.

President Reagan, the Congress and the budget deficit

The fate of the Energy Plan raises the question of whether the experience was typical of the modern Congress. Was President Carter's difficulty with the Congress a reflection of his personal inadequacies, or did it indicate a more fundamental problem in the ability of the Congress to deal with the nation's pressing difficulties. As you will have noted in Chapter 4, the Carter administration is viewed by a wide spectrum of opinion in the United States as having been fairly incompetent politically, and consequently there are several observers who are inclined to blame President Carter and his staff, rather than the Congress, for the demise of the Energy Plan. President Reagan, by contrast, cannot be dismissed in a similar manner. His two administrations are seen in a very different light, and his relations with the Congress, although they fluctuated over the eight years, were considered broadly satisfactory. Nevertheless, one of the most awkward domestic problems that confronted the Reagan administration, the federal budget deficit, remained unsolved throughout his period in office. It is a problem that has not gone away and continues to haunt President Bush. Moreover, the Congress had instituted reforms during the 1970s in order to give both the Senate and the House more effective control over the federal budgetary process (see Section 5.4). So why did a popular and successful president, along with Representatives and Senators who were far better informed than their predecessors over budgetary issues, fail to deal with the federal budget deficit.

The emergence of the federal budget deficit as a major national problem took place during the 1980s, although some of the underlying reasons can be traced back to the sharp increase in federal expenditures that began during the Kennedy administration(1961–63) and continued through the Great Society of Lyndon Johnson (1963–69) and the Nixon administration(1969–74). Spending by the federal government rose from $340.4 billion (expressed in constant 1982 dollars) in 1960 to $528.7 billion (constant 1982 dollars) in 1974 – an increase of 64 per cent in real terms during those years, and it has continued to rise. Between 1976 and 1988 there has been a further increase, again in real terms, of approximately 66 per cent. This rapid growth in federal expenditure was not fully matched by revenues, and as a result there has been a sequence of budget deficits. Indeed there have been only two years between 1958 and 1991 when the budget has been in surplus, the last surplus occurring in the fiscal year 1969. However, until the 1980s the deficits were broadly acceptable, either because they were not excessively large, or because there was a belief that they could be reduced in subsequent years. The 1980s, by contrast, saw a rapid and apparently uncontrollable increase in the federal budget deficit. The deficit in 1979 was $52.7 billion (expressed in constant 1982 dollars), and by 1983 that figure had grown to $200.7 billion (again in constant 1982 dollars). What were the causes of this development?

The reasons are relatively easy to establish. In 1981 the Reagan administration adopted the prescriptions of neo-conservative economics (see Chapter 4), and proposed a very substantial reduction in the rate of tax. The President and his economic advisers believed that this was required to 'liberate' the American economy from the then current regime of high taxation, and this in turn would release the productive energies of the economy. At the same time President Reagan proposed a substantial expansion in the defence budget, a process which had in fact begun in the Carter administration but which the Reagan administration intended to accelerate sharply. There was broad bipartisan agreement within the Congress for increasing military spending, as there was for reducing taxes, and both these elements of the administration's strategy were endorsed by the Congress. However, the consequence of reducing revenue and increasing expenditure simultaneously is to increase the size of the deficit. Somewhat belatedly, the Congress became aware of the dimensions of the problem it had created. It was confronted by three alternatives.

First, as urged by the Reagan administration, it could impose reductions on non-defence expenditure of approximately $100 billion, which would reduce the deficit substantially. Unfortunately if Congress had endorsed this strategy it would have created profound political difficulties for itself. The difficulties arose from the fact that by the 1980s almost three-quarters of federal expenditure was relatively uncontrollable by the Congress. These expenditures were uncontrollable, and they continue to be, because they are tied to programmes which do not require annual authorization. For instance, payments to individuals from such federal programmes as social security or medicare are automatically indexed to the cost of living. Again pensions, both military and civilian, are adjusted annually for inflation. These and similar programmes are known as entitlements, which are adjusted for cost of living increases without any need for congressional approval. They 'run on automatic' and are difficult to control. They require changes in the authorizing legislation, which is most improbable in the congressional political climate. Of course, any spending programme is controllable if the political will exists to exercise control. However, the experience of the 1980s and indeed previous decades suggests that few members of Congress have the political will to reduce the expenditure of these popular spending programmes. So if there were going to be significant reductions in non-defence expenditure in 1981 and 1982, the full weight of these reductions had to be borne by a narrow band of 'controllable' programmes, with potentially grave consequences for them. Inevitably the beneficiaries of these programmes lobbied their Senators and Representatives intensely and effectively, with the result that while the Congress agreed to some reductions, the cumulative total was insufficient to compensate for the tax cuts and increased military spending.

The second alternative available to the Congress was to rescind, in part or whole, the tax cuts and the larger defence budget, neither of which found favour with Senators, Representatives or their constituents. It should be noted that towards the end of Reagan's first term, the rate of growth in defence expenditure began to slow as a result of congressional reluctance to approve the Reagan administration's defence budget proposals. But these were reductions in the rate of growth: the defence budget continued to increase but not as fast as the administration desired.

The third option was to let the deficit grow. The Congress selected this option and the deficit grew inexorably. Why did the Congress choose to go down this road? President Reagan's Director of the Office of Management and the Budget (OMB), David Stockman, captures the lack of congressional concern: 'Deficits create many winners and few losers...Every legislator is in a position to confer benefits on his or her favorite constituencies and the incentive for any individual legislator to refrain from such behaviour is virtually nonexistent.' However, when the deficit reached over $200 billion in the 1983 fiscal year, the option of letting the deficit expand ceased to be available. If the deficit continued to expand or was even maintained at this level, it would threaten the very financial stability of the United States and thus of the entire international monetary order. The potential for economic disorder was so great that the Congress finally did act in 1985.

In December 1985, the Congress passed the Balanced Budget and Deficit Control Act, otherwise known as Gramm, Rudman, Hollings or G-M-H after its three co-sponsors. The objective of the Act is suggested in its title, namely to end the federal deficit. However, the process through which G-M-H seeks to achieve its objective does not allay any doubts, and indeed to some extent increases them, about the Congress as a constructive legislative body. Even though the Congress recognized the grave dangers of a large and continuing deficit, the mechanisms of G-M-H sought to place the political responsibility as far away from the Congress as was possible. Originally the Act required the United States Comptroller General of the General Accounting Office to issue a report, setting forth the level of reduction required in each fiscal year. The Comptroller General was delegated virtually absolute discretion over which programmes will be affected. The President was then required to implement the reductions specified by the Comptroller General. The Congress had little role to play.

There are, of course, evident dangers with automatic mechanisms. The reductions may be imposed at best insensitively, and at worst randomly and damagingly, although Senators and representatives were willing to take that risk if these procedures protected them from constituency pressures. Undoubtedly the desire to liberate themselves from local interests while reducing the deficit was the driving force behind G-M-H. Its appeal certainly did not derive from the quality of thought that lay behind the Bill.

One of the co-sponsors, Senator Warren B. Rudman, described it as 'a bad idea whose time has come'. Nor did it gain support from a long and careful consideration, for it passed, quite extraordinarily, without any committee hearings.

The haste and willingness of the Congress to delegate powers that are normally jealously preserved can only be explained by the level of concern over the deficit and by the realization that constituency pressures would not allow members of the Congress to resolve the problem. Unfortunately, for Senators and Representatives that is, the Supreme Court in 1986 found the delegation of authority to the Comptroller General to be unconstitutional. After the Court's decision the Congress was unable to distance itself from the awkward political decisions that have to be taken in order to eliminate the deficit. Consequently G-M-H has made far less progress in reducing the deficit than was anticipated when the Act was passed in 1985, because Senators and Representatives are unwilling to confront the political ramifications that will follow any serious attempt to reduce the deficit. The deficit continues and it is as pressing a problem for President Bush as it was for the Reagan administration.

The emergence of the budget deficit in the 1980s and the inability of the Congress to deal with it throughout the decade does not enhance the institution's reputation as a constructive legislative body. While there are those who believe that this is a major problem for the political process, the Founding Fathers would not have shared this view. Instead, they would have taken considerable comfort from the parochialism of the Congress. They would have been pleased to see the Congress represent local interests so avidly. Above all, the Founding Fathers would have been satisfied by the effective representation of minority interests.

5.2   Legislation

The Congress has not been an institution that has responded quickly to the nation's legislative needs. However, until the 1930s, as was noted in Chapter 4, the Congress did provide the legislative answers – perhaps not as rapidly as many would have wished, but the answers nevertheless were congressional. However, as the arena of federal government activity grew enormously in the 1930s, the Congress's capacity to formulate responses to ever rising demands directed towards the federal government was clearly inadequate. The presidency, with the assistance of a vastly enlarged bureaucracy and subsequently the Executive Office of the President, appeared to be the only branch of government able to respond to these demands, and the Congress acquiesced.

But why did the Congress acquiesce? There were several reasons, all linked by the fact that the political conditions were inappropriate for the exercise of congressional power. The crisis of the Great Depression made the Congress and the nation turn to the presidency almost in desperation for a solution. The Second World War similarly created the conditions for presidential domination of the nation's affairs. After the war the emergence of a consensus on domestic and foreign policy resulted, once again, in a disposition on the part of the Congress and the electorate to allow the President considerable latitude in the formulation of policy. In other words, the political climate from the 1930s to the end of the 1960s was conducive to a presidential ascendancy, and the Congress accepted this as a fact of political life.

This, however, should not be read to mean that Congress was willing to endorse all presidential initiatives throughout these four decades. The Senate and the House, for all the reasons outlined above, did not do so. Indeed, in the arena of domestic politics most of the Presidents during this period faced considerable difficulties in getting legislative approval for their programmes. Roosevelt did indeed have great success between 1933 and 1937, but was unable to persuade the Congress to pass a major piece of domestic legislation after 1938. His successor, Truman, did not fare well, an experience shared by Kennedy. Only Eisenhower, who did not have a controversial legislative programme, and Johnson, who did, can be deemed to have had a record of legislative achievement. So presidential domination did not mean automatic congressional assent. It did mean, however, that the debate was conducted on presidential terms. It was presidential proposals that were rejected or amended. The congressional role was usually essentially reactive and perhaps subordinate. But the conditions that produced the presidential ascendancy changed in the aftermath of Vietnam and Watergate. The end of the post-war consensus brought in its train an embattled presidency with a far more assertive Congress that embarked on a series of congressional reforms which attempted to reclaim for the Congress a significant role in policy formulation. However, before the recent reforms are explored, it is important to examine the internal organization of the Congress.

The internal structure

L. C. Dodd, writing in 1981, believed he could identify three distinct periods in the history of the Congress. There was a period of confrontation (1789–1860), one of expansion (1876–1910), and an era of consolidation (1920–65). The missing years in Dodd's schema were ones of particularly dramatic change in the nation's life (Dodd, 1981). While it is not the intention here to trace the changes within the Congress since 1789, it is nevertheless important to note that the internal structure and organization has not remained constant over the past two hundred years. The Congress's internal practices have reflected both the institution's changed role and developments in the political process at large. Consequently, alterations to procedures have occurred at periodic intervals. Interestingly, the most significant developments have affected the two principal loci of power, the committee system and the party leadership.

The committee system

To some extent, the Congress has always relied on its committees. In particular, the House of Representatives with its large membership has always been a somewhat unwieldy body, uneasy with its ability to deal with legislation and other substantial issues on the floor of the House, and has been willing to devolve its collective responsibility to its committees. The Senate has maintained a tradition of floor debate, but even so its committees are the nerve centre of its legislative process. The power and importance of the committee system was noted by Woodrow Wilson and several others at the end of the nineteenth century and, if anything, the position of committees has been enhanced during the twentieth century. There are currently fifteen standing committees in the Senate and twenty-two in the House.[2] Their structure, as Table 5.1 indicates, approximates that of the executive branch, although there is not an exact fit. Inevitably, the total number and the areas of policy-making have altered over time to accommodate the expanding responsibility of the federal government, but the power of the committees derives from a number of factors which have remained stable.

The first is that all proposed legislation is sent to the appropriate standing committee. In turn, the committee will give one of its sub-committees the task of making a detailed investigation of the Bill. When the sub-committee has completed this it will report back to the committee which, after considerating the sub-committee's views, will in turn report to the floor of the House or Senate. It is usually the case that a committee's view on a Bill will be accepted by either body, although the Senate and House do retain the authority to reject or amend the committee's recommendations – an authority that is exercised with only the greatest caution, for the committees provide the Congress's expertise. Thus the committee system is the critical element in the legislative process.

The second factor which sustains the importance of the committee system is that Senators and Representatives invest a great deal of their time and political energy in the committee structure. They hope to obtain committee assignments which are germane to the interests of their constituents, for obvious reasons. They also hope to obtain a place on one of the more prestigious committees, for there is a hierarchy of committees. Ways and Means and Appropriations are particularly prestigious in the House, while Finance and Foreign Relations have always been eagerly sought in the Senate. Their institutional sense of success is to a considerable extent measured by their committee assignments. So how do members of Congress obtain the most desirable assignments?

Seniority

Until the reforms of the 1970s, seniority or length of service was the principal determinant of committee allocation and had an equally great impact on the exercise of power within the committees. The adoption of the seniority rule in 1911 was the result of a successful attempt to lessen the authority of the party leadership, and especially the power of the Speaker of the House of Representatives, who is the leader of the majority party. Representatives wanted to take away the Speaker's discretionary powers to advance the careers of those he favoured and replace it with a neutral and automatic mechanism. They succeeded in their immediate objectives: the power of the Speaker was diminished sharply, but some of the consequences of their action were unexpected. The seniority rule could be and was applied automatically, but its impact was not neutral. It favoured those members who came from areas where one of the two parties was dominant and who consequently did not have to face a serious general election campaign. Of course, they were still liable to be challenged in their party's primary election, but even if this was the case, they still only had to contest one real election and not two. The result was that there were specific

Table 5.1 Senate and House: standing committees and sub-committees, 100th Congress, 1986-88

Committees	Number of sub-committees
Senate	
Agriculture, Nutrition and Forestry	8
Appropriations	12
Armed Services	6
Banking, Housing and Urban Affairs	7
Budget	0
Commerce, Science and Transportation	6
Energy and Natural Resources	6
Environment and Public Works	4
Finance	9
Foreign Relations	7
Governmental Affairs	8
Judiciary	9
Labor and Human Resources	7
Rules and Administration	0
Veterans' Affairs	0
House of Representatives	
Agriculture	8
Appropriations	13
Armed Services	7
Banking, Finance and Urban Affairs	8
Budget	0
District of Columbia	3
Education and Labor	8
Energy and Commerce	6
Foreign Affairs	8
Government Operations	7
House Administration	6
Interior and Insular Affairs	6
Judiciary	7
Merchant Marine and Fisheries	5
Post Office and Civil Service	7
Public Works and Transportation	6
Rules	2
Science and Technology	7
Small Business	6
Standards of Official Conduct	0
Veterans' Affairs	5
Ways and Means	6

Source: *Congressional Quarterly*

beneficiaries from the seniority rule. Within the Democratic Party those who represented the urban areas of the northern industrial states, and especially the South, gained from the application of the seniority principle. In the Republican Party, Senators and Representatives from the agricultural states of the Mid-West and the mountain states of the West rarely found themselves dispossessed by Democrats. The net effect was that these regions were disproportionately represented within the most important committees.

Moreover, the seniority rule applied even more rigorously to advancement within each committee. The chairman of a committee was automatically the most senior member of the majority party, and until the recent reforms the chairmanship bestowed various and substantial benefits. A chairman, before the powers were trimmed, controlled the agenda, the composition of the sub-committees, the manner and timing of public hearings, and the use of Congress's own professional staff allocated to the committee. Committee chairmen were, therefore, the most influential members of the Congress before the recent reforms. Because the Democratic Party controlled the Congress for all but four years between 1930 and 1970, they were invariably Democrats and disproportionately from the South. Southerners were overrepresented on the more important committees and had far more chairmanships than their numbers warranted. In the four decades up to the 1970s the Congress provided the extraordinary spectacle of an institution where a relatively small percentage of its members wrote the rules, set the tone and established 'the folkways' – the style of operation and behaviour (Matthews, 1960).

But did this southern domination matter? The unequivocal answer is yes. It mattered because the politics of the South, in these years, was very distinctive. The South was less industrialized than the rest of the nation, less heterogeneous both religiously and ethnically. But above all, the politics of the South were the politics of race. Southern politics were driven by the desire of a majority of the white population to maintain racial segregation and the subordination of black southerners. The sum of these characteristics made the South atypical. Its concerns and desires were on the whole different from the rest of the country and very different from the remainder of the Democratic Party. From the New Deal onwards, the Democratic Party had drawn an increasing percentage of its electoral support from those who lived in the metropolitan areas, labour unions and the ethnic minorities, including blacks. Moreover, these voters were far more important to the party in presidential elections than the South. Consequently, successive Democratic Presidents – Roosevelt, Truman, Kennedy and Johnson – dependent on these voters and anxious to reward them for their past support and ensure their future allegiance, proposed legislation which was attractive to them: urban renewal programmes, minimum wage legislation and, in general, the further expansion of the welfare state. These proposals, however, were not on the whole attractive to southerners, who used their hold on the committee system to prevent them being passed. They had a considerable degree of success.

The combination of the committee system and the seniority rule created a Congress resistance to reform, a fact which was frequently and understandably deplored. In the circumstances it was not surprising that the seniority rule had few supporters outside of those who were its beneficiaries, and, as a result, it was changed. But in retrospect, and despite its manifest inadequacies, it did provide one valuable service to the Congress. It gave the Congress an inner club, an establishment who could exercise a degree of control. They could enforce, to a limited extent, their will on the Senate and House. The committee chairmen, on the occasions when they were in alliance with the leadership of both parties, could make the Congress appear a coherent, even if obstructive, body. This was no mean achievement, for with the reform of the seniority rule and the limitations imposed on the power of chairmen, that coherence disappeared. The party leadership was not able to impose that order by itself.

The party leadership

The influence of party in the Congress has been a long-term secular decline. Perhaps the high point of party influence was the period after the American Civil War, but even then the degree of control and influence that the leadership could impose was curtailed by the need of members of the Congress to tend their constituency interests. Nevertheless, at the turn of the twentieth century, the party leaders were the most important individuals in the Congress.

The Speaker of the House of Representatives was especially powerful, as he had the authority to allocate committee membership and chaired the key Rules committee. The Rules committee selects those Bills that can continue through the legislative process. If the committee fails to allocate a 'rule' to a Bill – the time for consideration in committee and for floor debate – the legislative life for that Bill is terminated. Although the purpose of the committee was, and is, to ensure that the legislative process in the House ran smoothly, Speakers such as the Republicans Nicholas Reed and Joseph Cannon used the committee to kill legislation of which they did not approve. However, in 1910 there was a revolt against the authority of the Speaker, and the office was stripped of its powers, including the chairmanship of Rules. The party leadership has never been quite the same.

Without the power to reward and discipline, the Speaker and the leader of the minority party, plus their counterparts in the Senate, the majority and minority leaders, have had to resort to a variety of other tactics. They have had to accept that their ability to influence their colleagues is limited. They could not impose their views but have had to rely on conciliation and persuasion. The collective leadership of both parties in both Houses have to convince their fellow party members that there is no conflict between the interests of their constituents and their party. The leaders' success therefore depends on personal qualities and political skills to create support and weave coalitions rather than on institutional authority. In the decades up to the 1970s, the party leadership also had to work in close concert with the chairmen of committees, which was not always an easy task.

So party leaders need to possess the ability to accommodate the widely disparate interests of the congressional party, the patience to massage the egos of the committee chairmen, the desire to be permanently available, and the willingness to do the little favours that would earn the gratitude of their colleagues. They need these and other qualities if their term in office is to be a success, though it is hardly surprising that few, since 1910, have possessed all of them. It is far more surprising that some have. Sam Rayburn, a Democrat and Speaker of the House from 1940 to 1961, bar four years when the Republicans controlled the House, was one of the few who did. His successors, all Democrats – John McCormack, Carl Albert , Thomas (Tip) O'Neill, Jim Wright and the present incumbent Thomas Foley – have not been quite such imposing figures. In the Senate, the most impressive majority leader in recent years was Lyndon B. Johnson (1955–61), who also possessed the same range of skills as Rayburn. Again his successors – Democrats Mike Mansfield, Robert Byrd and the current majority leader George Mitchell, and non-Republicans Howard Baker and Robert Dole – have not had quite the same impact as Johnson. Both Rayburn and Johnson had outstanding political skills. They had a finely tuned sense of their respective institutions and an extraordinary ability to gauge the mood of their colleagues.

Nevertheless, it must be said that life was easier for Rayburn and Johnson during their terms in office. It was, no doubt, a testament to their abilities that the 'inner club' of committee chairmen were, on the whole, allies rather than opponents, but at least there was an 'inner club'. Furthermore, there is a question over the nature of their success. Rayburn and Johnson did indeed maintain a semblance of unity within the congressional Democratic Party. They papered over the chasm that existed between the northern and southern wings, but they did so at a cost. They sought to postpone contentious issues which divided the Democrats. If they could not avoid them, they tried to defuse the issues. Civil rights, for instance, was bypassed in the 1940s, and when it could not be overlooked it arrived before the Congress in the anodyne form of the 1957 and 1960 Civil Rights Act, which even white southerners could tolerate. Under Rayburn and Johnson's leadership, the congressional Democratic Party was not united over substantial policy issues. The party was deeply divided and no individual, however adept and able, was going to heal the rift, but at least they did not exacerbate these tensions and helped to conceal the full dimensions of the troubles. This was a substantial achievement, but it was the extent of their achievement, and it is an indication of the powerlessness of even the most 'successful' congressional leaders.

5.3 Congressional oversight

The ability of the Congress to check and balance the presidency is in part dependent on its powers of oversight. Congress not only has a legislative obligation under the Constitution, it also has the responsibility of reviewing the activities of the executive branch. This latter duty is known as 'congressional oversight'. The oversight function is normally carried out by the standing committees, although the most dramatic instances of congressional oversight are those investigations carried out by special committees. One such example was the Senate Select Committee on Campaign Practices, which investigated the Watergate affair. A further instance, in the aftermath of Watergate, was the examination of the role of the Central

Intelligence Agency (CIA). Both of these investigations were conducted in a highly charged political atmosphere and neither committee could be accused of being insufficiently rigorous. Indeed, if anything, they were deemed to have been over-zealous.

However, Congress does not usually carry out its oversight activities in the glare of national publicity. Legislative oversight is normally routine, and if it is carried out by one of the standing committees, there is no adversarial relationship between federal bureaucrats and members of Congress. The relationship between the officials of the executive branch and members of Congress is generally good, though some would say too good. Bureaucrats cultivate members of Congress and vice versa. Both gain from an understanding relationship. The bureaucracy protect their funding and prevent hostile investigations. Senators and Representatives ensure that the bureaucracy is sympathetic to any request they make on behalf of a constituent. It is, in the main, a cosy relationship, which partly explains why the Congress was and continues to be unwilling to reduce federal expenditures to the level desired by the Reagan and Bush administrations. It is an intimate relationship, which helps to account for presidential suspicion of the federal bureaucracy and which prevents effective oversight. But it is a relationship which members of Congress sustain because they find it helpful in their constant and permanent obsession of keeping their voters happy.

5.4 Congressional reform

The congressional reforms of the 1970s were driven by the attempt to achieve two not necessarily compatible objectives. The first was to reclaim some of the power and authority lost to the presidency in the preceding forty years. The political climate of the 1970s, conditioned by continuous revelations of presidential misbehaviour, offered the Congress an opportunity to assert itself, an opportunity which the Congress seized. The second objective was, in a sense, to 'democratize' the internal organization of the Congress – a desire which was felt strongly by the junior and newly elected members of the Congress who chafed at the power of committee chairmen and the hierarchical structure imposed by the seniority rule. Undoubtedly, part of their resentment can be put down to envy, that they would not be able to wield the instruments of congressional power for some time.

But a far more substantial problem with the extant congressional structure was that it complicated the relationship of members with their constituents. They had to take into account the views of those in positions of power, over whom they had no sanction. On the other hand, committee chairmen could, if they wished, make life awkward, if not difficult, for junior members. This distracted Senators and Representatives from tending their constituency fences, and sometimes erected tensions and conflict between constituency interests and congressional realities. Junior members of both Houses wanted to curtail the powers of chairmen and make them more amenable to their wishes. The result of this wish to 'democratize' the Congress and assert its authority resulted in a series of reforms, of which the most important were the following:

The War Powers Resolution. In 1973 the Congress overrode President Nixon's veto to pass the War Powers Resolution. It was designed to prevent the commitment of American military forces without congressional approval. Accordingly, under the Resolution, a President, apart from when the Congress had issued a declaration of war, could only commit US armed forces in a national emergency. Even then, any such action had to gain congressional agreement within sixty days. If the approval was given, a further thirty days could be granted, at which point, after ninety days, the Congress could terminate the military action – a decision which, under the Resolution, the President could not veto.

The Budget and Impoundment Control Act. The Congress's reliance on the presidency for budgetary information and economic analysis was deemed by many observers to be its most serious weakness as an effective policy-making institution. As a result, in 1974 the Budget and Impoundment Control Act was passed, which formed Budget committees in both the House and Senate, but perhaps most importantly created the Congressional Budget Office (CBO) with its own professional and specialist staff, which liberated members of Congress from their dependence on the executive. However, the experience of the 1980s with its ever increasing deficits does not suggest that these reforms will produce appropriate and sound budgetary policies.

Congressional staff. The CBO was only part of a striking increase in the number of professional staff employed by the Congress. The reasons that lay behind the formation of the CBO in 1974 also lay behind the formation of the Office of Technology Assessment in 1972, the expansion of the General Accounting Office and the restructuring of the Congressional Research Services, namely to provide Congress with its own independent source of information and analysis. Furthermore, the number of personal aides to Senators and Representatives almost doubled in the 1970s, as did the staff allocated to the committees. By the late 1980s the Congress employed over 40,000 staff for its committees, members' offices and support agencies such as the CBO. The number of personal staff has grown enormously to almost 18,000. The increase in congressional staffing expanded the capacity of the Congress to carry out policy analysis and evaluations of presidential initiatives. This growth has improved the capability and responsiveness of the Congress, although there are mounting concerns over the sheer size of this expanding congressional bureaucracy.

Internal reforms. In 1973 the Democratic members of the House of Representatives, meeting in a party caucus, took a momentous decision: they voted to end the automatic use of the seniority principle for the appointment of committee chairmen. Instead, chairmen would be nominated by the Steering and Policy Committee of the Democratic caucus and then be subject to election by a secret ballot of the whole party. The decision lost some of its impact when the caucus approved the nomination of all the senior members of the various committees. However, in 1975, three incumbent chairmen were defeated and the absolutism of seniority was ended.

In the reforming fervour of 1975, the Democratic caucus also prevented chairmen of important committees from serving as chairmen of other major committees. Furthermore, they ensured the more equitable distribution of sub-committee assignments, a development which took on an additional importance after the 1973 'sub-committee bill of rights'. The 'bill of rights' devolved a considerable element of the power of the committees to the sub-committees and, at the same time, substantially reduced the control of the committee chairmen over the sub-committees. The long reign of the committee chairmen, if not ended, was drawing to a close. Although these changes initially applied only to the Democratic Party in the House, the Republicans in the House and both parties in the Senate also bowed to the reforming impulse.

5.5   Congress in the 1980s

By the start of the 1980s the balance of power between the President and Congress had undoubtedly altered. The Congress was far more assertive, less willing to accept presidential direction, and more able to question and challenge presidential policy. It had released itself from its dependence on the executive branch. It now possessed both the political willingness and the resources to provide its own legislative answers on an array of issues. But, paradoxically, at the moment when it shed its deference to the presidency and strengthened its professional staff, it also weakened its ability to take collective action. Institutional power had been dispersed. Seniority was overthrown, and committee chairmen were no longer the autonomous powerful figures of the past. By the 1980s there were fewer – and very few indeed – institutional sanctions over Senators and Representatives. They were now free to respond to their constituents' interests. The institutional restraints were not a barrier to satisfying their constituency demands. The Congress was more than ever, by the 1980s, an institution composed of 535 individuals seeking local guidance. Its ability to act in concert, which was never considerable, was reduced. So at one and the same time, the Congress had gained the capacity to be a constructive, legislative body but was less able to use it. The experience of the 1980s reflected the inability of the Congress to act effectively. It was apparently unable to deal effectively with budgetary issues. It seemed increasingly responsive to local rather than national concerns. The influence of special interests appeared to have strengthened. Despite these inadequacies it can be predicted safely that barring a crisis, economic or political, the Congressional practice and behaviour will be relatively stable in the 1990s. If changes do occur, they will be gradual and incremental. The Founding Fathers would approve.

Notes

1. The direct election of Senators by voters, rather than by state legislatures, was brought about in 1913 by the Seventeenth Amendment. Nevertheless, the politics of the Senate, like those of the presidency and the House, was affected by the growing populism of American society long before the ratification of the Amendment.
2. Apart from the Standing Committees, there are Select Committees whose principal task is usually investigative. Joint Conference Committees are composed of members of both Houses who have the responsibility of ironing out all the differences between the Senate and House version of the same Bill. Joint Committees are also composed of members of both Houses and most of them are concerned with examining issues over the long term.

References

BRYCE, J. (1889) *The American Commonwealth*, 2 vols, New York, Macmillan.

DAVIDSON, R. H. (1969) *The Role of the Congressman*, New York, Pegasus.

DODD, L. C. (1981) 'Congress, the Constitution and the Crisis of Legitimation', in L. C. Dodd and B. I. Oppenheimer (eds) *Congress Reconsidered*, Washington DC, Congressional Quarterly Press.

FENNO Jr, R. F. (1978) *Home Style*, Boston, Little Brown.

MATTHEWS, D. R. (1960) *US Senators and Their World*, New York, Vintage Books.

MAYHEW, D. R. (1974) *Congress: The Electoral Connection*, New Haven, Yale University Press.

SUNDQUIST, J. L. (1981) *The Decline and Resurgence of Congress*, Washington DC, The Brookings Institution.

WILSON, W. (1956) *Congressional Government: A Study in American Politics*, New York, Meridian Books (first published 1885).

Further reading

ABSHIRE, D. M. and NURNBERGER, R. D. (eds) (1981) *The Growing Power of Congress*, Beverly Hills and London, Sage.

HINCKLEY, B. (1978) *Stability and Change in Congress*, New York, Harper and Row.

MANN, T. E. and ORNSTEIN, N. J. (eds) (1981) *The New Congress*, Washington DC, American Enterprise Institute.

RIESELBACH, L. N. (1986) *Congressional Reform*, Washington DC, Congressional Quarterly Press.

SUNDQUIST, J. L. (1986) *Constitutional Reform and Effective Government*, Washington DC, The Brookings Institution.

6   Parties, Elections and Interest Groups

In 1796 George Washington warned his fellow citizens of the dangers that lay ahead. As his second term of office drew to a close, Washington delivered his Farewell Address to the nation. It was an address that could only have been made by a member of the generation that had lived through the turbulence of the Revolution, the instability of the Confederation and was now aware of the fragility of the new Republic. His fears were not his alone, and the fear that exercised him and others the most was the rising tide of partisanship in the country. Washington deplored 'the baneful effects of the spirit of party generally [with] its alternate domination of one faction over another, sharpened by the spirit of revenge natural to party dissension'. But if the spirit of party was allowed nevertheless to infect the conduct of government, then he foresaw grave consequences for the nation:

> It seems always to distract the public councils and enfeeble the public administration. It agitates the community with ill-founded jealousies and false alarms; kindles the animosities of one part against another; ferments occasionally riot and corruption, which finds a facilitated access to the government itself through the channels of party passion.
> *(Richardson, 1897, Vol.1, pp.218–19).*

Unfortunately for Washington, his warning had come too late, for at the very moment that he was informing his fellow citizens of the danger of party, the first American party system was in place. Washington's fears, justified or not, had been overtaken by events. 'The Constitution against party', to use Richard Hofstadter's striking phrase, had produced, paradoxically within a few years of its existence, the 'first modern party system in any nation' (Hofstadter, 1969; McCormick, 1967, p.91). Why did this come about?

6.1   The origins of the party system

It is a profound historical irony that those mechanisms which the Founding Fathers built into the Constitution to prevent the instruments of government falling into the hands of any one faction, were also the cause of the emergence of national parties. The Constitution very deliberately dispersed power between the states and the national government and between the institutions of the federal government for all the reasons outlined in Chapter 2. The result was a fragmented governmental structure, where control resided in numerous and disparate hands, with little co-ordination and much hostility between its constituent elements – a position which could only be overcome, in part, if those of a similar persuasion could capture the presidency and dominate the Congress and the state governments. This realization dawned early, and by the 1790s there were two national parties, the Federalists and the Republicans, who intriguingly were the forerunners of the Democratic Party. This must not be understood to mean that there was an absence of political activity in the 1780s, for there was not. American society was already heterogeneous. There were divisions – racial, religious, social and economic – and inevitably there was tension and conflict which found political expression, but at state level. The Constitution, however, had erected a new national arena with new rules, and the Federalist and Republican parties were a response to this development. So what distinguished the Federalists and Republicans from the groups that operated at state level?

The first and most obvious distinction is that they were national parties concerned with national issues. Should the federal government underwrite the debt incurred by the states and, if it did, how should it be funded? Was there a need for a national bank? These and other national questions consumed the attention of the two parties. Secondly, these parties had to extend their horizons beyond the state boundaries. They had to draw support from all regions and sections, although the support was not uniform. The Republicans were particularly strong in the South and among farmers and planters, while the Federalists' strongholds were located in New England and among those involved in commerce. But the composition of the two parties leads to the third and the most important distinction. Both parties, but especially the Republicans, soon became aware of the dangers of exclusivity. They realized the need to increase their support, for without a broadly based coalition neither party would have a realistic chance of winning the presidency and gaining a majority in the Congress. Moreover, if a party did not have a realistic possibility of electoral success then its very existence might be in jeopardy. Indeed, the failure of the Federalist Party to widen its coalition led to its demise by the 1820s; its successor, the Whigs, suffered a similar fate by the 1850s.

The Republican Party, more adept and more in sympathy with the developing pattern of American life, flourished in its second guise as the Democratic-Republican and finally as the Democratic Party. The modern Republican Party was formed in the 1850s during the death throes of the Whigs and the prelude to the Civil War. Since then, control of the Congress and the presidency has alternated between the Democratic and Republican parties. Both these contemporary parties have absorbed the lesson of the Whigs and the Federalists, and in those periods when they have failed to heed it, they have suffered electorally. But in the drive to be broadly based coalitions they have developed characteristics which are, if not unique, then distinctive.

6.2   The characteristics of the party system

The most notable feature of the national American parties has been, and still is, the absence of a programme. By contrast with their counterparts in other Western liberal democracies, the Democrats and Republicans programmatically are remarkably eclectic. Once every four years the parties adopt a platform at the presidential nominating conventions, but this platform is vague, couched in generalities, and available to a variety of interpretations. But even when the platform is specific, it embraces a remarkable diversity of proposals which rarely form a coherent entity. Neither of the two national parties has developed a continuing and distinctive perspective on the conduct of the nation's affairs. Instead, the parties, apart from a few memorable occasions, have not sought to emphasize their policy differences. The American parties, unlike those in Western Europe, have not presented the electorate with alternative sets of beliefs and policies, however blurred. What, then, accounts for this phenomenon?

Perhaps the first element of such an explanation lies in a political culture that has proven infertile to an argument over the ownership and control of private property, an argument central to the politics of several Western European societies. The United States has not experienced a powerful socialist tradition, hostile to private ownership and anxious to replace it with some form of public ownership. There has not been such a division in the American political culture around which political parties could cluster. Of course, this does not mean that there have been no socialists. Indeed, there have been and are several socialist parties, but they have existed, apart from one brief period in the early twentieth century, at the periphery of American political life. A socialist tradition and party failed to enter the mainstream of politics because of the relative weakness of an American working-class consciousness, a consciousness which did not develop as strongly as in Europe because of the competing claims of racial, ethnic and religious attachments. Moreover, the absence of feudalism, so important to nurturing and developing a class consciousness, did not exist in the United States (see Chapter 1 for a fuller discussion). It should also be pointed out that while these reasons primarily account for the failure of a socialist movement to take root, several attempts to form socialist parties and organize unions were frequently met with hostility, violence and suppression.

The absence of a divide over private property should not be taken to indicate that there have been no debates or arguments over the ownership and control of particular institutions and industries, for there have been. Those who have felt aggrieved about the ownership and the exercise of that ownership have turned, throughout the history of the Republic, to the political process for redress. For instance, in the late nineteenth century, farmers complained vociferously about their 'exploitation' by the railroad companies and wanted government to control the charges that these companies could levy. Also in this period there were widely expressed fears over the growth of the trusts and monopolies, which resulted in the passage of the Sherman Antitrust Act of 1890. During the Great Depression there were calls to regulate and monitor certain significant sectors of the economy, including the financial markets.

Nor has there been an overriding hostility, in principle, to public ownership. There has been a range of projects over the last two centuries which have been funded and administered by either the states or the federal government. These projects include the Tennesse Valley Authority, a large-scale development of flood control, land reclamation and energy generation, which commenced in 1933 and is considered by many to be a model of public enterprise. So governmental intervention in the economy has existed as long as the Republic, and has occurred in various forms. But the intervention has been a specific response to a specific demand and not the result of a widespread hostility to and suspicion of private ownership.

Governmental regulation of the economy, public ownership and private enterprise have coexisted within the American political culture. The consequence for the political parties has been that both the Democrats and the Republicans, depending on the precise composition of their coalition, have urged and resisted governmental intervention in the economy. Farmers, especially those in the Mid-West, have traditionally been Republican, and their demands for lower railroad charges or, currently, their desire for federal subsidies for their crops have been channelled through their party. Similarly, Democrats, who command the allegiance of most citizens in the large metropolitan areas, have been the principal advocates of urban redevelopment. Moreover, Democrats who wish to succeed in agricultural constituencies have been only too anxious to endorse the farming community's demands on the political process, while Republicans who contest the large industrial cities of the North East and the Mid-West are not hesitant to support those government programmes which assist their electorate. Thus no single party has been the party of governmental intervention, and no party has been continually hostile to it. The central division over private property which has given the parties of several Western Europe states their relative programmatic consistency has been absent in the United States, and its absence has contributed to a party system characterized by a lack of programmatic commitment.

A second factor which also helps to account for this phenomenon is that programmatic commitments would make life difficult for the parties; they would jeopardize the surface unity of the vast and disparate coalitions that are the Democratic and Republican parties. Since the 1860s both of them, to a greater or lesser extent, have drawn voters from all sections of American life.

The Republican Party, which was anti-slavery and pro-Union, emerged victorious from the Civil War. Until the 1930s and the Great Depression, it was the nation's majority party. Most Americans from all walks of life, apart from southerners, voted Republican, and as a result that party dominated the electoral process, winning all but four of the presidential elections between 1860 and 1932.

The Democrats, during these six decades, were less of a national party. They suffered as a consequence of their identification with the southern cause during the Civil War, although in the South, at least among the whites, this was also a source of their electoral strength. The Democrats were not an exclusively southern party; they were also able to attract support from those states which bordered the South, once again overwhelmingly among whites, and furthermore they had pockets of electoral support in the burgeoning industrial areas of the North and Mid-West, especially among Catholics, and in particular Irish Catholics. But even if the Democratic coalition was not as extensive and heterogeneous as that of the Republicans, they nevertheless faced the task of accommodating the various elements of their coalition, which was never an easy task. Indeed, on several occasions both parties failed to pacify all their various sections. In 1912, a split within the Republicans led to the election of Woodrow

Wilson, and in 1924 and 1928 the Democrats were so divided over whether to nominate the Catholic, Al Smith, for President that the party suffered particularly heavy electoral defeats. The problem of accommodating all the sections of the Democratic Party soon became even more difficult as a consequence, paradoxically, of the party's success.

The Great Depression and the New Deal brought, in their train, disenchantment with the Republicans and a corresponding increase in the electoral attractiveness of the Democrats. Jews, Catholics – apart from those who were Irish – other ethnic groups, northern blacks and the growing union movement came under the Democratic umbrella, and when the Democrats could add these new voters to their existing supporters, victory was assured. Between 1932 and 1968, the Democratic Party lost only two presidential elections, and then only to a candidate, Dwight D. Eisenhower, who was a national hero. Its control over the Congress was continuous through this period, except for four years. But if this sequence of Democratic victories suggests that the task of maintaining the cohesion of this coalition was easy, it would be misleading, for it was profoundly difficult. The interests of the constituent elements frequently diverged and were often antipathetic – and this not only applied to white southeners and northern blacks.

By the 1960s, many northern white ethnic groups were increasingly unhappy over the policies of 'busing' and affirmative action (see Chapter 3). They were also disenchanted with the incidence of crime and disorder in the urban areas, for which they blamed the inner-city blacks and ineffective policing. Indeed, the rise to prominence of the 'social' issues of crime, law and order, and the widespread availability of materials deemed to be pornographic, made blue-collar white voters uneasy with a party they believed was too sympathetic, rightly or not, to the interests of disadvantaged blacks, Hispanics and other non-white minorities. Nor were the tensions confined to race. For instance, the states of the South and South West, which had long been bastions of Democratic strength but were anxious in the period after the Second World War to attract industry to a relatively non-industrial region, attempted to create a 'congenial' business atmosphere by restricting substantially the ability of unions to organize, a policy which was bitterly opposed by labour unions which were very influential in Democratic circles in the northern industrial states. Race relations, unionism and crime were just a few of the issues that strained the fabric of the Democratic coalition; they were the tip of an iceberg, albeit a large tip. Inevitably these tensions preoccupied the party's congressional leadership and those who sought the party's presidential nomination, for electoral success depended on party unity. Thus, reconciling the factions and establishing a *modus vivendi* between them became the party leadership's principal task. In such circumstances programmatic consistency offered few advantages. It would inhibit compromise, reveal divisions, and highlight the discordant character of the Democratic coalition. By contrast, the eclecticism of party platforms and the blurring of policy differences gave the Democrats a greater possibility of maintaining a unity, however fragile and shallow.

Throughout this period the Republicans, although less diverse a coalition, were preoccupied with similar stratagems to maintain their unity.

Republican Party platforms, like their Democratic counterparts, were a means of attaining the widest degree of support, and consequently sacrificed coherence for acceptability.

Since the late 1960s, the two parties have become more evenly balanced electorally, although the competition between them has been structured somewhat curiously. The control of the presidency and the Congress has not alternated frequently, which might have been expected given the relatively fine balance that has existed between the parties over the past quarter of a century. Rather the Republicans have dominated the elections for the presidency, while Democratic control of the Congress has not been impaired significantly. This is an unusual pattern, which has no real precedent. One explanation, or at least an element in the explanation, for this phenomenon, is the very substantial advantages attached to incumbency. Senators and Representatives, regardless of party, have resources or access to resources which are denied to their challengers. Interest groups of all kinds have shown over the recent past a far greater urgency to cultivate the politician in office rather than a potential alternative. The sitting members of Congress are able to further or indeed hinder the objectives of interest groups, and so groups direct their energies and resources towards them. Accordingly they channel their support to the incumbent, which usually ensures that the Senator or Representative is able to fund his or her campaign more easily and lavishly than any opponent. Moreover there are other advantages of office that enable the office holder to maintain a far higher profile with the electorate; recent electoral history suggests that this is a decisive advantage. Incumbency is therefore part of the explanation for this curious pattern of results that has emerged since the late 1960s and it is particularly important for congressional elections. It has far less impact on presidential elections, where a more significant factor is the disintegration of the 'New Deal coalition'.

This coalition was the source of the Democrats' hold on the White House, but during the last two decades it has seen substantial defections to the Republicans. In particular, southerners plus blue- and white-collar voters have supported Republican presidential candidates, notably in 1972, 1980, 1984 and 1988. Indeed, the South, which used to be the most reliable and consistent regional component of the Democratic coalition, has now become the most Republican region, at least at presidential level. Democratic candidates did not carry one southern or border state in 1972, 1984 or 1988, and were only more successful in 1976, and to a lesser extent in 1980, because Carter was a southerner. But despite five out of six defeats for the presidency, the Democrats have continued to dominate the congressional elections in the South and elsewhere. They have won control of both houses of the Congress repeatedly, apart from the Senate in 1980, 1982 and 1984. It is a recurrent phenomenon of recent years that the American electorate appears determined to return a Republican to the White House, while wishing to ensure that the Democrats retain control of the Congress. Neither party has established a decisive ascendancy over the past two decades. So if the 'New Deal coalition' is in terminal decay, there is no apparent replacement that is about to dominate American electoral politics. Rather the division of spoils looks likely to continue, with the Democrats apparently unable to threaten the Republican hold on the White House but equally likely to retain their lock on the Congress. Both parties have been able to create winning coalitions for one of the branches of government but not for the other. It has no historical precedent.

Nevertheless, both parties continue to remain vast coalitions and as such they are still governed by the imperatives of being coalitions, with all the continuing consequences for policy and programme. Even the Republican Party under Reagan and Bush is far more heterodox both in policy and in composition than it might appear at first glance. Despite suggestions from its friends, and interestingly its opponents, that since 1980 the Republican Party has adopted a far more consistent position on a number of issues, in practice the Party continues to contain a number of voices. Moreover if there is any conflict between consistency and constituency, then consistency is usually the loser. Certainly during the first Reagan administration, when the President and his closest advisers were ideologically at their most confident, they were anxious to create the impression that in the realm of economics it was the role of the international and domestic markets to determine the supply, demand and price of goods and services. Government had little role to play, the 'judgement' of the markets were sovereign. However, whenever the 'judgements' of the markets proved to be unhelpful to the industries and services located in their districts or states, Republican Senators and Congressmen sought to overturn these 'judgements' through the institutions of the federal government, and they frequently found a sympathetic response from the Reagan administration. Farmers, who have traditionally been predominantly Republican, have always found the federal government sympathetic to their perennial problem that the market price for agricultural produce is inadequate for their requirements. The Reagan administration, in the manner of its predecessors, was prepared to assist farmers especially during the slump in commodity prices in the early 1980s. Again the administration was sympathetic to those industries who were unable to compete with their foreign competitors. Although the administration usually claimed that its actions in imposing restrictions on the access of foreign producers to the US market was a retaliation for the unfair trade practices of other governments, it did indeed place such restrictions on a number of products. The semi-conductor industry was able to convince the administration of the necessity of such action against its Japanese competitors, although most informed commentators on the industry believed that the fundamental problem of the American manufacturers arose primarily out of their comparative inefficiency and not out of any unfair practices. Furthermore, the administration was prepared to condone a number of 'voluntary' agreements, notably in the automobile industry, which protected domestic manufacturers from the full force of overseas competition.

The Bush administration has operated with a similar degree of flexibility, although it must be noted that the President and his closest advisers have never been quite as anxious as their predecessors to establish their ideological credentials. The Bush administration has established a more pragmatic persona. It has sought to create a more accommodating and malleable personality. Nevertheless the President, particularly during the election campaign, appeared to set certain firm policy objectives. One of these was a commitment not to raise taxes. However, by 1990, with growing pressures to lower the budget deficit, the administration was considering a variety of devices to increase the federal government's revenue. Although the administration was determined to avoid raising the levels at which income tax was levied, it was prepared to consider a range of other strategies which included either new or higher taxes. The reason for this change by the Bush administration was simply the result of a political calculation, that the failure to control the deficit was more electorally damaging than reversing the President's position. In the annals of American political history, it was no more than one further instance where programmatic consistency succumbed to the reality of constituency politics and the primacy of electoral success.

This portrait of the two major American parties as vast and disparate coalitions with no coherent sets of beliefs in some senses raises more questions than it resolves. If a programme has not unified these coalitions, what has? Are there, and have there been, any differences between the parties? On what basis do voters choose between the Republicans and Democrats? How have the leaders managed to conciliate and accommodate the enormous array of interests that shelter under the umbrellas of the two national parties, and if they have, at what cost? These are questions that need to be answered.

Patronage

To take the first question, what indeed has held the two parties together over the last one hundred years? One answer has been the control of government and its consequent benefits. The control of the presidency in tandem with congressional majorities has traditionally meant rewards for the party faithful, rewards that have come in various guises. First, it has meant appointments to federal office. Presidents have within their gift, though subject to senatorial approval, a host of federal appointments, from Cabinet officers and federal judges to those who occupy lesser positions; and Presidents have used this power of patronage to repay political debts. Those who have established their political credit with the President, usually through supporting his candidacy, have expected and normally received appointments either for themselves or to be allocated on their advice. This transaction of electoral support in return for presidential appointment has traditionally transcended the political beliefs of the participants.

The history of American political parties is redolent with examples of Presidents trading in the currency of appointments with those who do not share their beliefs. The Democratic Party, in particular, provides several striking instances. As was noted in Chapter 5, most Democratic presidential candidates have been drawn from the party's northern and liberal wing, but victory in the presidential election could not be secured without the assistance of conservative southern Democrats. Accordingly, and despite disagreements over a range of policies, these candidates courted the southerners, and in the event of their victory, repaid this support. President Kennedy, for example, despite his explicit and proclaimed commitment to civil rights, appointed several southerners and notable segregationists to senior federal appointments, including one to his Cabinet and several as federal judges. This should not be interpreted as doubting Kennedy's commitment to civil rights but should be seen as an indication of an enduring political practice. Kennedy's appointees were not a statement of his belief over civil rights but were a debt being repaid to particular southern Democrats for his victory in 1960. Every President has traded in the same currency, which has provided some of the cement in party coalitions.

Appointments are one element of this currency; federal expenditure is another. The federal government currently spends $1,000 billion a year; a considerable percentage of this is expended on purchasing goods and services, which politicians attempt to attract to their constituencies. If an army base is to be constructed, they want it to be in their district or state. If a defence contract is to be awarded, they wish it to be given to a local contractor. A new research installation or land reclamation project arouse the same emotions. How are these decisions made? Undoubtedly, some of them are made on the appropriate criteria. However, a significantly large proportion of them are not decided by military requirements or the logic inherent to the project. Observers of American politics frequently note that the allocation of governmental expenditure is a consequence of political, rather than industrial or military, imperatives. As with appointments, expenditure is part of a political currency. It is a reward of political office, a fruit of victory, and as such has maintained the cohesion of the parties. Patronage has allowed parties to be a diverse mix of interests because it provides a tradeable unit of currency. Favour for reward, support in return for appointment; in such circumstances programmatic coherence can be left aside.

How voters decide

If the currency of patronage does explain, in part, why the two parties over the past hundred years have maintained their cohesion, it does not explain on what basis the voters make their choice. After all, the politicians of both parties can be expected to look after their constituences, so what accounts for party preference? How do voters distinguish between the two parties?

To most non-American observers, the differences between the Democratic and Republican parties do not appear substantial. Indeed, it is a commonplace that they are remarkably similar, and the reason for their similarity is that they do not divide on ideological grounds in the manner of parties in most other Western democracies. However, within the United States, the absence of these ideological differences has not led to a comparable evaluation. The two parties are not seen as identical twins but have developed distinct, if somewhat simple, personas. In part, these personas have been historically cumulative. For instance, even fifty years after the Great Depression, the Republican Party is still affected by its association with it. Similarly, the political success of the New Deal in coping with the Depression continues to give the Democrats a residual benefit. The fact that the four occasions on which the United States has been involved in a war during the twentieth century have occurred under Democratic Presidents, continues to be noted by the electorate. Of course, it would be a gross exaggeration to say that the Democratic and Republican parties are seen as the parties of war and depression respectively, but nevertheless their personas incorporate their history.

The perception of the two parties is also affected by the composition of their coalition. The post-New Deal Democratic coalition of ethnic and racial minorities, the inhabitants of large industrial conurbations, union members and the less affluent farmers, created the sense that it was the party of the little man and woman, the defender of their interests. The Republicans, by contrast, are commonly seen as representing the interests of the more affluent and of business corporations. Again, these are very simple identifiers, but they are not unimportant and they are reinforced by beliefs that the Democratic Party 'stands for' the redistribution of income, the extension of the welfare state and increased governmental expenditure, while Republicans are concerned about the level of taxation and the sheer size and weight of government. These are not sophisticated distinctions and are not always borne out in practice, but studies of the American electorate tend to show that it is simply not very sophisticated: 'The American public has a very unsophisticated view of political matters characterized by an inability to consider such matters in broad abstract terms' (Nie et al., 1979, p.37). So these rather simple differences do help to explain the basis on which Americans vote, but they do not provide a full and adequate account. However, the numerous studies of voting behaviour do offer a more complete explanation, although it must be noted that those who have conducted the surveys and analysed the results are not always in agreement and can arrive at very different conclusions. Nevertheless, there is a measure of common ground.

A key element in most explanations of American voting behaviour is the notion of party identification, whereby most of the electorate, despite – or perhaps because of – their lack of sophistication, have developed a strong psychological attachment to one of the two major parties. Why have they developed such an attachment? The most probable answer to this question offered by Campbell et al. (1960) in their study of The American Voter, and by others, is that voters have been guided towards that attachment by their parents and that it has been reinforced by relatives, neighbours and other social networks. But, of course, the matter cannot be left there, for why did their parents have such a sense of party identification? To answer this question we cannot simply turn to the grandparents and then back to the 1790s, as this would suggest that once identification was established it was then automatically transmitted generationally, in which case the very first parties would still be flourishing.

The voting study surveys instead mediate the notion of party identification with a theory of critical elections. Put simply, the theory of critical elections suggests that there have been events in American history of such enormous societal magnitude that they have rewritten the extant political rules. Old party loyalties, and indeed parties, have disappeared and been replaced by new ones. These extraordinary events have been few and far between, but the Civil War was one of them and the Great Depression another. In these periods of tumult, new attachments were forged. As was noted above, both of these events brought in their train a realignment of American party politics, in one case ushering in a period of Republican domination, and in the other replacing those Republican loyalties with Democratic ones. So 1864 and 1932 were *realigning* elections. In the aftermath of a new alignment those presidential elections won by the newly dominant coalition such as 1936, 1940, 1944, 1948, 1960 and 1964 were *maintaining* elections, while those elections lost by the majority party such as 1952 and 1956 were *deviating* elections.

How, then, are the presidential elections after 1964 to be classified? The Republicans have won five out of six of these elections, so have they been deviating elections? The answer is no, but neither do those who study electoral behaviour believe that the last six elections presage a realignment in party identification. As was noted above, the pattern of results, with each of the parties establishing a 'lock' on one of the branches of government, is unusual and suggests that neither party has achieved dominance. A Republican majority has not emerged, although that party now has greater electoral support than at any time since the 1920s. The achievement of winning five out of the last six presidential elections is no mean feat. The Democrats have far more substantial problems, which are discussed below. But the immediate future is likely to see a continuance of the past two decades, with intense party competition and no overall party dominance. However, there have been certain developments that are worth noting and which may suggest that traditional patterns are changing.

Surveys of the American electorate have detected some important trends in voting behaviour that do not coexist easily with the portrait of the voter as not particularly interested or knowledgeable in politics but with strong attachments to one of the two political parties. First, there does appear to be an increasing number of voters who are interested in issues and who cast their ballots according to their understanding of the issues and the candidates' response to them. They do not constitute a vast number and their importance can be overstated, but they do exist and they are better educated and have higher incomes than the electorate as a whole. The second trend, which may well be allied to the rise of issue-voting, is the gradual decline of party identification (see Table 6.1).

Table 6.1 Party identification, % of electorate in presidential election years 1952–84

Affiliation	1952	1956	1960	1964	1968	1972	1976	1980	1984
Strong Democrat	22	21	21	26	20	15	15	18	18
Weak Democrat	25	23	25	25	25	25	25	23	22
Independent Democrat	10	7	8	9	10	11	12	11	10
Independent	5	9	8	8	11	13	14	13	7
Independent Republican	7	8	7	6	9	11	10	10	13
Weak Republican	14	14	13	13	14	13	14	14	15
Strong Republican	13	15	14	11	10	10	9	9	14
Apolitical, Don't Know	4	3	4	2	1	2	1	2	2

Source: University of Michigan Survey Research Center/CPS/NES. Survey Research Center

There has been a perceptible, if slight, reduction in the number of those Americans who identify with the Democrats or Republicans, a phenomenon that political scientists refer to as *party dealignment*. Are there particular categories of voters who are especially responsible for party dealignment? Once again, those who see themselves as Independents are disproportionately affluent and more highly educated.

Furthermore, the lowest levels of party identification are registered among voters under the age of 24. The growing disenchantment with parties does appear to be concentrated particularly among younger voters and those with higher incomes and more education, a development which does not bode well for either party. So why has this disaffection taken place? What accounts for party dealignment? Are the Democratic and Republican parties unable to represent the full spectrum of American interests and opinions? The answer to these questions may emerge from an examination of the internal structure and organization of the parties.

6.3   Party organization

The internal structure and organization of the Democratic and Republican parties have altered dramatically during the twentieth century. In the early decades of this century the language used to describe the two parties was littered frequently with terms such as 'corruption', 'bosses', 'machines' and 'smoke-filled rooms'. Collectively, these words and phrases created a picture, and a broadly accurate one in the large metropolitan areas, of the party as a political machine. These machines, such as the famous Tammany Hall in New York, were organized on a hierarchical basis, with a political boss at the apex, who was usually, but not invariably, a corrupt figure who used the political power of the machine for private financial gain.

The machine's political power arose out of the loyalty of voters to it, a loyalty purchased by the help given by the machine to its heavily immigrant electorate in coping with the vicissitudes of urban American life. In return for these services the machine gained substantial electoral support, which was frequently enhanced by a degree of corrupt voting practices. It controlled the process of party nomination and usually had little difficulty in winning the November election for its chosen candidate. Moreover, because the political boss could rely on a solid base of electoral support within his city, he was also an important player at both state and national level. Bosses were the inhabitants of the smoke-filled rooms at the presidential nominating conventions. They could deliver votes both at the convention and in the presidential election. Consequently, they were courted by candidates and rewarded by Presidents.

However, the power and influence of the machines had begun to wane by the early decades of this century due to the impact of two developments. The first was the growth in welfare services provided initially by the state governments and subsequently by the federal government, services which were available without payment and which consequently diminished the importance of the assistance provided by the machines. The second development, and perhaps the more significant one, was the drive to democratize the internal structure of the parties.

The Progressive reforms

The origins of the desire to change lay in the Progressive movement that emerged in the late nineteenth century. The Progressives sought, among other objectives, to end the widespread corruption and venality in American public life, a state of affairs which they blamed on the power of the political machines. Accordingly, they proposed a series of reforms intended to end the machines' control of the electoral process. They suggested a variety of devices and procedures to achieve this objective, including the referendum, but the Progressive reform that has had the greatest impact on the parties has been the primary election.

The primary election was designed to transfer control of the nomination process from the boss and the party hierarchy to the electorate. It was supposed to democratize the parties and the party hierarchy to the electorate. It was supposed to democratize the parties and return power from the smoke-filled rooms to the people. Thus, in those circumstances where more than one candidate seeks the nomination of the Democratic Party, the party's nominee is chosen by an election – a primary election – which either the entire electorate, or at least that percentage of it registered as Democrats, is eligible to participate. The precise rules governing the eligibility to vote in primaries can, and do, vary considerably between states, but even in those states where the rules are more restrictive, the advent of the primary election fundamentally changed the rules of the game. The nomination process was no longer in the gift of the party machine. The boss could no longer use the party nomination for public office as a reward for past service to the machine. Nor could he use it as an incentive to spur his subordinates, or use it as a unit of currency in his political dealings.

The primary election transferred the nomination process to a public arena which was accessible to a variety of actors and interests outside the machine's control. Initially the machines may have had advantages in this arena. They had organization and electoral experience, but as their power eroded, for the reasons noted earlier, these advantages did not prove decisive. Opponents of the machines could, and did, successfully contest primary elections. As a result, the bosses did not automatically control the process of nomination, a fact which broke the power of the machines and hastened their demise. By the 1950s the few machines that remained, with the sole exception of the Daley machine in Chicago, were pale and ineffective shadows of their earlier selves. By the 1970s, even the Chicago machine, after the death of Richard Daley, was itself in its final death throes. So the primary election helped to end the era of machine politics in the United States, but its impact did not end along with the political bosses.

Primaries have had very similar effects on party organizations other than machines. Even those organizations that were not corrupt and accessible to ordinary democratic and Republican voters have discovered that the primary election removed their control of the party nomination. Nominations were no longer guaranteed through party service. The primary was open to any candidate, with no requirement of party service. Of course, a record of party commitment might well be an advantage to a candidate, although the experience of the past several decades does not suggest that it is an overwhelming advantage. There are examples, far too numerous to recount here, of both Democratic and Republican candidates, with no history of party attachment, who nevertheless have won the primary election. Consequently, the logic of joining and working for a party organization diminished. As the use of primary elections became more widespread, party organization across the United States began to disintegrate. By the 1970s all fifty states used a form of primary election for most local state and federal offices. The consequences for party organizations, as Ehrenreich (1986, p.47) has recently noted, have been severe:

> The Democratic party, which was once thought to be an essential ingredient of the two-party system, has gone underground. To be perfectly non-partisan about all this, I should say that the existence of the Republican party has also been in doubt for some years now. There are no known Republican volunteers, or in most places local headquarters.

So what has replaced the vacuum left by the decay of party organizations?

Candidates

To a considerable extent, candidates have replaced parties as the central influence in political campaigns. Candidates have become the principal actors in the electoral process. Their abilities and personalities are now critically important factors in any American election. When they enter a primary election, they must, if they wish to succeed, create their own campaign organization. They must raise the campaign finance through their own efforts and recruit volunteers on the back of their own enthusiasm. They have to make the decision to hire the three crucial figures of recent American elections: the political consultant, the opinion pollster and the media consultant. Interestingly, these services used to be supplied, albeit in a less sophisticated form, by party organizations, but since their demise, the task of political and campaign advice has been, in a sense, privatized. The private companies who offer the advice and whose numbers have increased dramatically over the past twenty years, are currently among the few organizations that have expertise, experience and constant involvement in the electoral process. Inevitably, their services are in considerable demand from candidates of both parties and all shades of opinion, who purchase those services for their own campaigns for the duration of the election.

So candidates construct personal campaign organizations designed for their own electoral success. These organizations either disband in the event of defeat in the primary, or after victory are expanded and enhanced to deal with the general election in November. Of course, after the victory in the primary election, the candidate becomes the official party nominee, though in a very real sense the nomination is merely a label. The nominees still have to rely on their own resources and organization. Party politics have become focused on the candidate. So what has been the consequence of candidate-oriented politics?

Some of the consequences for the presidency, Congress and the public have been discussed in Chapters 4 and 5. Of the other effects perhaps the most striking is the fact that this type of politics expands the differences between parties in American and those in other Western democracies. Because parties in the United States have lost control of the nomination process, they have also blurred their collective identity, which in any case was always somewhat unclear. The primary election, while democratizing the party, has introduced a certain random and almost idiosyncratic element into the two parties at state and national level. For instance, in 1980 a member of the Ku-Klux-Klan won the Democratic Party nomination for a seat in the House of Representatives. Similarly in Louisiana, a former official of the Ku-Klux-Klan won the Republican nomination for the House of Representatives, although he was denounced by officials of the national Republican Party. Somewhat more bizarrely, in 1986 two members of a group whose proclaimed beliefs include the allegations that the former Secretary of State, Henry Kissinger, is a Soviet agent and that Queen Elizabeth II is the co-ordinator of an international drug trafficking cartel, nevertheless won Democratic nominations for two public offices in Illinois, including that of Lieutenant Governor. These examples, though not isolated, are untypical, but they nevertheless illustrate the fact that the control of nominations is in the hands of an electorate capable, if only occasionally, of making eccentric selections. Thus the parties do face a dilemma over internal democracy and the unpredictability that appears to be a consequence of it. The parties also face the dilemma over the process of presidential selection.

The same drive for democratization has affected the procedures of presidential nomination, although interestingly it was somewhat slower in manifesting itself in this arena. As recently as 1964, only seventeen state parties chose their delegations to both the Republican and Democratic presidential nominating conventions by primary election. The remaining states used a variety of other devices. By 1980, thirty-five state Democratic parties and thirty-four Republican parties had opted for primaries, although by 1984 the Democratic figure had fallen to twenty-five and the Republican number declined to thirty. In 1988 several southern states held their primaries on the same day. The event became known as Super Tuesday. The intention was to make candidates, particularly in the Democratic Party, take the interests of the South into greater consideration. The constant modification of the primary process will almost certainly continue. In 1992 the California primary, which traditionally has been held on the final day of the primary season in early June, will be brought back to a date in March, in order to give that state's election greater impact in the nominating process. But whatever the exact number of primaries or precise configuration of dates and states, the primary election has become the key mechanism in the presidential nominating process. Well over 60 per cent of the delegates to the 1984 Democratic National Convention were chosen by primary election and the figure in 1988 was approximately the same (Crotty and Jackson, 1985, p. 14).

In addition to the greater use of primaries, both parties, but particularly the Democrats, wanted to make their convention more accessible to those groups that were traditionally underrepresented: women, blacks, other ethnic minorities and younger voters. In order to do so, from the late 1960s onwards the party undertook to reform those practices which would inhibit such a development. The cumulative effect of the reforms and the primaries did indeed create a more open nomination process, as the history of the last four conventions demonstrates.

In 1972 the Democratic Party chose Senator George McGovern, a liberal and passionate critic of the Vietnam War, and in an important sense a political outsider who had little support from the established interests within the Democratic Party. He was not the candidate of the unions, the black or Jewish interest groups, or the professional politicians. In 1976 the nominee was Governor Jimmy Carter, a moderate to conservative southerner, but who also aroused the same lack of enthusiasm as McGovern from the major interests that operated within the party. Both Carter's and McGovern's success was due to their victories in the primaries, which, in Carter's case, was all the more remarkable as the proportion of the population who recognized his name only six months before the convention was barely 2 per cent. In 1980 Carter was renominated without any degree of enthusiasm after a strenuous and testing primary campaign with Senator Edward Kennedy, and in 1984 Carter's Vice-President, Walter Mondale, a liberal of the traditional Democratic variety, won the nomination. He did so only after a bitter primary campaign against another outside, Senator Gary Hart, who, like Carter, had minimal national recognition before the campaign began in earnest.

In 1988 the nomination was won by yet another candidate who had no national reputation. Michael Dukakis had been a successful governor of Massachussets but was unknown nationally. The primaries allowed him to establish a credible candidacy and his victories in the late primary elections against the Reverend Jesse Jackson, the only black candidate, secured him the nomination.

On the Republican side, the openness of the system almost permitted Ronald Reagan, another outsider – at least in 1976 – to break one of the unwritten rules of American political life, namely that an incumbent President cannot be denied renomination. In 1976 he barely failed to wrest the nomination away from President Gerald Ford after a series of victories in the later primaries. It was his strength in the primary elections in 1980 that gained him the nomination in that year and in 1984 President Reagan's renomination was unopposed.

In 1988 Vice-President George Bush won the nomination, but only after a series of bitter elections. The contests against Senator Robert Dole, the Republican leader in the Senate, appeared at one stage to have damaged permanently the Bush candidacy. Even the very considerable advantage of being the incumbent Vice-President in a successful administration does not guarantee a nomination, at least without a serious challenge.

There can be little doubt about the accessibility of the presidential nominating process. Indeed, in some respects it is even more open than those for state and congressional elections because there has been a degree of federal funding for primary election campaigns since the Campaign Reform Act of 1974, which lessens the dependence on private contributors. But this accessibility has been bought at a cost to the parties. The candidates chosen by the Democratic and Republican parties do not indicate a confident and stable party system, but the reverse. The democratization of the nomination process has allowed the parties to be captured temporarily by particular factions. There has been no sense of continuity. The candidates have become the party at national, state and congressional level, and no longer possess even the minimal unity that they previously shared. In these circumstances it is not surprising that there has been a measure of disaffection with the parties, a degree of dealignment. This growing unhappiness with the Democrats and Republicans perhaps explains, in part, the low level of political participation in the United States and the dramatic growth in the number and activities of interest groups.

6.4   Political participation

It is one of the paradoxes of American political life that a party system that places such a high premium on party democracy nevertheless attracts such little response at the ballot box. By comparison with virtually every other Western democracy, the percentage of Americans who vote – one important indicator of political participation – is very low. The turnout in the 1984 presidential elections was 53.2 per cent and continued the steady decline since 1960. The average figure for the off-year congressional elections in 1974, 1978 and 1982 was less than 40 per cent. In the United Kingdom, voter turnout in a general election is regularly over 70 per cent, and in some other European countries 80 per cent is not an unusual figure. So what accounts for the difference?

Some of the discrepancy can be accounted for by the problem of voter registration, which in the United States is more complicated than in most European countries and where the burden of registration is placed on the individual and not on the government. Furthermore, the right to vote is not only dependent on age, but also on length of residence and, in some states, on evidence that the person registering has voted at least once in five years. 'It is, in part, because of these requirements that the voter turnout rate in the United States was, and is, one of the lowest among the developed democracies' (Conway, 1985, p.93).

But the legal requirements to register do not fully explain the differential. There are explanations which do give a reasonably convincing account of why turnout is declining; these are based on the evidence of considerable variation in turnout between the constituent elements of the electorate. Whites are more likely to vote by some 10 per cent than blacks. Other ethnic groups, Hispanics for instance, are less inclined to vote than blacks. Turnout among college-educated voters is appreciably higher than among those who have only attended high school or grade school. Young voters have far lower turnout rates than their elders, and those who identify strongly with one of the two parties turn out in higher numbers than those who do not so identify. But those categories of voters who have low turnout rates, such as those aged under 24, members of ethnic minorities and those who do not identify with parties, are a growing percentage of the electorate, which explains the steady decline in the rate of turnout.

This does not account for the fact that turnout in the United States is lower across the entire social spectrum. Some commentators lean towards explanations of voter alienation among the dispossessed, while others are inclined to view Americans as being overly absorbed in their private lives and thus less disposed to care about public acts of political participation. The legacies of Vietnam and Watergate are also offered as an explanation, as is the disintegration of the American party system. But there is no commonly agreed explanation for the low voter turnout, which remains a puzzle. It is interesting to note, though, that alongside these low and declining percentages of Americans who vote, there has been a vast growth in interest group activity, a development which suggests that interest groups provide an arena for participation that is proving increasingly attractive and fruitful.

6.5   Interest groups

In the 1830s, Alexis de Tocqueville commented on the enthusiasm of Americans to join organizations: 'In no country in the world has the principle of association been more successfully used or applied to a greater multitude of objects than in America' (de Tocqueville, 1966, p.135). It is an observation that continues to hold true. In 1985, there were over 18,000 interest or pressure groups, which was not only a testament to the enthusiasm of Americans to join such organizations, but also to the diversity of American society, a characteristic which has been one of the themes of this book. These groups or organized interests both reflect and arise out of this diversity. There are several hundred organizations which are based on ethnic or national origins, and nearly a thousand religious groups. There are several thousand concerned with educational and cultural matters. The single largest category, though, are business and trade interest groups, which comprise approximately 20 per cent of the total; this reflects their power and influence but also illustrates the array of commercial activities and the variety of occupations and professions that exist within the United States. Between 1960 and 1980 the attractiveness of organized groups of all kinds increased. The number of such organizations grew by 60 per cent, and perhaps even more significantly the number of these interest groups that were represented in Washington doubled.

So clearly Americans not only find it congenial to belong to an interest group, but, increasingly, a significant percentage of them believe that they need such an organization to represent them in Washington. So how effective are interest groups? How important are they in the American political process? Before these questions are examined, it may be useful to consider some of the principal categories of interest groups and how they function.

Business groups

The number of business and trade groups indicates their collective power, but such a large number is rarely, if ever, united. The business interest groups are not a monolith. There are associations representing small businesses, such as the National Federation of Independent Business, and those which reflect the views of large corporations, of which the National Association of Manufacturers is the most important. The US Chamber of Commerce, with its local and state branches, represents over 200,000 individual businesses of varying size. Interestingly, these collective associations have traditionally not been particularly influential in Washington, in part because the very largest corporations have their own representation. For instance, General Electric the largest US electrical company with interests from consumer appliances to aero engines, maintains a Washington staff of 130. Other major corporations have bureaux of a similar size, and they are the business groups that wield the greatest influence in Washington. They have a powerful impact on policy-making, a fact which is observed in Chapters 7 and 8.

Unions

The comparative weakness of American unions was noted in Chapter 1, and they are consequently less important players in the political process than business groups. However, they are not insignificant. The single most important union organization is the AFL-CIO (the American Federation of Labor and the Congress of Industrial Organizations) which represents ninety-six unions with fifteen million members and whose voice inevitably carries weight, particularly with Democrats. However, the unions, like the business groups, are not a monolithic entity. Some large unions, such as the Teamsters, which represents truckers, are not in the AFL-CIO and they can, and do, support policies and candidates opposed by the AFL-CIO. Furthermore, unions have to face the reality that they represent a declining percentage of the workforce and that their membership is overwhelmingly concentrated in the industrialized North East and Mid-West, areas whose political influence is on the wane.

Professional associations

Some of the most powerful interest groups fall into this category. The American Medical Association (AMA), the organization that represents doctors, has had the most significant impact on the making of health policy. For several decades it successfully resisted the intervention of the federal government in medicine. When its objections were overcome in 1964, the AMA nevertheless ensured that Medicare was tailored for the financial benefit of its members. The American Bar Association and the National Education Association, which represent lawyers and teachers respectively, have also been notably powerful players in Washington.

Agriculture

Historically, farm organizations have been the most powerful of all. Their influence has undoubtedly been enhanced by the fact that farmers were, and are, overrepresented in the Congress and particularly the Senate. Whatever the reason, the main farm organizations, the American Farm Bureau Federation, the National Farmers' Union and the Grange, have always found politicians very receptive. In recent years, commodity organizations that promote cotton, tobacco, etc. have sought representation in Washington, as well as the large corporations involved in agriculture, known as agribusinesses.

Public interest

There has been a rapid growth in those groups which do not pursue their members' narrow economic interest. Since the late 1960s, those organizations interested in promoting the public interest have seen their memberships rise very sharply, with a commensurate rise in public attention. Some of these groups have developed a high public profile and on some issues a considerable degree of public influence. For instance, on matters concerning the environment, the Sierra Club is an important actor in the policy-making process. Other notable groups are Common Cause, which concerns itself with the accountability of government, and Public Citizen, founded by Ralph Nader, which frequently exposes the inadequacy of government regulation.

Single-issue groups

There is a degree of difficulty in deciding what constitutes a single-issue group. Is, for instance, the environment a single issue, or do environmentalists take a stand on several policy questions such as nuclear power, clean air and chemical waste? With this caveat in mind, there has been a striking growth in single-issue interest groups, a growth which has received substantial publicity as the issues, on the whole, have a high public consciousness. There is no better illustration of single-issue politics than the problem of abortion, which has aroused enormous controversy and intense political activity since the early 1970s. Interestingly, the pro-life or anti-abortion groups had the greater impact on the political process in the aftermath of the *Roe* v. *Wade* decision. In part this was due to the fact that the pro-choice or pro-abortion groups wanted to maintain *Roe* and the status quo, while the pro-life groups had to make the running in order to reverse the position. But now that the Supreme Court has apparently given the individual states a greater role in formulating the rules over abortion (see Chapter 3), the pro-choice groups have been far more active and vociferous.

The Washington lobby

In one sense, Washington has been and continues to be, the traditional arena of interest group activity. As the scope of the federal government's activities has expanded, not surprisingly the number of interest groups represented in Washington has also grown. So the congenial and intimate Washington lobby of the 1960s has been replaced by one with a far larger and more diverse membership.

Apart from the many new groups, the most striking phenomenon has been the specialization of lobbying. An increasing number of groups no longer rely on their internal resources to promote their interests, but hire the services of professional lobbyists, who have shed their somewhat shady personas and have been transformed into key figures in Washington. They are usually individuals who have had recent experience in government and are assumed to have an intimate knowledge of both people and procedures. However, the most important point to note about the rise in professional lobbying is that it is a function of the growth and complexity of the federal government. As the government's activities have increased, so has the need for an expertise to understand the processes and procedures and the implications of legislation. Again, as the claims on government have grown, any one claim can be lost in the welter of competing demands, unless it is brought to the attention of the relevant institutions and people. The lobbyists offer expertise and access, and interest groups clearly value both.

Political action committees

It has always been the case that interest groups have sought to affect the outcome of elections. Accordingly, they have contributed time, energy and money to achieving their desired objective. Until 1974, the regulations that governed campaign finance were widely ignored, and there were no effective limitations on the level of campaign contributions. However, the abuses of Watergate led to the 1974 Federal Campaign Act, which not only introduced a system of federal funding for presidential elections, but also imposed limitations on campaign contributions to congressional elections, of a maximum of $5000 for any one primary campaign and a further $5000 for any one general election campaign. These new restrictions led to a very sharp rise in the number of political action committees (PACs), which were already in existence but were not seen as especially useful forms of organization. However, the restrictions on campaign funding led to a reassessment of the value of PACs. The new laws were devised to prevent any candidate receiving more than $5000 in each phase of the campaign. However, a further $10,000 could be given to a PAC formed to support the candidate, and if several PACs were formed they too could be the recipients of contributions. Moreover, there was no limit on the amount of money that a PAC could spend in support of, or opposition to, a candidate. Unsurprisingly, the number of PACs has grown by over 1000 per cent since 1974.

Has the rise of PACs adversely affected one of the two parties? The answer is broadly no. The business and corporate PACs which receive and spend the largest percentage of contributions distribute their money fairly evenly between the two parties. The union PACs favour the Democratic Party. However, it is noticeable that the more conservative PACs, such as the National Conservative Political Action Committee (NICPAC), are more adept at raising money and are more effectively organized. Nevertheless, they have not had quite the impact on the electoral processes that they claim, and there are signs that liberal PACs have closed the gap in terms of organization and efficiency.

Interest groups in the political process

Interest groups have always been an important constituent element of the American political process. Since the creation of the Republic, they have attempted to influence policy in the state capitals and Washington, as well as opinion at the grass roots level. They continue to do so, but in some senses interest groups appear to have moved to the centre of the political stage. Their influence used to be mediated by the parties, the traditional vehicle of mass representation. But as the parties have disintegrated, the role of the interest group has loomed larger. Understandably, a growing percentage of Americans, responding to the plight of the parties, have felt the need to be represented effectively by interest groups, a development which is understandable but also disturbing. The strength and power of an interest group depends to a significant extent on its financial resources and organization. Unfortunately, there are those Americans who do not have access to such resources and who are unable to organize, or, if organized, are not able to muster the money and energy to be effective advocates of their cause. To some extent the ballot has been supplanted by the professional lobbyist. The growth and influence of interest groups has, to a degree, altered the configuration of power in the political process, a development that is evident from Part 2 of the book.

References

CAMPBELL, A., CONOERSE, P., MILLER, W. and STOKES, D. (1960) *The American Voter,* New York, John Wiley.

CONWAY, M. (1985) *Political Participation in the United States,* Washington DC, CQ Press.

CROTTY, W and JACKSON III, J. (1985) *Presidential Primaries and Nominations,* Washington DC, CQ Press.

EHRENREICH, B. (1986) 'The Liberals' Disappearing Act', *Mother Jones,* Vol. XI, No. III.

HOFSTADTER, R. (1969) *The Idea of a Party System. The Rise of Legitimate Opposition in the United States 1780–1840,* Berkeley, University of California Press.

McCORMICK, R. (1967) 'Political Development and the Second Party System', in W. Chambers and W. Barnhem (eds) *The American Party Systems,* New York, Oxford University Press.

NIE, N., VERBA, S. and PETROCIK, J. (1979) *The Changing American Voter,* Cambridge, Mass., Harvard University Press.

RICHARDSON, J. (ed.) (1897) *Messages and Papers of the Presidents,* 10 vols, Washington DC, Government Printing Office.

TOCQUEVILLE, A. DE (1966) *Democracy in America,* London, Fontana (first published 1835).

Further reading

CIGLER, C. J. and LOOMIS, B. (eds) (1985) *Interest Group Politics,* Washington DC, CQ Press.

LADD, E. (1982) *Where Have All the Voters Gone? The Fracturing of America's Political Parties,* 2nd edition, New York, W. W. Norton.

POLSBY, N. (1983) *The Consequences of Party Reform,* New York, Oxford University Press.

POMPER, G. (1980) *Party Renewal in America,* New York, Praeger.

WILSON, G. (1981) *Interest Groups in the United States,* Oxford, Clarendon Press.

Part 2
The Making of Public Policy

7   The Politics of American Foreign Policy

Ever since America emerged from the Second World War as a global super-power, foreign and national security matters have come to acquire an exalted status in the nation's political imagination. This is not unrelated to the fact that, as President Kennedy warned, policy is formed with a constant awareness that 'one mistake could cost all our lives'. This alone would pro-vide an unequivocal justification for exploring how foreign and national security policy is formulated. But it is also the case that the foreign policy process offers extremely rich insights into the dynamics of public policy for-mulation more generally. It reflects to a remarkable degree the complex forces which shape the particular characteristics of American politics; it is, in large part, a microcosm of the political system at work. Moreover it illus-trates starkly the disjunctures between the policy making process and the principles of American liberal democracy. Indeed, for many reasons this inherent tension between political ideals and political praxis is particularly acute in respect of foreign and national security affairs. For in an age in which Presidents have acquired the ultimate power 'to lisp the alphabet of annihilation', the question of democratic control of government has devel-oped an urgent and chilling relevance.

7.1   Domestic politics and the foreign policy process

Traditionally foreign and national security policy have been conceived as arenas of state activity which should not be subject to the vagaries of domes-tic politics. Since foreign policy is concerned with the furtherance of the national interest and ultimately national survival in a hostile world so, tra-dition has it, must it be above politics. Echoing this sentiment the late Sena-tor Jackson once remarked that 'in matters of national security, the best politics is no politics'. Underlying such a prescription is a belief in foreign policy as the calculated pursuit of national power and advantage in an anar-chic world, a project which could be readily undermined through the intrusion of moral, parochial or domestic political considerations. This 'real-politik' tradition, however, has never sat comfortably alongside the ideals of American liberal democracy. In part this is because the 'amoral' character of 'power politics' has always been in direct conflict with the nation's perceived historical mission as the primary advocate of liberal democratic values in a largely un-democratic world. In addition 'realpolitik' demands executive control over the formulation and implementation of foreign policy to ensure that politics does not intrude and corrode the national purpose. Such a requirement stands in opposition to the constitutional separation of powers in American government which makes the executive and legislative branches 'partners' in the determination of foreign and national security matters. Finally, in a political culture which emphasizes individualism, plu-ralism and ethnicity the notion of a singular 'national interest' is regarded with great sceptism. For there has never been complete domestic agreement on the ends for which foreign policy should strive except perhaps for the two decades following the end of the Second World War. A domestic political consensus on foreign policy, as Destler has indicated, is more the exception than the norm (Destler *et al.*, 1984).

Despite the logic of 'realpolitik' and the desires of many politicians in practice foreign and national security policy have never been insulated from domestic politics. The notion that 'politics stops at the waters edge' is therefore more myth than reality, more prescription than description. Indeed, since the Vietnam War and more recently the demise of Cold War rivalry, foreign and domestic politics have become increasingly inseparable. A number of factors have contributed to this apparent trend.

As Chapter 4 argued, the war in Vietnam shattered the fragile cold war consensus which underpinned post-war foreign and national security policy. Containment of communism was no longer accepted by many Americans as the guiding principle of foreign policy. In the aftermath of the Vietnam War, liberal-internationalism, which aimed to make the world safe for democracy, appeared decidedly tarnished. Isolationism gained political ground and a new phrase entered the political vocabulary: neo-isolationism. This was not unconnected with a deepening concern that America's superpower role was corroding the foundation of its democratic system. The 'imperial presidency' was no longer perceived as an historical accident but increasingly as a natural product of excessive foreign entanglement. The late 1970s witnessed moves in Congress to contract America's global commitments and to reduce the defence establishment. But neo-isolationism did not gain the ideological high ground. Instead foreign policy drifted between the competing claims of a tarnished liberal-internationalism, an emerging new cold war conservatism championed by Ronald Reagan, and neo-isolationist tendencies. Even with the advent of the first Reagan administration in 1981, which was committed to a new cold war conservatism, the domestic politics of foreign policy was characterized more by disagreement than consensus.

One consequence of this erosion of the post-war elite consensus was that foreign policy became embroiled in an intense ideological and increasingly partisan debate. Suddenly the agenda of foreign policy, which for most of the post-war period had been taken for granted, became highly politicized. This was connected with more dramatic shifts in the character of domestic politics, in particular the rise of the New Right and its militant new 'cold war conservatism'. The New Right rejected many of the key assumptions underlying post-war foreign policy. In a somewhat curious 'repackaging' of the early Eisenhower administration's 'New Look' foreign policy of the 1950s, the 'New Right' challenged the political efficacy of containment. The strategy was condemned because it placed the US on the defensive and, since it was primarily reactive in character, advertised America's moral and military weakness in the face of growing Soviet influence around the globe. The New Right dismissed the accepted ways of doing business with the Soviets. Particularly caustic disapproval was reserved for the Kissinger–Nixon strategy of *détente*, which was conceived as the beginning of the decline of American power in the world. President Carter's emphasis on human rights too was regarded with disdain in what became the resurgence of a new 'realism'or 'realpolitik'. With the election of Ronald Reagan a new agenda emerged: the priority was achieving military superiority and the reassertion

of American power and influence in the world both to counteract a perceived growing Soviet threat and to promote American values abroad. As a
result, foreign policy became much more highly politicized and inextricably
woven into the fabric of domestic political debate.

This occurred just as Congress, concerned to eliminate the last vestiges
of the imperial presidency in the aftermath of the Watergate affair, had
strongly reasserted its role in the foreign policy process. Although Congress
had always actively participated in the formulation of policy, it had,
throughout much of the cold war period, acquiesced in the accretion of
power by the executive. But reacting against this, it began in the 1970s to
recover its influence and to re-establish its rightful constitutional role. By
various legislative means, such as the passage in 1973 on the War Powers
Act, it began to reclaim lost authority in the making of foreign policy. Major
setbacks for presidential policies became commonplace as Congress interfered across a spectrum of foreign and defence matters. Among the most
famous was the Senate debate over the ratification of SALT II in 1978–9. In
order to avoid a humiliating defeat President Carter was forced to withdraw
the treaty from Senate consideration despite the fact that it had already been
signed by himself and General Secretary Brezhnev. But there were, and continue to be, many more episodes in this reassertion of Congressional power.
Clearly this has contributed directly to the increasing politicization of foreign policy issues. More importantly, though, this resurgence of congressional activism has accelerated the 'democratization' of the foreign policy
process. Both these developments have been reinforced by significant
changes in the nature of international politics.

Throughout much of the post-war period, international politics was
conceived by academics and policy-makers alike as a power game played
only between governments. In this 'realist' view, security and military power
dominate the political agenda. But in the environment of the 1970s, and
1980s when the West was submerged in economic crises, this 'realist' view
seemed somewhat anachronistic. To many Americans, the real threat to
their own prosperity was not Soviet 'expansionism' but rather the more tan-
gible problems of high oil prices, Japanese imports, the export of capital and,
with it, jobs. The nation's economic vitality seemed to be under threat with
the growth of new centres of economic power, in Europe and Japan, as well
as new forms of economic power, such as multi-national corporations,
which were exporting capital and with it jobs to Latin America and the
Pacific region. Across the country from the factory floor to the gas pump,
more and more people were affected by, and began to protest against, the
increasing vulnerability to international economic and political forces. This
had profound political ramifications. Most obviously it undermined the traditional separation of foreign and domestic policy. As Paarlberg notes
(Paarlberg, 1970), foreign policy became 'domesticated'. Policy-makers began
to talk about 'intermestic' affairs: those issues (such as trade, finance, pollu-
tion, energy, terrorism, human rights, drugs, etc.) which overlapped the foreign and the domestic policy boundaries. At times these new 'intermestic'
issues swamped the foreign policy agenda, pushing other matters aside. Foreign policy-making, too, appeared to take on a more open and democratic
character as the policy-making arena expanded to embrace a diverse array of

organized interests. It also became highly politicized, for the issues with which it was now concerned often affected the political and economic interests of a diverse range of domestic constituencies.

If foreign policy has become more domesticated, it follows that domestic, rather than international, political conditions shape, more than ever before, the conduct of the nation's relations with the outside world. Although it would be absurd to ignore the fact that alliance ties, political commitments and the web of strategic relations in which the United States is enmeshed do have a special influence upon its foreign and national security policies, they have not been the pervasive influence. Since the 1970s, the foreign policy establishment has had to adjust to a new and dynamic political environment. Moreover, the transformation of Eastern Europe, following the revolutions of 1989, and the ending of the 'Cold War' have made the basic thrust of the nation's post-war containment strategy largely redundant. As a consequence the US enters a new decade confronting powerful domestic political pressures to restructure its foreign and national security policies not least because lower defence spending will allow resources to be devoted to domestic programmes and to pressing policy problems such as the budget deficit. A great 'national debate' is now underway exploring the future options for the nation's foreign and military strategy in the context of the more polyarchic and interdependent global system of the 1990s. Without doubt this debate will be permeated by domestic political considerations. It will also visibly reflect the growing public attention devoted to the new range of 'intermestic' issues such as drugs, the environment, trade, economic welfare, etc. Whilst the future strategy guiding American foreign policy may be somewhat uncertain it is nonetheless evident that domestic politics and foreign policy will remain (for the foreseeable future) inextricably bound together. This is hardly surprising since it merely confirms Wolfe's (1984) observation that 'rather than America's global participation shaping its political system, the unique American political system has shaped America's imperial behaviour'.

7.2   The structure of foreign policy-making

George Kennan, the father of containment, noted in 1948 that it was impossible for foreign observers to comprehend Soviet foreign policy from the outside. Over three decades later the same observation could equally be made of the United States, since the process has become incredibly fragmented and complex. In answering the question, 'who makes American foreign policy?', it would therefore seem sensible to begin by sketching in the formal, constitutional structure of power before attempting to describe the actual policy process.

As many experts have recognized, the structure of American government is ill-suited to the requirements of traditional diplomacy. The problem, according to Charles Bohlen, is simply that 'the American system of the separation of powers was not designed for the conduct of foreign affairs' (quoted in Rubin, 1985, p.251). On occasions, the resolution of international issues demands secrecy, decisive action and political flexibility, qualities which are hardly encouraged by the separation of powers. This structural division of power and sharing of responsibilities between the two branches of government can have catastrophic consequences for the conduct of foreign policy. Perhaps the most famous example is the Senate's refusal to ratify the Versailles Peace Treaty in 1919. On questions of foreign policy, it often appears that there are two governments in Washington, each at different ends of Pennsylvania Avenue. However, it is generally accepted that it is the President who initiates policy. This gives the executive branch a degree of primacy in the making of foreign policy, although this should never be exaggerated.

The executive and foreign policy

A tally of the President's constitutional powers tells us little about the actual powers of this office. Whilst the Constitution grants authority to the President to negotiate treaties, make Ambassadorial appointments and be Commander-in-Chief of the Armed Forces, such authority is subject to congressional review. The emergence of the 'imperial presidency' did not develop because of the Constitution but rather in spite of it. Successive Presidents, unchallenged by Congress, simply accreted power to their office by invoking the claims of national security, domestic exigencies, or executive privilege. Moreover, science bequeathed Presidents the ultimate power over the nation's destiny, by transforming the office into the 'Nuclear Presidency'. Clearly Presidents do have enormous powers in relation to foreign and national security matters, but most are formally unacknowledged in the Constitution.

Presidents sit atop of a huge, diverse and complex foreign and defence policy apparatus. It is hardly surprising therefore that one popular image of the White House is of an institution besieged by bureaucratic and political pressures, with the President struggling to control the direction taken by the foreign policy 'machine'. Although a popular image, it is not entirely accurate. In fact, Presidents have many instruments at their disposal for imposing their policy priorities upon the foreign policy apparatus. Presidents, subject to some congressional review, choose their Cabinets. They decide who is to fill the influential Cabinet offices of Secretary of State (SOS), of Defense (SOD) and of the Treasury (SOT). They also appoint, within certain constraints, the heads of all the key agencies such as the Central Intelligence Agency (CIA) in the foreign policy nexus. Of course, their choice of incumbents, as Chapter 6 described, will reflect the political balancing act which the electoral process encourages. It will also depend on the style of foreign policy management they wish to establish. Thus President Nixon chose William Rogers as his Secretary of State precisely because he did not have expertise in foreign affairs and so would not oppose the centralization of decision-making in the White House. As Henry Kissinger recounts, 'few Secretaries of State can have been selected because of their President's confidence in their ignorance of foreign policy' (Kissinger, 1979, p.26).

Besides making appointments to the great offices of state, Presidents also surround themselves, in the Executive Office, with their own personal foreign policy advisors. Chapter 4 has pointed to the paramount significance of the President's Special Assistant for National Security Affairs (SA) in shaping foreign policy. From Woodrow Wilson onwards, Presidents have relied considerably upon personal advisors. With the creation of the National Security Council (NSC) and the post of the SA, this practice has been institutionalized. But what is interesting is that since the Nixon administration, the SA and NSC staff have expanded their authority enormously, at times virtually coming to dominate the foreign policy scene. This would appear to be an irreversible development. Both President Carter and Reagan came to office pledged to curtail the powers of the Special Assistant, yet, under both Presidents, the position of the Special Assistant remained central to the formulation and execution of foreign policy. Indeed, under Reagan the SA and his staff were given unprecedented autonomy to the extent that during 1985 and 1986 they operated an independent foreign policy which came to light in what is now referred to as the 'Iran–Contra affair' or 'Irangate'. Without the knowledge of the State Department or Congress the President's SA and members of the NSC staff, including Colonel Oliver North, attempted to trade arms with Iran in return for the release of American hostages. In addition, the proceeds from the arms sales were used to illicitly supply the US backed Contra rebel forces in Nicaragua with arms as part of a strategy to circumvent a Congressional veto on military supplies. For almost two years the SA's office carried out a covert foreign policy which was in complete opposition to the established policy of the US government. The 'Irangate' scandal was a further episode confirming the powerful role of the SA in the determination of foreign policy as well as the limits to democratic control of that office. The SA's particular status and role in the policy making hierarchy derives essentially from the fact that all Presidents crave independent advice on foreign and national security questions; independent in the sense of not being 'infected' by the bureaucratic and parochial interests of any executive agencies.

What gives SAs their particular influence over policy is both their direct access to the President and the fact that their main function is to service the needs of the National Security Council. Today this is the central interdepartmental coordinating body for foreign and national security policy and in the public mind 'is the most exalted committee in the federal government' (Destler, 1977). It consists of the Secretary of State, the Secretary of Defense, the Director of the Central Intelligence Agency, the Special Assistant, the President and the Vice-President. Originally it was established (in 1948) to provide the primary institutional mechanism for co-ordinating national security and foreign policy within the executive branch. However, rather than becoming the collective decision-making body which its designers envisaged, it has become another vehicle for expanding presidential influence over foreign policy. It has facilitated the creation of a strong specialist foreign policy staff chosen by the President. At its height in the Kissinger period, the NSC staff numbered over fifty people. Since then Carter, Reagan and Bush have employed a smaller, although not substantially smaller, number of staff. In most administrations, the NSC has not been a formal decision-making body, although there is some evidence that President Bush has returned to a more traditional interpretation of its role: as the primary arena for foreign policy coordination (Williams and Miller, 1990). For the most part the NSC has been the forum in which major foreign policy issues are discussed and debated, as under Kennedy and Johnson, and as a mechanism for reconciling severe inter-departmental conflicts on key issues, as occurred under the Reagan administration. In general fundamental decisions on core issues of foreign policy appear to be decided elsewhere.

Most Presidents shun the formal structures of decision-making, such as the NSC and the Cabinet, preferring instead informal and *ad hoc* arrangements involving their closest advisors. President Johnson established his famous Tuesday 'luncheon club' at which policy issues were hammered out. Kennedy had a small coterie of personal advisors, including his brother Robert. This tradition has continued in all successive administrations. Moreover, since the Nixon–Kissinger period, the Special Assistant has always been a key participant in these informal arrangements. The foreign policy structure in the White House would thus appear to bear most resemblance, as Destler (Destler *et al.*, 1984) has suggested, to the traditional relationship between the king and his courtiers: formal position and formal roles are less significant than access to the king; those with access have influence and power, but the king has supreme authority. In both Reagan administrations, for example, many key foreign policy issues appear to have been decided collectively by the President, the Secretary of Defense and the Director of the CIA. However, the monarchical analogy is somewhat misleading, since beyond the inner sanctums of power in the White House is a massive foreign policy bureaucracy upon which Presidents depend for information and the implementation of policy. Since it has such a pervasive role in the policy process, it is examined separately at greater length in this chapter.

To summarize: the structure of foreign policy-making in the executive branch might best be envisaged as a series of concentric circles with the President at the centre. Surrounding the President, at one remove, are the President's closest personal advisors, including the SA who also heads the NSC staff. Beyond is the NSC, its staff and the various heads of government departments, particularly the Secretaries of State, Defense and the Treasury, the Director of the CIA and the Chair of the Joint Chiefs of Staff (JCS). Beyond that are the many government departments whose responsibilities impinge upon questions of foreign and defence policy, which today encompasses virtually the whole federal government.

The legislature and foreign policy
As emphasized in Chapter 2, the Constitution framed a sharing of powers between Congress and the executive in the making of foreign policy. Throughout its history, except in conditions of national crisis, Congress has not neglected the exercise of these formal powers. Today no President can pursue a foreign policy initiative successfully without, as a first requirement, mobilizing congressional support. For Congress has become increasingly assertive in the formulation of foreign and national security policy. The passage of the War Powers Resolution in 1973 signified the beginnings of a major shift in the balance of power between Congress and the Executive. In confirming the constitutional role of Congress in decisions relating to the nations involvement in war or international hostilities, the War Powers Resolution symbolized the emergence of a new era in Congressional–Executive relations. Presidential primacy in the making of foreign policy was no longer regarded so benignly as it had been in the past.

Chapter 5 discussed the key factors which contributed to this reawakening of congressional power. Two of these demand particular mention here. First, the breakdown of the bipartisan approach to foreign affairs, in the aftermath of the Vietnam War, forced Congress into a more activist role. Congressional politicians exploited this situation for their own political purposes since it was a new career opportunity which few could resist given the powerful re-election imperative. Second, many members of Congress were besieged by constituency and organized lobbying as communities were buffeted by the international economic crises of the 1970s and 1980s. These two factors together combined to persuade Congress to adopt a more interventionist role in the making of foreign policy.

While some have argued that executive dominance of the foreign policy process is just another swing of the pendulum away, there is considerable evidence to suggest that 'what we are experiencing is a revolution that will not be unmade' (Franck and Weisband, 1979). In other words, the last two decades have witnessed evolving structural change in the power relations between Congress and the executive. Moreover, the ending of the Cold War and the arrival of a new agenda of intermestic issues appear to confirm a permanently interventionist role for Congress in the determination of the nation's foreign policy. Several developments within Congress too have been critical in crystallizing this structural change including the abandonment of the seniority system; the decline of party unity; the ascendancy of the committee system; the fragmentation of political parties; and the meteoric growth of congressional staff with professional expertise in foreign and national security matters. All these developments have enhanced the salience and importance of Congress in the formulation of foreign policy. Executive dominance of the foreign policy arena is without doubt largely a thing of the past.

The Supreme Court and foreign affairs
Like the silent hound in Conan Doyle's story the 'Hound of the Baskervilles' the Supreme Court has been curiously absent from the foreign policy making arena. Although its jurisdiction encompasses foreign and defence policy questions, to the extent that these raise constitutional issues, the Supreme Court has tended to avoid those matters which demand judgements on the proper constitutional conduct of foreign affairs. Apart from the 1971 Pentagon Papers judgement and the Chaddha judgement in 1983 (each of which raised issues concerning the limits to executive and legislative authority in respect of foreign affairs), the Court has focused its efforts on primarily domestic matters. This has simply reinforced the implicit convention that the question of 'who should make foreign policy' is an issue best resolved in the political, as opposed to the legal, arena.

From structure to processes
Throughout much of the post-war period up until the final stages of the Vietnam War, the structure of foreign policy-making was decidedly hierarchical in character. Presidents, in general, had primacy both within the executive branch and over Congress. The notion of the 'imperial presidency' captured the essence of this power structure well. But since the mid-1970s executive dominance of foreign policy has been challenged by a host of

developments which, as noted above, have created a complex pattern of relations between the major institutional actors in the foreign policy drama. Answers to the questions, 'who makes American foreign policy?' and 'how is it made?', are therefore no longer quite so simple or straightforward.

In part the answers to these 'who' and 'how' questions depend upon making some distinctions between types of foreign policy decisions. In their analysis of foreign policy-making Spanier and Uslaner (1982) isolate three broad types of decisions: those concerning intermestic issues; those involving national security issues; and crisis decisions. Each of these three types of decisions, they suggest, has different characteristics and each displays distinctive policy-making styles. But they also share some common features such as the significant role of bureaucracy in shaping policy outcomes.

Intermestic issues, as noted earlier reflect the growing interdependence between American society and the outside world. Consequently it is exceedingly difficult to disentangle the foreign from the domestic. In matters of trade, monetary, environmental and drug policy, to isolate just a few issues, domestic and international considerations are virtually inseparable. International developments impinge directly on American society and domestic decisions can have significant international repercussions. Generally 'intermestic' issues involve policy questions that are both distributive in character (i.e. some sections of society gain from the policy decisions taken whilst others may lose) and have a differential impact across society such that those directly affected may vary considerably from issue to issue. Policy-making is therefore best characterized as *pluralist* or *neo-pluralist* in that decision taking is a product of bargaining and accommodation between groups within and outside the institutions of government.

National security policy, however, involves matters which impact upon the whole nation rather than particular sections of it. It is solely concerned with organizing and managing the defence of the 'state' against external threats to its integrity and challenges to vital American interests around the globe. Consequently policy making, in theory at least, is assumed to transcend parochial and sectional interests. Decision making therefore tends to become the joint preserve of the military and civil experts. In comparison with intermestic issues the policy-making arena, except on the most controversial issues, is much less accessible to general pressure group activity. Characterizations of the policy making process thus tend to highlight the primary role of the military-industrial complex or the 'Iron-Triangle' as the exclusive determinant of policy outcomes.

By comparison, crisis decisions imply an even more restricted decision-making arena. This is because crisis situations have unique characteristics in that they exhibit a critical element of surprise, a perceived high level of threat, and have to be resolved in an extremely short time span. This implies small group decision-making and accordingly ensures crisis management is the almost exclusive preserve of the White House. For these reasons the processes of decision-making in a crisis situation are quite unique bearing little resemblance to policy-making on national security and intermestic issues.

In the remainder of the chapter this threefold typology of decisions will be used to explore the dynamics of the foreign policy process and to offer some tentative answers to the big 'who' and 'how' questions raised at the beginning of this section. But first some discussion is warranted of the one ingredient common to all policy-making: bureaucracy.

7.3   Bureaucratic determinants of foreign policy

Presidents, as Sorensen has remarked, 'rarely, if ever, make decisions — particularly in foreign affairs — in the sense of writing their conclusions on a clean slate' (quoted in Allison, 1971, p.80). Though they often come to office with the desire to create a 'new look' to foreign policy the bureaucracy is only too keen to remind them that existing commitments, policies and practices cannot be dismissed easily. This fact often makes Presidents intensely suspicious and at times distrustful of the foreign policy bureaucracy. Indeed some Presidents have regarded the foreign policy establishment as doggedly hostile to their grand policy designs and the source of potential policy sabotage. Certainly this is how President Nixon perceived the State Department (DOS). The eruption of conflict between the White House and the State Department for control of foreign policy is a very visible feature of the contemporary policy-making process, for Presidents desire to innovate, while bureaucracy is designed primarily to consolidate.

Presidents and the foreign policy bureaucracy

Upon coming to office in 1969 President Nixon, together with his SA Henry Kissinger, made it clear that they considered bureaucracy to be a dead weight on the foreign policy-making process. Both perceived the foreign policy apparatus as slow to reach decisions, unimaginative, obsessed with continuity, resistant to radical change, unable to plan, and believed that it frequently confused bureaucratic self-interest with the national interest. In his memoirs Kissinger recalls that 'a large bureaucracy, however organized, tends to stifle creativity. It confuses wise policy with smooth administration ... it favours the status quo' (Kissinger, 1979, p.39). These characteristics were considered incompatible with the administration's desire to reshape American foreign policy and to establish a new international order. Consequently, both Nixon and his SA took immediate steps 'to isolate the bureaucracy from the policy making process almost entirely, centralizing decisions to an unprecedented degree in their hands' (Gaddis, 1982, p.302). In their key policy decisions on strategic arms control, *détente* and China, Nixon and Kissinger bypassed the bureaucracy of the Departments of State and Defense almost completely. Moreover, through the 'backchannel system' Kissinger maintained direct personal communications with foreign leaders and foreign ministers like Soviet Foreign Minister Gromyko.

At times the compulsion to exclude the bureaucracy, particularly the State Department, from both policy formulation and implementation created bizarre situations. On one issue Nixon conspired with Soviet Foreign Minister Gromyko to keep information from his own Secretary of State whilst during the Strategic Arms Limitation Talks (SALT) negotiations Kissinger 'expelled' a 'spy' from his own staff 'recruited by no less august a body than the JCS' (Gaddis, 1982, p.304).

Whilst the Nixon–Kissinger era is remarkable for the intense distrust between the White House and the bureaucracy, it is not atypical. A recent study of the DOS concluded, 'White House mistrust of State and its search for alternatives have been familiar features of the Washington scene for so long as to seem the norm rather than some heretical deviation' (Rubin, 1985, p.140).

In both the Carter and the first Reagan administrations the DOS continued to be marginalized in the foreign policy process. Despite the fact that both Presidents came into office committed to enhancing its role in the policy process, both ended up attempting to neutralize its influence. The major casualties in this struggle were the Secretaries of State — six in the decade 1973 to 1983. Alexander Haig lasted only a mere eighteen months, resigning because of irreconcilable differences with the Reagan White House over the management of foreign policy. This desire on the part of the White House to control foreign policy contributed directly to the gravest political crisis experienced by any administration since the Watergate scandal and the ensuing resignation of President Nixon. The Irangate affair (mentioned previously) involved the White House in conducting a parallel foreign policy towards Iran and Nicaragua completely bypassing the State Department and in direct conflict with official policy. Irangate demonstrated quite unambiguously the scandalous excesses of the White House in its attempts to control foreign policy. It was only during the later part of the Reagan administration, in the aftermath of Irangate, that the DOS, under the leadership of Secretary of State George Schultz, began to reassert its role in the policy making process. A more stable and cooperative relationship between the White House and DOS ensued with the latter becoming increasingly paramount in the determination of policy. The 'Schultz era', as Nitze refers to this period, established the foundations for a more constructive relationship between the White House and State. A legacy which has informed the foreign policy style of the Bush administration too.

As part of a general strategy to make the bureaucracy more responsive to Presidential priorities both Carter and Reagan made political appointments not only, as is traditional, to senior positions in the bureaucracy but also more unusually to the lower tiers of management. In the case of the Reagan administration this was aimed at 'combating resistance from a Foreign Service they saw as a hotbed of liberalism' (Rubin, 1985, p.204). Technology also offers a potential instrument for controlling the bureaucracy. Some Presidents have exploited the capabilities of the White House Communications Agency to snoop on departmental communications with the outside world. Indeed there are cases where National Security Council staff have even read incoming DOS cables before they have reached the relevant desk to which they were addressed. Such actions illustrate the obsession which some administrations have had with controlling the bureaucracy lest it control them. But is such an obsession justified? What substantive power and influence over the foreign policy process does the bureaucracy actually possess? Can the bureaucracy really subvert a President's policy initiatives?

The influence of bureaucracy upon foreign policy
Bureaucracy is an inescapable feature of modern government; it is indispensable. Presidents are therefore dependent on it for the success of their policies. Because of this it has come to have a profound influence on the policy-making process. Indeed, some have suggested that foreign policy is largely bureaucratically determined. That is an extreme position. A more

accurate assessment is that the foreign policy bureaucracy, which embraces he State Department, the Department of Defense, the CIA, the Department of Commerce and the Treasury together with those domestic agencies whose activities have an international dimension, has a unique influence over the formulation and implementation of policy. That influence in part derives from the nature of bureaucracy and in particular from the fact that it has its own priorities and its own clientele to placate.

Although Presidents may formally take the key decisions on foreign policy matters, it is often the bureaucracy that has set the agenda or defined the problem to be resolved. Both Kissinger and Nixon recognized this and it underlay their determination to exclude the bureaucracy from the formulation of policy. They understood only too well the experience of the Johnson administration which had become embroiled in Vietnam partly as a result of accepting the 'expert' advice of the DOS and the DOD. Besides influencing the policy agenda the bureaucracy has a crucial role in providing information upon which decisions are taken. On any major issue Presidents have to rely upon the CIA, the DOD and the DOS for detailed or technical information. But the way such information is packaged and presented can have a significant impact on what decisions are taken. Thus in the late 1950s intelligence estimates indicated a 'missile gap' with the Soviets. Partly as a result of this a massive expansion in strategic nuclear forces was sanctioned by the President, a course of action which the Air Force had been pressing for some considerable time. The information later turned out to be wildly inaccurate, mainly because of the very conservative assumptions built into the estimating process by the military analysts. By that point the missile procurement programme had gained its own momentum. Similarly, in the early 1980s, intelligence information indicated the emergence of a 'window of vulnerability' in which US land based nuclear forces would become increasingly susceptible in future years to a disarming Soviet first strike. This 'window of vulnerability' thesis stimulated a major national debate on strategic nuclear policy one of the consequences of which was the Reagan administration's massive strategic nuclear modernization programme. As the decade came to a close the notion of 'strategic vulnerability' was being seriously questioned in what appeared to the general public as a replay of the earlier 'missile gap' scare. Both these cases confirm Rourke's assertion that, 'The ability of bureaucracies to channel information into policy deliberations provides substantial leverage with which to affect the shape of decisions' (Rourke, 1972, p.26).

Beside providing information, a major function of the bureaucracy is to ensure that the decision-makers have a decent range of policy options before them when considering any particular issue. Not surprisingly in drafting the menu of policy options officials can sometimes influence the decisions that emerge, since in practice the Goldilocks principle is often applied: one option that is too extreme, one option that is too weak, and one option that is just right but just so happens to coincide with bureaucratic priorities. Effective choice over policy may thus be removed from the President and his Cabinet colleagues. During the early period of the Reagan administration the Pentagon, according to Talbott (1985), operated this technique quite effectively in connection with arms control issues. As a consequence the President was dissuaded (to the delight of the DOD) from making any meaningful arms control proposals. In extreme circumstances, particularly in crisis situations, Presidents or Secretaries of Defense may be left with no realistic options from which to choose such that they are reduced simply to giving a symbolic imprimatur to pre-existing bureaucratic decisions. Thus, for example, in the event of a nuclear crisis, all the various strategic options and commands are preplanned and preprogrammed in the complex architecture of the Single Integrated Operational Plan. The President would be forced to choose from this 'menu' and, like the German van Schifflen plan in 1914, the means could easily come to define the ends, rather than vice versa. Presidential choice is therefore reduced to the minimum by the Pentagon's strategic nuclear planners.

Officials have many other resources at their disposal to influence policy outcomes. They can mobilize political support either within the rest of the foreign policy bureaucracy or within Congress. For powerful departments such as Defense, which spends huge amounts of money in many constituencies across the country, eliciting congressional support on an important issue is not difficult. However, for the DOS, which has no political constituency in Congress and is even actively disliked, obtaining wider domestic support is exceedingly difficult. Nonetheless it is able at times to utilize its strong diplomatic connections with other foreign governments to bolster its position on vital internal policy debates. It frequently 'invites' them to make their views known by lobbying Congress or making representations to the White House. In this way the Reagan administration was pushed by the DOS and European governments, in the early 1980s, towards developing an arms control initiative with respect to theatre nuclear weapons deployment in Europe. This manipulation of 'transgovernmental' bureaucratic allegiances, for the purposes of influencing internal policy debate, has become increasingly evident, particularly in the economic and technical spheres. In the late 1970s, for example, the US Agency for International Development (AID) sought the support of foreign aid agencies in the other major Western governments in its internal battles with the US Treasury over international debt relief. A strong transgovernmental coalition developed which was successful in providing AID with sufficient political support, through lobbying in Washington, to get the President to override the Treasury's opposition to a new international debt relief scheme to help the world's poorest nations.

Perhaps the aspect of the foreign policy process most vulnerable to bureaucratic influence is not so much the formulation of policy as its implementation. All organizations develop standard operating procedures for putting decisions into effect. As the Admiral informed Defense Secretary McNamara after the decision to impose the naval blockade on Cuba in 1962: 'Now, Mr Secretary, if you ... will go back to your offices the Navy will run the blockade' (Allison, 1971, p.132). But the discretion involved in implementing decisions allows the bureaucracy to revise policy in ways which cohere with its own interests and priorities. Policy outcomes thus may not correspond entirely with the intentions or desires of Presidents or their advisers. Kissinger, for example, found it impossible to get the Commerce Department to attach political conditions to trade with the Soviets, as his *détente* policy required, because this conflicted with established departmental policy to keep trade and politics separate. In general the foreign policy bureaucracy has considerable latitude with respect to the implementation of policy and so over eventual policy outcomes.

By its nature the foreign policy bureaucracy is not a passive agent of its political masters; it shapes their actions in manifold ways. Each department has its own goals, its own policy programmes, its own particular clients to placate, and its own parochial view of the national interest. This often leads to conflict. Policy-making then becomes a bureaucratic battleground.

Foreign policy as bureaucratic politics

During the early years of the first Reagan administration intense bureaucratic conflicts erupted between the Defense Secretary, the Secretary of State, the JCS and the head of the Arms Control and Disarmament Agency (ACDA) over strategic arms control policy. Indeed, one study of this period refers to it as 'untrammelled bureaucratic warfare' (Talbott, 1985, p.233). In numerous NSC and inter-agency co-ordination meetings the conflict between, on the one hand, the Defense Department and the ACDA, who were opposed to arms control, and on the other the JCS and the State Department, who supported it, raged for months with no clear resolution. Each opposing faction attempted to persuade the President and his closest advisers of the merits of their policy proposals. In effect the President became an arbiter between these competing bureaucratic interests rather than an informed participant in decision-making. Policy on strategic arms control became the product of bureaucratic politics, of politics within the government machine.

Both the structure and the complexity of modern American government encourage bureaucratic politics. The power to take decisions is effectively dispersed among a vast array of bureaucratic actors throughout the government machine. Moreover, the complexity of most foreign policy issues has actively assisted the expansion of the decision-making arena to embrace most of the federal bureaucracy. Because officials in different bureaucracies have different priorities, goals and interests, a given policy problem will evoke quite distinctive sets of policy responses. Policy formulation thus tends to reflect the dynamics of bureaucratic politics.

As Krasner observes, notions of bureaucratic politics merely transfer 'the logic of pluralism to policy making within governments' (Krasner, 1978, p.27). *Pluralism* stresses the fragmentation of power and influence in the American polity. It views public policy as the product of pressure group politics in which competing groups attempt to ensure that their interests are promoted or protected. Policy-making therefore involves forging bargains and compromises among conflicting interests to produce some overall consensus on an acceptable course of action. The test of a good policy is that it can be agreed rather than that it maximizes particular goals.

In all these respect politics within government shares some of the characteristics of pluralism. But what is distinctive about politics within government is that in general the players in the game are individuals like the Secretaries of State or Defense, not groups, and their interests are defined by their bureaucratic allegiances and affiliations. For instance, during the first Reagan administration, the State Department desired a negotiated solution to the turmoil in Central America; the CIA lobbied for the expansion of covert activities; and the Defense Department sought increased military assistance to bolster the military forces in the region. These conflicting priorities were resolved in a compromise solution which appeared to the outside world as incoherent and contradictory but within the administration was perceived as a rational outcome. Such a situation is not unique or unusual since the struggle to achieve a consensus between conflicting bureaucratic interests leads to a policy process that is highly disjointed and incremental in character: disjointed because in reality foreign policy problems, as in the case above, are segmented between different bureaucracies; and incremental because the natural attachment of each organization to existing policies makes it unlikely that they will agree to anything other than marginal adjustments to their established policies.

Although power may be fragmented within government, it is certainly not equally distributed among the bureaucratic participants in the foreign policy process. The natural hierarchy of bureaucratic organizations gives some bureaucratic players much greater control over policy outcomes than others. Thus the Secretary of State has more influence over the direction of US–Latin American relations than the lowly desk officer for Haiti. Equally, some departments, by virtue of their sheer size, resources and capabilities, have much more power than others. Thus, in general, the Pentagon, which consumes almost one-third of all government spending, has considerably greater potential power in the policy process than the State Department. But power is also issue-specific: the influence of each agency varies from issue to issue depending upon its expertise. Thus on international financial matters, such as the Third World debt, the Treasury, because of its expertise, will have considerably greater influence in policy deliberations than the State Department or any other department except perhaps the Office of Management and the Budget. Yet on other issues, such as defence policy, it will only have a marginal involvement. But what of the President's power to determine policy decisions?

In one sense the President is no more than another player in the pulling and hauling which is the 'game of bureaucratic politics'. But Presidents are undoubtedly special players since, as has already been noted, they choose the other key players and are the focus of much of the play. Yet on many issues Presidents may be uncommitted and will act as arbiters between the conflicting interests, ensuring that consensus solutions are sought. In 1969 President Nixon sanctioned a modified Anti-Ballistic Missile Programme as a final compromise between the demands of the military and the arms controllers in his own administration. The President was the ultimate arbiter between these conflicting interests and negotiated a consensus on what appeared the least politically damaging policy option.

However, on some issues Presidents have deep political commitments and extensive personal knowledge which informs the establishment of very clear foreign policy priorities. Carter, for instance, was genuinely committed to altering radically US policy on human rights whilst Reagan sought to roll back Soviet influence in the Third World. All Presidents seek to proclaim their own foreign policy doctrines in order to provide a general set of principles to guide the policy process. The most famous is perhaps the Truman doctrine which laid the basis for the whole post-war military containment of the Soviet Union. In comparison, the Reagan doctrine established the principal of US assistance to pro-Western forces of liberation in the Third World. By formulating such doctrines Presidents avoid simply acting as passive arbiters among the warring factions of their own administrations but rather become intensely powerful exponents of their own policy priorities. They participate in the bureaucratic tussle exploiting their extensive patronage, their political allies and appointees in the bureaucracy, to shape both the formulation and the implementation of policy in the desired direction. In this respect Presidents, although only one further player in the policy-making arena, are in every respect 'a superpower amongst many lesser but considerable powers' (Allison, 1971, p.162).

Bureaucratic politics has important consequences for traditional notions of democratic control of foreign policy. If it is the case that policy is primarily the result of bureaucratic infighting or bureaucratic imperatives, what then is the value and purpose of elections? How accountable is the bureaucracy for its activities? In response to these questions it is important to recognize that foreign policy is not forged simply by the interplay between Presidents and bureaucrats, however senior. Undoubtedly bureaucratic politics can help explain policy outcomes, but it cannot do so by itself. As Destler has warned, too much 'concentration on what happens within the executive branch may lead to a neglect of the broader national politics of policy making' (Destler, 1974).

7.4   The 'democratization' of foreign policy

With the transformation of the foreign policy agenda in the 1970s, a plethora of new issues has arisen which have expanded considerably the potential for greater public participation in the foreign policy-making process. These new 'intermestic' issues, like that of energy discussed in Chapter 4, straddle the domestic and foreign divide and are symptomatic of an increasing interdependence between America and the world outside. Since, in general, these issues are distributive in nature, such that policy outcomes affect (often unequally) the material welfare or political interests of different sections of society, they tend to exhibit pluralistic modes of decision-making. Policy is therefore the product of political interaction and bargaining between Congress, organized interests and the bureaucracy. This is particularly well illustrated by one central episode in the story of 'détente'.

A central feature of détente in the 1970s was 'linkage': trade and co-operation with the Soviets was to be made conditional upon their good behaviour. In an effort to give it substance the Nixon administration proposed granting the Soviets preferential treatment in trade and commercial matters. But this had to be authorized by Congress. In proposing the necessary legislation the administration became enveloped in a major conflict with Congress, together with a coalition of powerful organized interests, which lasted for over two years and eventually contributed to the demise of détente. The conflict arose from the so-called Jackson–Vanik amendment, attached by Congress to the administration's trade legislation, which required that no preferential trade status could be granted to communist countries which restricted emigration. This amendment was specifically designed to pressure the Soviets into reversing their policy with respect to Jewish emigration. It was supported by a coalition of organized interests, including the American Federation of Labor and the Congress of Industrial Organizations (AFL-CIO), and the Federation of American Scientists, co-ordinated by various Jewish pressure groups such as the Jewish Defense League and the American Conference on Soviet Jewry. Within Congress it gained momentum since elections were approaching. Moreover, opponents of *détente* perceived this as a unique opportunity to undermine the whole Kissinger–Nixon strategy. As the political battle raged, Soviet dissidents too became involved writing letters direct to US Congressmen.

But there was also powerful opposition to the Jackson–Vanik amendment. A coalition of business and commercial interests, including the National Association of Manufacturers, the US Chamber of Commerce and the East–West Trade Council, lobbied hard against its passage. Soviet industrialists and officials came to Washington to lend support to their American commercial partners. Even General Secretary Brezhnev made a direct appeal to Congress.

Within the administration there was a heated bureaucratic debate. The Department of Commerce opposed the amendment since they perceived that expanding foreign markets was a top priority given the US trade deficit. In opposition the Defense Department supported it since they objected to potential transfers of sensitive military technology to the Soviets. Both Kissinger and Nixon strenuously fought the amendment too since they considered its passage would undermine their whole *détente* strategy. Following intense negotiations between Kissinger, Senator Jackson and the Soviets, a compromise was reached between the opposing groups, which included some modifications to Soviet emigration policy. Despite this, the Jackson–Vanik amendment was passed in 1974. Congress, pressured by domestic organized interests, effectively demolished one of the key foundations of Kissinger's new world order.

This particular episode illustrates nicely the capacity which Congress and organized interests have to check presidential foreign policy initiatives. It would also appear to characterize pluralist democracy at work in as much as it reflects a disjointed process embracing the conflicting demands of organized interests, the formation of opposing coalitions of political interests, the functioning of elected representatives in aggregating and representing constituency and private interests, the role of the executive in mediating and facilitating the accommodation of conflicting interests, and the emergence of a final consensus which reflects the demands of the political 'market-place'. But just how far does this classical pluralist account explain the foreign policy process on most intermestic issues? In brief, not very convincingly, for the various reasons suggested below.

Congress and intermestic issues

In Chapter 5 Congress was described as being concerned mainly with the articulation of 'local' and parochial interests. Paradoxically, it is this parochialism which has, in part, driven it to reassert its role in the making of foreign policy. For as growing interdependence has made their constituents more vulnerable to developments and events abroad Congressional politicians have been forced to take a more active role with regard to foreign affairs. Over the last two decades Congress, largely through internal reform and the expansion of its professional staff, has developed the capabilities to be more assertive in this sphere. In comparison with legislatures in other liberal democratic states, Congress now has enormous influence over the making and implementation of foreign policy.

Exploiting its power to legislate, authorize federal expenditure, and oversee executive activities, Congress has expanded its authority over foreign policy matters. Moreover, because of the increasing specialization within its committee system and the massive increase in committee staff with foreign policy expertise, it has been able to utilize these powers quite effectively. It is no longer the uninformed or ignorant body which Presidents have often claimed it to be. Indeed, the close relationship between congressional staff and their counterparts in the bureaucracy often ensures that members of Congress are as knowledgeable on the details of specific issues as are the bureaucrats. Similarly, Congressional politicians whose political constituencies rely upon defence related industries or have significant ethnic populations tend to develop a very sophisticated knowledge of those dimensions of foreign or national security policy which directly impinge upon their constituent's welfare or interests. Politicians from New York, for instance, tend to acquire a deep appreciation of Middle East policy because of the large Jewish vote, whilst those from California or Washington state (which are home to significant defence related industries) develop strong interests in national security policy.

The combination of a sophisticated capacity to shape foreign policy with the increasing salience of intermestic issues on constituency agendas has drawn a number of responses from Congress. There have been and continue to be successful attempts at constraining the exercise of presidential power. Despite the Chaddha judgement Congress continues to act as if the legislative veto were intact by inserting legislative constraints on executive discretion into a range of foreign policy legislation. Alongside attempts to constrain the executive, it has adopted a more aggressive stance with respect to the actual formulation of policy.

The key congressional actors in shaping foreign policy are the committees; in particular the Senate Foreign Relations, House Foreign Affairs, and Senate Armed Services Committees. But with the expansion of the policy agenda many other committees now have jurisdiction over foreign policy matters. What has strengthened the role of Congressional committees in the policy making process is the enormous growth in the number of sub-committees, combined with a staffing and expertise which in some areas outflanks that of the executive. The traditional view that Congress is too large and unwieldy to make policy has been challenged by these developments. For in some circumstances the modern committee system is equipped to do just that: to initiate policy rather than simply to react. During the Carter administration, the Senate Government Operations Committee introduced and successfully piloted legislation through Congress to reform radically the bureaucratic structures, rules and procedures governing nuclear exports. In the mid 1970s international trade policy was hammered out between the administration and the Senate Finance Committee before being negotiated in Tokyo. Throughout the same period, too, congressional committees cut the defence budget and carved out new defence priorities. Indeed, as will be discussed later, in some cases the committees can be considered an integral element of the executive policy system.

Relying upon its powers to hold the executive accountable, together with its authority over government spending, Congress is able to wield considerable influence not just over policy formulation but also the policy agenda. During the early 1980s, at the height of the Second Cold War, the nuclear freeze movement attracted much public support. Responding to this the House of Representatives voted overwhelmingly for a unilateral freeze on nuclear weapons production and development. Simultaneously it reduced the Pentagon's spending plans for nuclear weapons procurement. Reflecting the public mood, Congress openly criticized the administration's arms control and nuclear weapons procurement plans. Although opposed by most Republicans in the Senate, these initiatives were an attempt by a significant vocal minority to impose an arms control agenda on the Reagan administration as part of a more conciliatory policy towards the Soviets. According to Talbott (1985), congressional pressure, combined with extensive public support for the nuclear freeze, eventually forced the administration into genuine arms control negotiations with the Soviets by breaking the bureaucratic deadlock within the executive branch.

An important ingredient in Congressional activism in the foreign policy arena is the primacy of constituency politics. Given the re-election imperative, should constituency interests be implicated in any policy issue, a member of Congress's automatic response will be 'to go to bat for his [sic] constituency'. Of course, exactly whose interests are given primacy will depend upon who lobbies the hardest, which in turn depends, for the most part, upon resources. This is often complicated by the fact that on many issues there is also likely to be a conflict between the demands of different groups within the same constituency. Thus farmers in the Mid-West wish to see grain exports to the Soviets to alleviate their mounting economic problems, but Christian fundamentalists in the same constituencies oppose such sales upon ideological grounds. Conflicts also arise between the material interests of different Congressional constituencies. In Chapter 5 it was argued that the divergent interests of the oil-producing and oil-consuming sates were partly responsible for the failure of Congress to pass President Carter's energy Bill. Both these illustrations suggest that Congress acts not just to articulate the competing demands of different interests but also functions as an aggregator of conflicting interests. Through its committee structures and internal politics, coalitions are forged, bargains struck, and compromises made. Of course this activity is heavily conditioned by the interventions of pressure groups and professional lobbyists.

Organized interests and intermestic issues

Pluralist theories stress the significant role of organized interests in supplementing the representative system with more direct communication between citizens and the government. Although historically the role of organized interests in the foreign policy process has never been as extensive as that in purely domestic affairs, the growth of intermestic issues has drawn many groups into the foreign policy arena. Ethnic groups like B'nai B'rith or the Jewish Defense League; sectional groups like the Committee on the Present Danger; and state governments, as well as foreign governments, now actively lobby Congress as well as the bureaucracy on those international matters which directly impinge upon their interests or concerns. On any day the corridors of the Dirksen Building or the Rayburn Building buzz with professional lobbyists and representatives of organized interests on their way to persuade the politicians of their case.

Because of the social structure of American society, ethnic groups have always had some influence on the direction of foreign policy. President Wilson's support for national self-determination in Europe in the wake of the First World War was largely induced by the vociferous European immigrant lobbies; Czechoslovakia, it is remarked, 'was invented in Pittsburgh' (Cunliffe, 1978). But the most dramatic and enduring, some would say entangling, connection between ethnic politics and foreign policy has been in relations with Israel. Here the Jewish lobby, which consists of a number of very powerful organizations, such as the B'nai B'rith, and the American– Israeli Political Action Committee, has ensured continuity in America's 'alliance' commitment to Israel despite, in recent years, considerable domestic unease with the relationship. Moreover, its impact has been felt across the whole policy agenda from human rights, trade issues, policy towards the Arab states, relations with the Soviet Union, and arms sales to the Third World. Other ethnic groups, although not as powerful, have influenced the direction of foreign policy too. Recent policy towards South Africa, particularly the imposition of economic sanctions in 1986, was shaped considerably by a spectrum of black groups, including the Black Caucus within Congress.

A rather dramatic illustration of the significant impact of ethnic politics on foreign policy occurred in the early 1970s. In 1974, following the Turkish invasion of Cyprus, Greek organizations mounted a massive lobbying campaign in Congress with the aim of establishing an arms embargo against Turkey. This raised highly sensitive strategic issues, since both countries were NATO allies and were central to Western security policy in the Eastern Mediterranean. Two countervailing lobbies of Greek and Turkish organizations, each supported by different patrons from within the foreign policy bureaucracy, pressed their case on Capitol Hill. Eventually Congress was persuaded by the more influential Greek lobby and an arms embargo was legislated against Turkey. This had undesirable consequences for the NATO alliance most obviously undermining its political unity and coherence. Ethnic politics, as this case demonstrates, can impose its own particular dynamic on the foreign policy process sometimes with highly unwelcome results.

Among the most powerful organized interests are sectional groups: that is corporate, labour and professional groups which arise out of the productive and economic divisions within society. In general, these groups tend to have considerable financial and organizational capabilities which places them in a very privileged position in their relationship with Congress or the bureaucracy. In the case of major corporations and business interests access to key decision makers on particular issues arises from a recognition that their private decisions can have important ramifications for both domestic and foreign policy. These groups can rarely be ignored since the big multinational corporations dominate the domestic economy and through their international operations condition the vitality of the world economy too. The expertise, resources and capabilities of the business community are frequently of critical value to politicians and policymakers. Sometimes they can be exploited as a conduit for government policy abroad. One infamous illustration of this occurred in the early 1970s when ITT (the International Telephone and Telegraph Company) was implicated, along with the CIA, in actively destabilizing the socialist Allende regime in Chile. It should therefore come as little surprise to learn that 'governments award to business managers a privileged position in the play of power in policy making' (Lindblom, 1980, p.74).

As Lindblom asserts corporate interests, more than other sectional groups, are a 'structurally privileged' group in that they obtain preferential access to the policy-makers and legislators. This 'privileging' is further compounded by the existence of discrete policy sub-systems in which participation in decision making is restricted to the most influential groups. For obvious reasons Congress and the bureaucracy tend to cultivate relations with the most powerful sectional interests in each policy sector with the result that a certain 'clientelism' develops in which some groups become 'insiders' in the policy-making process while others, with equally legitimate interests at stake, are often marginalized. If unchecked clientelism effectively undermines democratic processes since policy-makers may become 'captured' by their clients to the extent that they are unable to express or pursue the broader public interest. The existence of clientelism also raises serious questions concerning the validity of classical pluralist explanations of the policy process. Trade policy is a particularly vivid illustration of both a policy sub-system and clientelism in operation.

In the 1930s, Congress devolved control over international trade matters to the President. But in the aftermath of the economic crisis of 1971, which symbolized the collapse of the post-war international economic order, Congress began to retrieve its authority with a vengeance. It refused, under pressure from business and labor groups affected by a surge of foreign imports, to provide the necessary legal authority for the executive to participate in forthcoming international trade negotiations under the auspices of the GATT (the General Agreement on Tariffs and Trade) in Tokyo. Congress, along with many business and labor organizations, feared the executive would yield to free trade pressures. Only after the President agreed to formal consultation with relevant congressional committees and the representatives of the major corporate and union interests did Congress sanction US participation in the Tokyo negotiations. A formal consultation procedure was written into the 1974 Trade Act, which gave the process legal backing. Accordingly throughout the Tokyo trade negotiations, the bureaucracy, congressional committees, corporate and union interests, including, for example, the National Association of Manufacturers, the Chamber of Commerce, AFL-CIO and others, collectively established policy goals and even formulated the US negotiating position on a number of specific issues. Representatives of all groups also participated in the actual diplomatic negotiations. Moreover, the Trade Agreements Bill of 1979, which was required to bring into legal effect the final trade agreements reached in Tokyo, was presented to Congress only when its detailed contents had been mutually accepted by the appropriate committee chairpersons, representatives of the executive branch and the sectional interests involved. Since under previously agreed procedures the Bill could not be amended further once its contents had been formally agreed by these key groups, its passage through Congress was largely a formality.

In this particular case policy making does not appear to correspond to the classical pluralist account of the political process introduced earlier. First, access to the policy-makers and legislators was effectively restricted to the major sectional interests implicated in the decisions. This meant that consumers, and others, were all but excluded. Second, it was not so much a competition between countervailing coalitions which shaped policy, as in the Jackson–Vanik amendment, but rather a process of mutual accommodation between experts representing different sets of organized interests. Indeed, the experts dominated the policy process. Third, the distinction between the public interest and private interests was decidedly blurred since the bureaucracy and Congress tended to articulate the interests of powerful corporate and labour interests. In these three respects, the nature of trade policy-making appears to diverge considerably from the pluralist blueprint of an open, competitive political system in which fluid coalitions and countervailing alliances of organized interest shaped public policy. Rather, policy-making on trade issues exhibits features of what Nordlinger has described as the 'distorted liberal state' (Nordlinger, 1981, p.157) in which the major sectional organized interests, particularly corporate interests, come to play a privileged role in the making and implementation of public policy.

Underlying Nordlinger's remark is an implicit *neo-pluralist* account of policy-making. *Neo-pluralists*, while accepting that policy emerges from a group competition, emphasize how the growth of government and the growth of corporate power have 'distorted' the political process. In particular they stress how corporate and major sectional interests have much greater, and a more 'institutionalized', access to politicians and policy-makers than do other organized interests. In effect they become 'insider' groups and are all but 'co-opted' into the federal bureaucracy. This is because they have the power to subvert government policy initiatives or the expertise that government needs to implement its programmes successfully. Moreover, the federal bureaucracy and politicians are highly dependent on the business community for generating the economic prosperity which is vital respectively to the success of their policy programmes or their own election chances. Consequently, the public policy agenda, as in the trade case, for the most part tends to reflect the priorities and preferences of the most powerful economic interests in society. Additionally, the complexity of most policy issues restricts participation in the policy-making process to those, both in government and outside it, with the necessary expertise. By definition this effectively excludes other interested parties.

But it would be a vast oversimplification to conclude that government simply acts to translate the demands of powerful economic interests into public policy irrespective of competing demands. For, as noted earlier, bureaucracy is very much a powerful organized interest in its own right. Within certain constraints the bureaucracy can operate quite autonomously pursuing its own bureaucratic goals and interests. Policy-making, according to neo-pluralists, should therefore be conceived in terms of a process of bargaining and accommodation between the experts from the bureaucracy, the dominant economic interests, and Congress within what is in effect a closed policy sub-system. This image is far removed from that of the open, competitive political struggle portrayed in classical pluralist theories of the policy process. As an interpretation of the trade policy process, neo-pluralism is undoubtedly more convincing than classical pluralism. Indeed across the spectrum of intermestic issues, which are primarily economic, financial or technological in nature, neo-pluralist accounts uniquely capture the essence of the policy-making process. This suggests that the 'democratization' of the foreign policy process has not been as pervasive as many have believed — a conclusion which is reinforced by an examination of how national security policy is determined.

7.5   Policy-making on national security issues

National security policy is concerned primarily with the acquisition of military capabilities and the use of force to defend the state from external threats to its territorial integrity, as well as to protect the nations global interests and its cherished ideal of a democratic way of life. To achieve these objectives a huge defence establishment has evolved, which in 1990 employed directly over 3 million Americans and consumed in excess of $300 billion, almost 29 per cent of the total federal budget. Regardless of the 'post-Cold War' restructuring of defence the Pentagon will remain (for the foreseeable future) a mammoth organization, with outposts across the globe and an expenditure (even after a 25 per cent reduction) greater than the total GNP of Belgium. Through its weapons procurement and research programmes it has and will continue to have a critical influence on the economic and technological vitality of the nation. Yet, because of its sheer size, the very nature of its responsibilities and the secrecy that necessarily shrouds much of its activity, it is less susceptible to traditional democratic controls than any other arm of the 'state'. To some critics the Pentagon is considered 'a state within a state'.

The military-industrial complex
In the period 1979 to 1986 defence usurped a growing slice of the nation's economic effort, increasing from 4.7 to 6.3 per cent of total GNP. Simultaneously, defence spending also pre-empted an expanding share of Federal expenditure whilst welfare spending declined in relative terms. The magnitude of the Reagan defence spending 'boom' was unprecedented in peacetime conditions and generated much public criticism for its profligacy. Yet by the end of the second Reagan administration it was becoming transparently obvious that continued real growth in defence spending was unsustainable in the context of a huge budget deficit and the nation's status as the single largest debtor in the world financial community. Thus even before President Gorbachev announced the ending of the Cold War the Pentagon's experts were already considering plans to reduce defence expenditure. In the post-Cold War world this process of retrenchment has been accelerated and

the once unthinkable prospect of considerable reductions in defence spending has become a central political issue. Politicians and organized interests openly debate the alternative domestic uses to which this 'peace dividend' could be put. The problem is that restructuring the defence establishment will be politically controversial since it will impose real costs and hardships on many communities across the country. The domestic politics of defence spending will therefore dominate the future debate on national security more so than perhaps at any time in the past.

Policy making on national security issues cannot be properly understood without some appreciation of the political economy of defence spending. The general macroeconomic trends in defence expenditure tend to conceal the dependence of specific industries and many local communities on defence contracts. Estimates indicate that somewhere approaching three million workers are in defence-related employment. Additionally if active and retired military as well as civilian personnel are included some 10 per cent of the entire working and pensioned population rely to some degree on defence expenditure. Moreover, in some industrial sectors defence contracts account for the single largest slice of output and, throughout the 1980s, the fastest growing area of demand. Many big corporations are significantly dependent on military purchases. Almost 50 per cent of Raytheon's production is military related accounting for 79 per cent of its profit whilst for Boeing the figures are 42 per cent and 94 per cent respectively (First, 1988). Furthermore, the 100 largest corporations receive almost 75 per cent of all defence contracts. Defence spending is geographically concentrated too. In recent years the new sun-belt regions (the South and the West Coast), which coincidentally have been the political home of the New Right, appear to have benefited most from the defence build-up. Military spending now penetrates every major sector and region of the economy with the consequence that few political constituencies can afford to ignore defence matters. In effect there exists an extensive and powerful network of political, corporate and labour interests spread across the nation which is motivated predominantly by the need to maintain defence spending.

Decisions on defence spending are for the most part made within a restricted 'policy community', or policy sub-system encompassing the Pentagon, congressional committees and the major defence contractors. Each of these three 'institutions' recognize that their self interests will be best achieved through a process of mutual accommodation and co-operation. Industry desires defence contracts to sustain profitability, politicians want jobs for their constituents, and the military requires weapons and services. In effect the core interests of these groups coincide more than they conflict. Consequently, over the years, informal relationships between industry, the politicians, and the Pentagon have been regularized and institutionalized in a form which facilitates the realization of their separate interests. This 'military-industrial complex' or 'Iron-Triangle' defines a mutually beneficial structure of informal relationships between Congress, industry and the Pentagon which permeates every single dimension of defence policy making. It is a distinctive policy sub-system which has an exclusive membership and its own characteristic form of politics. But how does this 'complex' shape policy outcomes?

In 1977, President Carter, against intense military and congressional opposition, cancelled production of the B-1 bomber, which was to replace an ageing B-52 strategic force. By 1980, procurement of the B-1 resurfaced on the policy agenda and the incoming Reagan administration sanctioned the construction of 100 planes, a decision later endorsed by Congress. The B-1 episode illustrates how military requirements, defined in this case by the Air Force, and the need to ensure the continuing viability of key defence contractors, in this case Rockwell International, together with the support of members of Congress whose districts were affected by its cancellation, combined to reinstate the programme. In many respects it epitomizes the robustness and the imperatives of the 'military-industrial complex'.

The operation of the 'military-industrial complex' reflects much more than a simple convergence of material interests between the military, industry and politicians. For each group assiduously cultivates and supports its 'partners'. Members of Congress with major defence contractors in their constituencies deliberately seek and retain membership of key committees, such as Armed Services and Appropriations, in order to safeguard constituency interests as well as their own political careers. In a rather honest acknowledgement of his motives for opposing cancellation of the Navy's A-6 Intruder programme one congressman stated: 'I'm the congressman from that district and I'm on the Armed Services Committee... It's my job, whether I think the A-6 is good or not, to support it.' (quoted in Adams and Humm, 1990, p.281). Similarly defence contractors tend to become incorporated into the Pentagon machine acquiring privileged access to the defence bureaucracy, so giving them a significant influence over military procurement plans. The frequent interchange of personnel between contractors and the Pentagon bureaucracy, often referred to as the 'revolving door', affirms their special relationship. Moreover, these same contractors spend huge sums of money lobbying Congress. In a similar vein, the Pentagon and contractors manipulate the awarding of defence contracts and sub-contracts to mobilize political support for their cherished programmes in Congress. One recent example of this occurred with the Stealth bomber programme. The Pentagon together with the lead manufacturers deliberately ensured that contracts were placed in as many Congressional districts as possible in order to establish a broad coalition of public and Congressional support to defeat any potential moves to cancel the programme.

Alongside these orchestrated links, members of the military-industrial complex also tend to share a common outlook on defence issues. In a recent study of the beliefs of foreign policy-makers, Holsti and Rosenau convincingly demonstrate that business executives share a largely pessimistic view of the Soviet worldwide military threat (Holsti and Rosenau, 1984, pp.108–13). Given this, it is not surprising that they should seek to maintain or expand defence programmes.

Despite the ideological and political affinities between the military, defence contractors and politicians, it would be absurd to conclude that there were never any substantive disagreements between them over defence issues. Conflicts have arisen over numerous policies and procurement programmes. On the B-1, for example, many members of Congress were unconvinced by the military case for the plane and made their objections public.

Within the Pentagon too there were intense debates among the different services about defence priorities. Whilst within the aerospace industry there was stiff competition between potential contractors and sub-contractors, as well as others pressing for the funding of alternatives to the B-1. These intra-service, corporate and intra-congressional rivalries, frequently surface in the case of major defence projects both because there are always alternative uses to which the Pentagon's resources can be put and much competition for the award of contracts.

Some defence issues, like the MX missile programme in the early 1980s, can generate much public controversy, with the consequence that the policy arena expands to include a diverse array of interested political players. In the case of MX, environmental groups, citizen groups from the Mid-West, promotional groups like the Arms Control Association, and others fought to have the programme modified or even cancelled. To some degree the opposition achieved its goals in having the programme curtailed, although it did not succeed in having it terminated. This particular case suggests that while on controversial defence issues the policy process may become more accessible for a broader spectrum of interests, the policy agenda, and policy outcomes, nevertheless tend to gravitate towards the preferences of the military and industrial elites. Like an elastic net, the military-industrial complex, when necessary can expand to accommodate the activities of diverse organized interests, whilst simultaneously ensuring that policy outcomes conform to the dictates of the dominant elites.

However with the demise of the Cold War the military-industrial complex is beginning to experience its own 'legitimation crisis'. The collapse of communism and the decline of Soviet power have removed both the ideological fear and the political justification underpinning public acceptance of continued high levels of military expenditure. As a consequence considerable reductions in defence spending have been proposed and the defence debate in the early 1990s will be dominated, as noted earlier, by questions of re-structuring and retrenchment. Of course this does not necessarily mean the demise of the 'military-industry complex' since it will remain central to the dynamics of defence policymaking. Indeed, the politics of defence re-structuring will illuminate more clearly perhaps than ever before the significance of the military-industrial interests in shaping national decisions on defence issues. For instance despite the Bush administration's decision to axe a number of military programmes in its first defence budget, the Congress with military and contractor support, had them reinstated even though public opinion was strongly behind the President. Reducing the defence budget may therefore provide a unique test of the power of popular democracy over the entrenched structures of the defence-industrial complex.

Policy making within the military-industrial complex provokes serious reservations concerning democratic control of national security policy. For it appears that participation in decision making is confined to a community of 'experts' whose interests largely reflect those of the military and the defence contractors, and politicians whose careers are dependent on the mainten-ance of the status quo. Policy-making on issues of weapons procurement and defence spending is therefore more accurately accounted for by neo-plural-ist, as opposed to classical pluralist, explanations of the policy process. But national security is not confined solely to weapons procurement or defence spending issues; it also involves the disposition and employment of military force for political purposes. Decisions on these matters tend to be even further removed from the effective organs of popular democratic control.

Defending the national interest

Since 1789 Presidents have authorized the use of military force abroad on average once every year (Hodgson, 1979, p.2). This does not take into account the numerous occasions on which force, including nuclear weapons, has been threatened but not employed. In all these instances force has been exploited primarily to achieve political ends: to defend or promote American interests or values abroad. This immediately raises questions about whose interests and whose values national security policy is designed to defend and promote. For it is clear that on some of the most critical occasions in the history of America's foreign relations, it has not been the public interest, as expressed in public opinion, which has informed the crucial decisions but rather, as with Franklin Roosevelt's assistance to the United Kingdom in 1941, the value judgements of key decision-makers.

As Commander-in-Chief of the Armed Forces, the President has sole responsibility for the employment and disposition of American military forces. From the White House Situation Room or from his airborne command post the President can control America's worldwide nuclear and conventional forces. Since the end of the Second World War the most prevalent use of force has been, as in the case of Grenada in 1983 and Panama in 1989, military intervention. In taking decisions about the employment of military force, Presidents are effectively beyond any direct mechanisms of democratic control, since, for obvious reasons, such decisions tend to be taken in secret. When President Reagan ordered the invasion of Grenada, the Congress and public were informed after the event.

In a study of American military intervention abroad Krasner (1978) concludes that Presidents can act as autonomous decision-makers, largely insulated from sectional interests or public opinion and driven by their own conception of the 'national interest'. But what informs presidential conceptions of the 'national interest'? According to Krasner, the answer is quite simply ideology. Indeed, he argues that national security policy in the postwar world 'must be understood in terms of ideology: leaders were driven by a vision of what the global order should be like' (Krasner, 1978, p.335). This 'vision' has never directly meshed with either American economic interests abroad or military concerns. Indeed, according to Russett and Hanson (1975), business tends not to be supportive of military interventionism, whilst recent evidence suggests that the military are much more cautious than politicians about the employment of force. In comparison Presidents, because they are often overtly concerned with the nature of the global order and America's position within it, are more easily persuaded to employ military force. It is therefore not so much a narrow conception of the national interest which has informed Presidential decisions to employ military force abroad but rather a desire to promote and realize a particular vision of a liberal world order — Pax Americana. As Krasner concludes, in the post-war period: 'Lockean liberalism was the key to American foreign policy; it was the desire to create a world order in America's image that led to the use of force' (Krasner, 1978, p.347). But how are we to account for this obsession with world order?

For much of the post-war era the obvious explanation is to be found in the endemic ideological rivalry with the Soviet Union. The division of the world into two competing ideological and economic systems imposed on all global political issues a zero-sum logic: a win for one side was a loss for the other. Accordingly the motivation to establish a liberal world order, or a Pax Americana, was rooted in the bipolar structure of the international system and the necessity to prevent by any means the expansion of the socialist world system. The resort to force is thereby explained in terms of the maintenance of 'Pax Americana' and the global struggle for power with the Soviets. But, whilst appealing, such an explanation is somewhat incomplete. The fact is that as the world's dominant or hegemonic capitalist power US foreign and national security policy was and continues to be crucial to the maintenance and reproduction of a global capitalist order. In the post-Cold War era this is even more so the case than in the recent past. Accordingly, *neo-Marxist* accounts of US foreign policy, stress that it is precisely because the US is the world's hegemonic capitalist state that its political leadership retains such a persistent preoccupation with the question of global order and stability. For as the hegemonic capitalist power, American foreign and national security policies play a crucial role in sustaining the international structures and conditions that contribute to the maintenance and reproduction of capitalism at the global level, particularly in the Third World. Moreover, the domestic economy is largely dominated by a relatively small number of huge multinational corporations which, in turn, are heavily reliant on world markets and opportunities for expansion abroad. Without a global economic order which assists the international expansion of American capital the domestic economy would be forced to make severe readjustments, which would effectively establish the conditions for a prolonged economic crisis. Together these various pressures impose both structural constraints upon the policy-makers as well as a certain logic on the policy making process. In effect the political leadership is 'persuaded' to provide the political and military conditions necessary for the maintenance of the global capitalist order which in turn is essential to the continued vitality of American economy.

Hemmed in by economic constraints, it is therefore no surprise to neo-Marxists that successive post-war administrations, whether Republican or Democrat, have followed broadly similar (but certainly not identical) national security policies. Such policies have always been premised upon maintaining a global defence posture, namely the use of military and economic assistance to keep allies and client states within the capitalist order, and where necessary the threat or employment of military force to ensure the achievement of these goals. But, as the 1980s have demonstrated, the domestic burden of maintaining a hegemonic role, including the enormous military establishment which goes with it, cannot be sustained indefinitely. In order to legitimize their national security policies every administration has played on the communist threat as a direct challenge to American 'interests' and 'democratic values'. Ideology provides an essential lubricant in the foreign policy process, legitimizing interventionary policies abroad which the public would not otherwise condone. Of course in the post-Cold War era, as the invasion of Panama in 1989 demonstrated, the appeal to democratic and liberal values, rather than the fear of communism, will become the dominant justification for the use of force abroad.

Clearly, a sophisticated neo-Marxist analysis would not deny that foreign policy results from the competition between various groups both within and outside government. The argument is a subtle one, for it acknowledges the complex and fluid politics of pressure group activity in the policy-making process but concludes that this is a much less significant determinant of policy outcomes than the constraints and requirements of being the hegemonic capitalist world power. Thus neo-Marxist approaches are incompatible with pluralist and neo-pluralist accounts of the foreign policy process, which emphasize the dominance of organized interests (whether public or private) in determining policy outcomes.

Neo-Marxism raises important questions about how far the democratic ideals of the political system are compromised by the requirements of capitalism. For it suggests that while Presidents and national security managers may act quite independently from particular business, corporate or economic interests, ultimately policy outcomes tend to reflect the requirements of sustaining and reproducing the basic structures of the domestic and international capitalist order. However, in some situations, such as a superpower crisis, the key policy-makers have a much greater degree of autonomy in decision making than even neo-Marxist arguments recognize.

7.6   Crisis decision-making and presidential primacy

On 22 October 1962 President Kennedy imposed a naval blockade around Cuba in an attempt to prevent the Soviets from placing any further ballistic missiles on this small island only 90 miles from the American mainland. He also demanded the removal of existing Soviet nuclear missiles. For the first time since the Berlin crisis of 1948, the prospect of direct military confrontation between the two superpowers appeared decidedly possible. Fear of impending Armageddon dominated the public mood in the West. However, the crisis evaporated almost as instantly as it had appeared. But its consequences were considerably more permanent. Since then, all Presidents have retained primacy over the management of foreign policy crises because of the enormous stakes involved.

Crisis management requires all the elements of sober, detached, rational decision-making; a clear identification of national objectives, a weighing up of alternative courses of action, and the controlled implementation of the most effective policy options. It demands secrecy, high-level diplomacy, the manipulation of threats, consistency, flexibility, and the mobilization of international support. Combined with the awesome political stakes involved, decision-making in a crisis is for good reason an exclusively presidential affair. As Walter Lippmann observed, in crisis situations the Americans have always preferred to 'trust the President rather than summon the Congress', because of the belief that the 'flexibility of one mind was superior to the inertia of many' (quoted in Thompson, 1960, p.43). The advent of nuclear weapons has reinforced this principle since, in a real nuclear crisis, there would be no time at all for summoning Congress.

The potentially catastrophic consequences of war in the nuclear age have forced all Presidents entering office to establish structures and procedures for dealing with crisis situations. Thus Kissinger, with Nixon's authority, established the Washington Special Actions Group; Carter created the Special Co-ordinating Committee, under the chairmanship of his Special Assistant, Brzezinski; and Reagan gave primary responsibility for crisis management to his Vice-President, George Bush. The organization of crisis management machinery has two implications for decision making processes. First, control over the formulation and implementation of policy is deliberately centralized in the White House Situation Room, located in the basement of the West Wing, from which Presidents and their closest advisers can observe events as they unfold. Second, decisions are taken within a small and closed forum consisting of individuals chosen by the President. Thus in the Cuban missile crisis all the key policy decisions were taken in EXCOM, an *ad hoc* body comprising the President's most respected colleagues and advisers. As a result, crisis decision-making has a number of distinctive characteristics.

In his classic study of the Cuban missile crisis, Allison (1971) has shown that the actions of any administration confronted by a crisis are not determined solely by rational calculation. For governments are not monolithic entities but rather agglomerations of large bureaucratic organizations. Each organization has its own priorities, goals and its own genuine prescriptions for dealing with the crisis in hand. Accordingly in a crisis, the heads of the major departments, such as the Secretary of State, the Defense Secretary, the Director of the CIA and the Joint Chiefs of Staff, through the established crisis management machinery, each provide the President with policy options and advice on how to proceed. Often he will be faced with conflicting policy prescriptions. During the Iranian hostage crisis in 1980, Carter was advised by his SA Brzezinski, backed by the JCS and the Secretary of Defense, to use military force. Cautioning against this Secretary of State Cyrus Vance, stressed the need for negotiation and diplomacy; and later resigned over the decision to take military action. Rather than the President's crisis management machinery fostering a comprehensive rational evaluation of competing courses of action, it often becomes the site of bureaucratic politics between different agencies. Decisions may thus arise less from a deliberate presidential choice than from the bargaining, compromise or consensus between the representatives of the different bureaucratic interests within the decision making form. In the Cuban missile crisis the decision to mount the blockade arose as a compromise between the advocates of military action and the proponents of a diplomatic solution. Crisis decision-making is therefore often suffused with its own high-level bureaucratic politics, although this is considerably constrained both by the need to take decisions quickly and the sobering consequences of the stakes involved.

Successful crisis management requires totally centralized control over the implementation of decisions as opposed to routine policy decisions which are implemented by the appropriate bureaucracy. So in a crisis the White House consciously attempts to maintain as much control over policy implementation as is technically possible, since any unintended action could have dire consequences. Through the worldwide military communications system the President, as Commander-in-Chief, can control the actual disposition and actions of American military forces abroad directly from the White House. Thus it was President Carter who gave the command to local American forces to launch the Iranian hostage rescue mission in 1980. Moreover, through the White House Communications Agency, the Presidents and his staff members can maintain 'real' time direct contact with other heads of government or their senior staff. During the Middle East crisis in 1973 Kissinger talked directly to Soviet Foreign Minister Gromyko two or three times a day. It is therefore possible for a President or his aides to bypass the State Department and bureaucratic machinery. Equally President Bush communicated directly with President Gorbachov and other Western leaders both prior to and in the immediate aftermath of the US invasion of Panama in late 1989. Such direct communication applies to diplomatic negotiations during a crisis. Kissinger, for instance, flew to Moscow at the height of the Middle East crisis to negotiate with the Soviets directly, while the Secretary of State remained ignorant of the discussions. With the revolution in modern communications technology the presidency has become more than ever before an operational one.

The relative autonomy of the presidency in the making and implementation of foreign policy is nowhere as acutely displayed as in crisis situations. Not only is policy formulated and directly implemented by the White House, but also the normal buzz of domestic politics is temporarily suspended as the nation rallies to support the President. Decision-making in crises therefore challenges the notion of democratic control of foreign policy; it forces an acknowledgement that the principles of liberal democracy may be incompatible with the process of foreign policy-making in the nuclear age. At best, as Dahl (1985) has argued, all that democracy can mean in such circumstances is 'democratic guardianship'; the President, elected by the whole nation acts as its temporary guardian.

7.7 Democracy and foreign policy in the 1990s

Since the 1970s the process of foreign policy-making would appear, on the surface, to have undergone a democratic transformation. The belief that foreign policy is best left to the executive has been swept away in the wake of Vietnam, Watergate and the Iran–Contra affair. Furthermore the domestication of the foreign policy agenda, the breakdown of elite consensus, and the complexity of contemporary policy issues have contributed to a more open and participatory policy process. However, as this chapter has indicated, the degree of effective participation and democratic control varies considerably according to the type of policy issue involved. It is least with respect to crisis decisions and the employment of military force, but greatest on those intermestic issues which now tend to dominate the foreign policy agenda. But in relation to the latter participation and democratic control is often restricted both by inequalities in the distribution of political and economic power and the structural constraints inherent in the nation's role as the world's dominant capitalist power, with the consequence that some aspects of foreign and national security policy tend primarily to reflect the interests of the most powerful elites. Even in the post-Cold War era the realities of the foreign policy process are not entirely in accord with the principles of liberal democracy.

References

ADAMS, G. and HUMM, R. (1990) 'The US military-industrial complex and national strategy' in Jacobsen, C.G. (ed.) *Strategic Power: USA/USSR*, London, Macmillan.

ALLISON, G.T. (1971) *Essence of Decision*, Boston, Little Brown.

CUNLIFFE, M. (1978) 'The public and the experts: American attitudes to the world outside' in Halle, L.J. and Thompson, K.W. (eds) *Foreign Policy and the Democratic Process*, Washington DC, University Press of America.

DAHL, R.A. (1985) *Controlling Nuclear Weapons: Democracy versus Guardianship*, New York, Syracuse University Press.

DESTLER, I.M., GELB, L.H. and LAKE, A. (1984) *Our Own Worst Enemy — the Unmaking of American Foreign Policy*, New York, Simon and Schuster.

DESTLER, I.M. (1974) *Presidents, Bureaucrats and Foreign Policy*, Princeton, Princeton University Press.

DESTLER, I.M. (1977) 'National Security advice to US Presidents: some lessons from thirty years' experience', *World Politics*, Vol. 29, No. 2, January.

FIRST, A. (1988) 'Military build up without a strategy' in Haftendorn, H. and Schissler, S. (eds) *The Reagan Administration: a Reconstruction of American Strength*, Berlin, W. de Gruyter.

FRANCK, T and WEISBAND, E. (1979) 'Congress as a world power', *Worldview*, October, pp. 4–7.

GADDIS, J.L. (1982) *Strategies of Containment*, New York, Oxford University Press.

HODGSON, G. (1979) 'Congress and American foreign policy', *Chatham House Papers No. 2*.

HOLSTI, O.R. and ROSENAU, J.N. (1984) *American Leadership in World Affairs — Vietnam and the Breakdown of Consensus*, London, Allen and Unwin.

KISSINGER, H. (1979) *The White House Years*, London, Weidenfeld and Nicholson.

KRASNER, S.D. (1978) *Defending the National Interest — Raw Materials, Investment and US Foreign Policy*, New Jersey, Princeton University Press.

LINDBLOM, C.E. (1980) *The Policy Making Process*, New Jersey, Prentice-Hall, 2nd edition.

NORDLINGER, E. (1981) *On the Autonomy of the Democratic State*, Cambridge, Mass., Harvard University Press.

PAARLBERG, R. (1970) 'The domestication of American foreign policy', *Public Policy*, Vol. 18, No. 2, pp. 245–64.

ROURKE, F.E. (1972) *Bureaucracy and Foreign Policy*, Baltimore, John Hopkins University Press.

RUBIN, B. (1985) *Secrets of State — the State Department and the Struggle over US Foreign Policy*, New York, Oxford University Press.

RUSSETT, B.M. and HANSON, E.C. (1975) *Interest and Ideology — the Foreign Policy Beliefs of American Businessmen*, San Francisco, Freeman.

SPANIER, J. and USLANER, E. (1982) *Foreign Policy and Democratic Dilemmas*, Boston, Houghton Miflin.

TALBOTT, S. (1985) *Deadly Gambits*, London, Picador.

THOMPSON, K.W. (1960) *Political Realism and the Crisis of World Politics*, Princeton, Princeton University Press.

WILLIAMS, P. and MILLER, C. (1990) 'The Bush administration's foreign policy review', pp. 82–101 in Pugh, M. and Williams, P. (eds) *Superpower Politics*, Manchester, Manchester University Press.

WOLFE, A. (1984) 'The irony of anti-Communism: ideology and interest in post-war American foreign policy', pp. 214–29 in Miliband, R., Savile, J. and Liebman, M. 'The uses of anti-Communism' in *Socialist Register* 1984, London, Merlin Press.

Further reading

GARDINER, L.C. (1984) *A Covenant with Power*, New York, Oxford University Press.

HALLIDAY, F. (1986) *The Making of the Second World War*, London, Verso, 2nd edition.

HOFFMANN, S. (1980) *Primacy or World Order — American Foreign Policy Since the Cold War*, New York, McGraw-Hill.

McCORMICK, T.J. (1989) *America's Half Century*, New York, John Hopkins.

SPANIER, J. and NOGEE, J. (eds) (1981) *Congress, the Presidency and American Foreign Policy*, Oxford, Pergamon Press.

8 US–Latin American Relations: Case Studies in the Making of Public Policy

On 27 April 1983 President Reagan addressed a specially convened Joint Session of Congress on the crisis in Central America. During this nationally televised address he expressed the fear that the 'communist' revolution in Nicaragua, unless checked by American action, would ultimately threaten the survival of democracy at home. Central America, like Vietnam before it, was portrayed as a crucial test of the administration's attempt to restore US hegemony over its Latin neighbours. At the same time the administration faced a more material threat from its southern neighbours in which credit, rather than US credibility, was the primary *leitmotiv*. Such was the hopeless indebtedness of the major Latin American countries to US multinational banks that a major default on debt repayments posed a significant source of potential instability to the whole US financial system. Throughout the mid-1980s these twin structural problems of political instability and financial indebtedness in Latin America purchased a pre-eminent place on the American foreign policy agenda. Moreover, the administration's policy towards Nicaragua unleashed the most controversial domestic political debate since the Vietnam War and with the revelation of the Iran–Contra affair brought the Presidency into disrepute much as the Watergate affair had done over a decade earlier. This chapter explores the political processes underlying policy formulation on these two key issues during the Reagan years. In doing so it aims to illustrate the complex dynamics of the foreign policy process in the context of two historical case studies about which a great deal is now known. Engaging directly with these specific cases offers a novel and interesting approach to fleshing out the more abstract arguments and theories introduced in the previous chapter and so to acquiring a deeper understanding of the determinants of US foreign policy.

8.1 Contemporary US–Latin American relations

Since the establishment of the Monroe Doctrine in 1823, US policy towards Latin America has always reflected the desire to prevent foreign political and economic penetration of the hemisphere, to ensure its internal political stability and, where possible, to encourage the emergence of pluralistic-type democracy. Over the years different administrations have given different relative priorities to these objectives, and policy has fluctuated erratically between military intervention and benign neglect. Similarly, the salience of Latin America in the concerns of US foreign policy makers has ebbed and flowed. During the early years of this century Latin America experienced the era of 'dollar diplomacy', in which successive administrations frequently intervened militarily in their neighbours' affairs to impose financial and political stability. There followed many decades of neglect, as the Cold War stamped its Eurocentric concerns on US policy-makers. Only the Cuban revolution in 1959 and the American response in the form of the Alliance for

Progress projected inter-American relations into the domestic political arena. But the growing political and economic burdens of the Vietnam War forced hemispheric relations into abeyance through the 1960s and 1970s. A period of benign neglect ensued, punctuated by bursts of compulsive action to protect American interests in the region, either through military intervention, as occurred in the Dominican Republic in 1965, or covert intervention which, in the case of Chile, contributed to the violent overthrow of the socialist Allende regime in 1973.

With the arrival of the Carter administration in 1976, concern over developments in Latin America revived. By then the trauma of Vietnam, and public contempt for the amoral character of US foreign policy during the Nixon–Kissinger era, had evoked a strong desire for a distinctly more principled approach to political relations with the Third World including Latin America. Carter's human rights policy, which mirrored a domestic desire for a moral foreign policy which promoted American values abroad, had a most profound impact on inter-American relations. Almost overnight military aid and arms supplies to several of America's long-standing political allies in Latin America were embargoed because of their domestic human rights abuses. Political relations with most of the major states, such as Brazil, Argentina and Chile, as well as with many smaller states such as Paraguay, El Salvador and Guatemala, were very seriously undermined. This was seized upon by the Republicans during the 1980 presidential election campaign. President Carter was vilified for alienating America's strongest allies in Latin America whilst ignoring Soviet and Cuban penetration of the hemisphere and accepting the socialist Sandinista revolution in Nicaragua as a *fait accompli*. Whether valid or not, Republican claims of growing Soviet influence in 'America's back yard' captured public attention and strengthened political pressures for a transformation in policy. Even before Reagan was inaugurated in 1981 conservative forces in American domestic politics had made Carter renege partially on his human rights policy.

Upon entering office in 1981, the first Reagan administration set about dismantling the Carter policy on human rights. Arms supplies to Brazil, Argentina, Chile and Central America were restored. Indeed an openly warm diplomatic embrace was afforded to these regimes for their strong anti-communist policies. Underlying the Reagan administration's approach to hemispheric relations was its virulent anti-communism and its sincerely held conviction that Central America, in particular, was an emerging battleground in the new cold war between the superpowers. Developments in Latin America increasingly took on a strategic significance, since they were interpreted as intimately connected to the East–West power struggle. In this context the administration's objections were to combat what it perceived as Soviet and Cuban inspired political instability in the region by reaffirming American hegemony in the hemisphere.

But Latin America's high profile did not arise simply because it was perceived as a key arena in the new cold war, but also because it touched upon the material interests of the broad Reaganite conservative coalition. Because of their proximity to the region the sun-belt areas (of the South and West), from which the New Right drew its political support, tended to be deeply concerned by events in Mexico and Central America. Fears of political instability and a torrent of illegal immigration fuelled conservative reactions. Furthermore, among corporate and banking interests there was a very clear recognition that Latin America remained a vital export and investment market for US business: the region accounted for the largest slice of US exports and investment outside Europe. Ensuring political stability and protecting US commercial interests were thus viewed as mutually reinforcing goals. But, particularly for the major US banks, Latin America's escalating indebtedness meant that the region could no longer continue to be awarded such a low priority in the nation's foreign policy, particularly given the change in administration.

Close political and ideological affinities between the New Right in the USA and the political and business elites in the major Latin American nations also contributed to reawakening the domestic political consciousness to the needs of the region. One vivid illustration of the significance of this transnational American lobby in shaping the administration's foreign policy occurred during the Falklands War in 1982. For, under immense political pressure from this lobby, the administration sought every possible opportunity to avoid alienating its Latin American allies. Initially it adopted an 'even-handed' approach and refused unqualified support to Britain, its long-standing NATO ally. Only when it became obvious that this policy would irreparably damage NATO did it finally abandon its disinterested stance. But even this was effected with a carefully choreographed diplomatic offensive, designed to placate its Latin American allies. More than any other event in the 1980s the Falklands episode demonstrated the paramount significance attached to hemispheric relations by the Reagan administration.

Whatever the causes of its attachment to Latin America in the 1980s, the thrust of the administration's policy was not startlingly innovative. Rather, what distinguished its policy towards the region from that of its predecessors was both its unashamed willingness, in the post-Vietnam era, to utilize coercive power in the pursuit of its policy objectives and its explicit attempts to impose liberal democratic institutions and free enterprise culture on Latin American states. But why did such policies arise? What forces influenced and fashioned the style as well as the substance of the administration's policy towards Latin America? Who controlled the formulation and implementation of policy? In the remainder of this chapter the answers to these questions will be sought by sharpening the focus to US responses to the Central America crisis and the debt problem. Both issues offer fascinating insights into the complex forces which fashion foreign policy. In accounting for these forces explicit consideration will be given to the various theories of the foreign policy process discussed in Chapter 7. Clearly, space constraints do not permit a rigorous evaluation of the relative explanatory utility of these different approaches. Nonetheless, a number of key analytical themes, which flow directly out of the discussion in Chapter 7, energize the case studies in question. In particular, the relevance of classical pluralist explanations of the policy process in respect of both these cases, is obviously an important theme. Furthermore, the compatibility of neo-pluralist analyses with the events described in the case studies is a further theme. Finally, some consideration is given to the question of whether neo-Marxist approaches provide any distinctive insights, not already apparent, into the nature of the foreign policy-making process. These questions and themes together provide the basis for analysing the case studies which follow.

8.2   Revolution in Central America

Throughout the 1980s the Reagan administration's approach to the crisis in Central America triggered the fiercest domestic political controversies since the early 1970s. Attempts to rally the nation behind an overt campaign to destabilize the (socialist) Nicaraguan Sandinista regime, which came to power in 1979, even rekindled unhealthy memories of Vietnam. At times fears were expressed of a deepening entanglement which would eventually, like Vietnam before it, corrode the legitimacy of the nation's political insti-

Figure 8.1

tutions. Moreover, few Americans understood why the administration had become obsessed with Central America, for there were no significant economic interests at stake, nor did developments in the region pose any direct threat to America's national security. Consequently, as the decade ended political opposition to its policies became increasingly vocal, driven largely by the implicit fear of military involvement. Opponents imposed humiliating congressional defeats on the President, disabled the effective implementation of his overt policy, and forced the administration to compromise on its policy objectives. Revelations of the covert Iran–Contra connection in 1986 severely undermined the administration's policy and irreparably weakened the Presidency. In many respects policy-making with regard to Central America in this period illustrates the fragmented and incoherent nature of the policy process as well as the incessant struggle of the executive to retain control over its own policy initiatives. It also partly confirms Krasner's observation that: 'In the American political system negative power prevails; one actor can block the initiatives of another but cannot carry through its own preferences' (Krasner, 1978, p.20).

Bureaucratic politics and US policy in Central America

For almost two years into the first Reagan administration, policy-making on Central American issues was confined to the bureaucracy and the White House nexus. Apart from the odd skirmish with Congress, over military aid and human rights violations in Central America, the administration's policy was rarely debated in public. But within the executive branch there was a deep split over both the goals to be pursued as well as the appropriate policy instruments. This culminated in an intense bureaucratic struggle, for control over policy-making. A compromise known as the 'two track' policy emerged, allowing conflicting hardline and dovish factions within the administration to pursue their own, in many respects contradictory, policies. Behind the 'two track' policy was serious internal political disagreement within the administration about how to deal with the mounting violence and political instability in Central America. The President and his closest advisers in the White House believed that the virtual war in El Salvador, which had claimed tens of thousands of lives, together with the growing political unrest in Honduras, were instigated by external forces. In particular, the Nicaraguan Sandinista regime, mainly because of its developing connections with Cuba and the Soviet Union, was perceived as the cause of this 'communist'-backed insurgency in the region. They also feared a domino effect, arguing that if the Nicaraguan revolution was allowed to succeed it would become a base for the export of socialist revolution to the 'fragile democracies' in the region, leading to the destabilization of Mexico, and eventually threatening democracy in the USA itself. To prevent this the White House sought to both 'roll back' communism in the region, by undermining the Sandinista regime, and to encourage the establishment of pluralistic-type democracies.

Almost in opposition to this strategy the State Department sought a combination of diplomatic pressure and direct negotiations with the Sandinistas. The objective was to persuade the Sandinistas to terminate all forms of assistance to the various revolutionary forces in El Salvador and Honduras. Underlying this strategy was a concern, which emanated from the

State's Bureau of Inter-American Affairs, that too aggressive a policy towards Central America would seriously damage diplomatic relations with the major Latin American states. A more interventionary stance, it was believed, would be condemned outright in the Organization of American States and would thereby weaken the legitimacy of US policy in the region. Assistant Secretary of State for Inter-American Affairs Enders convinced Secretary of State Haig that the Nicaraguans could be persuaded to adopt a more 'acceptable' domestic and foreign policy by a combination of aid, diplomatic pressure and negotiation. In particular, he believed that the Sandinistas would agree to terminate assistance to the rebel forces in El Salvador in return for the US withdrawing its support for the counter-revolutionary forces (the Contras) in Nicaragua. However, although Haig impressed this diplomatic approach (the Haig–Enders strategy, as it became known) upon the other members of the National Security Council (NSC), it was received with considerable scepticism.

Among the sceptics was Secretary of Defense Weinberger and the Director of the CIA, Casey. Weinberger perceived the Central American problem primarily in terms of national security. Deep concern was expressed that most of the nation's oil came through the Caribbean and that something approaching 50 per cent of its trade flowed through the Panama Canal and the Caribbean basin. This posed a serious strategic vulnerability in either peace or war. An equally serious threat to national security, it was argued, would clearly arise if the Nicaraguans offered the Soviets, or their Cuban allies, a base on the Atlantic or Pacific seaboard, for this would give them a military foothold on the mainland. Consequently, Weinberger recommended the President to take a tough line on Central America. Short of overthrowing the Sandinistas, the DOD sought to bolster the military forces in the republics adjoining Nicaragua, providing them with increased quantities of military aid, both in terms of hardware and training, whilst simultaneously strengthening the US military presence in the area. However, the Joint Chiefs of Staff were somewhat diffident about the latter and made clear their opposition to any direct military intervention. This provided the CIA with a convenient rationale for promoting covert action against the Sandinistas.

With the arrival of the Reagan administration the CIA had taken an increasingly active role in both the formulation and implementation of foreign policy. Its budget had been considerably increased and it had expanded its Directorate of Operations (which was responsible for covert activities) as part of the administration's general policy to combat Soviet activities in the Third World. Furthermore, it had vital political resources in the battle over Central American policy, since it controlled flows of intelligence information to the President and the NSC, as well as having considerable discretion over its own operational activities. The new Director of the CIA viewed the deteriorating political situation in Central America as a fundamental threat to US strategic interests in the region. CIA intelligence reports stated that the basic cause was not internal economic and political conditions but Nicaragua itself. This despite the fact that as Rubin notes, 'During the Carter administration ... CIA reports played down Nicaraguan involvement in El Salvador' (Rubin, 1985, p.121). Itching to demonstrate the effectiveness of his new investment in covert operations, the CIA's Director was able to persuade the President of the value of covert activities in achieving, without any irritating congressional interference, the desired policy goals. However, not all members of the NSC were convinced that this was a politically astute policy.

It was not until November 1981 that a tacit consensus on Central American policy emerged in the NSC. This 'two track' compromise effectively allowed each major bureaucratic actor in the drama to implement their own independent foreign policies in the region. With the help of the Argentinian government the CIA began busily recruiting, organizing and training the Contra rebel forces to counter the Nicaraguan Sandinista forces. The Defense Department sought and prosecuted a considerable militarization of the region, expanding military aid and assistance to Honduras and El Salvador, while the State Department engaged in direct negotiations with the Nicaraguans and increased the diplomatic pressure on them by closing off all loan and aid facilities. Because of the divergent objectives of the different agencies involved and the lack of any effective interdepartmental co-ordination of their initiatives, the administration's policy towards Central America appeared both incoherent and contradictory. However, by 1983 several developments forced a fundamental review of policy. First, there was a change in key personnel. A new Secretary of State, a new Deputy Secretary of State for Inter-American Affairs and a new Special Assistant to the President for National Security Affairs had taken office. In addition, the President had appointed a new adviser on Central America in the form of Ambassador to the UN Jeane Kirkpatrick, a staunch neo-liberal. Second, in late 1982 revelations about the CIA's secret war against Nicaragua provoked a torrent of domestic protest against both the methods and the objectives of Reagan's policy. Third, the situation in El Salvador had become critical, with government-based 'death squads' terrorizing the population in the war against the 'leftist' guerrilla forces. Political unrest also began to spread to both Guatemala and Honduras. Finally, negotiations with Nicaragua reached an impasse largely because of the disarray in American policy. The State Department 'retired' to facilitate an independent Latin American initiative, through the Contadora group (comprising representatives of Colombia, Mexico, Panama and Venezuela) which sought a diplomatic solution to the region's political problems through a negotiated peace treaty. In combination all these factors contributed to the President's Special Assistant for National Security requesting, in January 1983, a complete reassessment of Central American policy. Consequently a special NSC working group was established to effect such a review.

During this policy review it became evident that the more hardline elements in the executive branch had been strengthened. In particular, the personnel changes in the State Department had left it much less sympathetic to the Haig–Enders strategy of negotiation. Returning from a visit to Central America, Special Adviser Kirkpatrick, pressed for increased aid to the Contra rebels and further reinforcement of the allied military forces in the region. This was seized upon by the CIA as endorsing further expansion of covert activity against the Sandinistas. At the same time the Defense Department was increasingly of the opinion that to provide adequate assistance and training to its military allies in the region would require an enhanced, it not virtually permanent US military presence. A new consensus gravitated towards a more aggressive policy embracing a deepening militarization of the region combined with an overt campaign to destabilize and perhaps topple the Sandinista regime.

Two developments flowed from this NSC policy review. First, it was without doubt a watershed, since US policy became progressively more coercive in character. An economic blockade was imposed upon Nicaragua in that the US Agency for International Development (AID) cut off aid; leverage was used in international financial institutions, such as the Inter-American Development Bank (IADB) and the World Bank, to terminate further lending; and trade was suspended by presidential executive order. In parallel there was a further expansion of the US military presence in the region and a massive increase in military aid to Honduras and El Salvador. By 1984 there were more than 11,000 American troops in the area and hundreds of military advisers. Most were based in Honduras, although many advisers were to be found in El Salvador. The military intervention in Grenada in December 1983 epitomized this 'militaristic' US response to the problems of Central America. As Fred Ikle, Under Secretary for Defense for Policy, indicated in late 1983, US policy 'must prevent the consolidation of a Sandinista regime in Nicaragua' (Rubin, 1985, p.227). But this could not be achieved without public debate, for in particular congressional funding was required.

A second development flowing from the policy review was the administration's conscious attempt to forge a domestic political consensus behind its revised policy. This began with the almost unprecedented step of the President convening a Joint Session of Congress, which was designed to impress upon the American public the seriousness of the situation in Central America whilst also marginalizing domestic opposition to the administration's policy. This was complemented by the creation of a special unit, called the Central American Policy Outreach programme, which sought to 'educate' public opinion on the dangers emanating from the 'communist threat' in Central America. An independent bipartisan Commission on Central America, headed by Henry Kissinger, was also established in the belief that it might endorse and thereby legitimize the administration's policy. When the Commission did report, in early 1984, it supported the general thrust of the administration's policy. However, it did not silence political opposition, particularly in the Democratic Party. Thus the administration embarked on various attempts to establish the perception, in the public mind, that opponents of its policy towards Central America were 'soft on communism' or even part of a 'communist conspiracy'. This in turn was exploited by the opposition since it appeared much like the beginnings of another 'McCarthyite' witchhunt. Quite unintentionally, by the mid-1980s the administration had succeeded in making Central America one of the most controversial issues on the nation's political agenda. It was even exploited quite successfully in the 1984 Presidential election campaign to galvanize right-wing support for the Reagan ticket.

Congress and Central American policy

Throughout 1983 and 1984 there was growing unease both in Congress and among the public over the administration's policy. All the opinion polls showed a decisive majority of the public against US policy in Central America: nearly 70 per cent thought the USA should keep out, and 80 per cent disagreed with any form of military intervention (Schneider, 1984, pp.22–3). This coincided with increasing opposition to defence spending. Opinion polls suggested that well over 60 per cent of the public desired substantial cuts in the defence budget, a degree of opposition not evident since the turmoil of the early 1970s (Capitanchik and Eichenberg, 1983, p.73). As Lipset (1985) observed, a substantial ideological gap was emerging between the administration and electorate with respect to foreign and defence issues. Congress reflected this growing disenchantment in its attempts to exert some control over the direction of Central American policy.

There were two mechanisms by which Congress sought to obtain leverage over the administration: through its powers to authorize federal expenditure and its oversight role. Its power to authorize spending in particular gave it considerable influence, in the years 1983–8, over the nature and scale of the administration's overt activities in Central America, the policy objectives being pursued, and mechanisms of policy implementation.

For its success the administration's policy depended upon it being able to provide military and economic aid to its allies in Central America, adequate funding of Defense Department and CIA activities in the region, and substantial financial military support to the Contra rebel forces in Nicaragua. All of these programmes were subject to congressional approval because they each involved federal expenditure. Consequently, congressional opponents of the administration's policy, which in the early years consisted of a broad bipartisan coalition, concentrated on denying the President's request for funding of its Central American policies. From 1985 onwards, there were increasingly acrimonious conflicts between the President and the Congress over funding requests. Each attempt by the administration to win funds to arm the Contra forces was defeated by Congress. Compromises were reached, such as that agreed in 1985 allowing the release of some humanitarian aid to the Contras, but even so Congress continued to oppose the provision of 'lethal aid' (i.e. military aid) to the rebel forces. The administration was therefore forced on to the offensive. Throughout March 1986 it mounted an extensive and sophisticated media campaign, with the assistance of various conservative organizations such as the Heritage Foundation, to persuade the House to vote through a $100m aid package for the Contra forces. With congressional elections in the offing, it was assumed that the opposition would be somewhat temporarily muted. In fact the President was forced to make fundamental compromises, but even then the House vote went narrowly against him. These continuing defeats had a marked impact on the conduct of policy, for it lacked the effective means to achieve its objectives; policy had to be readjusted. Following a particularly crushing defeat in 1985, an exasperated President remarked that: 'We have got to get to where we can run a foreign policy without a committee of 535 [the combined membership of the Senate and House] telling us what we can do' (*Keesings Archives*, 1985, p.33968).

Despite this initial setback the President stepped up the political pressure on Congress throughout 1986. The question of military aid to the Contras had now become a litmus test of executive primacy in the making of foreign policy. Representatives in particular became the targets of a highly organized and insidious lobbying campaign designed to capture votes for the administration's policy. Given forthcoming Congressional elections the prospect of being presented by opponents as 'soft on communism' weighed heavily on many Congressional politicians. Their situation was not eased either by the apparent strengthening of ties between Moscow and Managua. These combined political pressures were sufficient to win the President enough support in the House to approve a $100m Contra aid package in June 1986. This was the administration's first major victory over Congress but it was extremely short lived. Just a few weeks after the President signed the aid bill into law in October the first revelations of the Iran–Contra scandal began to break in the media. Once the full details of the scandal became public the President found it impossible to overcome Congressional opposition to further military aid to the Contra forces in Nicaragua. Indeed, in March 1987 Congress refused to release the second branch of the June 1986 aid package. This event symbolized the transitory and pyrrhic nature of the Presidents only substantial victory over Congressional opponents of the administration's policy. Throughout 1988, despite several attempts, Congress refused requests for military aid, although it did grant humanitarian and non-lethal aid to the Contras but only after political compromises had been made. By the fall of 1988 the administration had come full circle in announcing that, during the remaining tenure of his office, the President would make no further requests to Congress for military aid for the Contras.

By making the release or approval of funding dependent upon the fulfilment of certain conditions, Congress acquired additional leverage over the administration's policy. Particularly with regard to El Salvador, Congress tied the approval of economic and military assistance to progress towards democratization and respect for human rights. Human rights violations were appalling: somewhere approaching 50,000 people disappeared in the period 1981 to 1985. A 'certification process' was therefore incorporated into aid legislation, whereby the release of funds was made dependent upon the State Department certifying to the Foreign Affairs Committee that El Salvador was moving towards more 'democratic rule'. This had an important influence on the administration's policy towards El Salvador, for it had to give greater priority to democratization even if only at a rhetorical level. As a result it encouraged and assisted the holding of elections in the country. Moreover, in 1984, the newly elected Duarte regime was pressured by the administration into initiating political and economic reforms which without Congressional influence might otherwise never have surfaced on the political agenda.

Alongside 'certification' Congress attempted to restrict the activities of the CIA in the region. Following revelations of the CIA's covert campaign against the Sandinistas, the Select Committee on Intelligence strengthened the Boland amendment previously incorporated into authorization legislation. This amendment stated that no CIA or Defense Department funds could be used either directly or indirectly to train, arm or support any forces conducting military operations in Nicaragua. As Foley notes '... the result was that the Democratic leadership in the House of Representatives had seized the initiative in this particular foreign policy area' (Foley, 1989, p.11).

Consequently the administration was forced to retreat, at least in public, from its commitment to toppling the Sandinista regime. However, as the evidence from the Tower Commission report into the Iran–Contra affair shows the White House circumvented the Boland amendment through its prosecution of a completely autonomous covert policy, privatized and hidden from public or congressional scrutiny.

Finally, by detailing exactly how authorized aid could be expended, Congress acquired some influence, albeit limited, over policy implementation. In granting humanitarian aid to the Contras in 1985 Congress specified that it could not be distributed through either CIA or Defense Department channels. As a result the administration created the Nicaraguan Humanitarian Assistance Office, attached formally to the State Department, as an institutional mechanism for distributing non-lethal aid to the Contras. Through such congressional action the State Department was encouraged to adopt a more enthusiastic approach towards diplomatic solutions to the Nicaraguan problem and had its position in the bureaucratic struggles over Central American policy strengthened.

Overall Congress acted as both a constraint upon and a participant in the executive policy formulation with respect to Central American affairs. It shaped policy objectives and the selection of policy instruments as well as the actual implementation of policy. But it was not successful in dislodging the administration from its primary desire to destabilize the Sandinista regime. Indeed, Lowenthal (1986) argues, that by 1986 the administration had settled 'into a low-intensity indirect war against the Sandinista government' by using the military forces in neighbouring Honduras and El Salvador as proxies. Nor was Congressional opposition able to generate a coherent alternative policy to that of the administration which also commanded majority support on Capitol Hill. There are echoes here of Krasner's observation, quoted earlier in the chapter concerning the realities of negative power in the American political system.

The significance of organized interests

Pluralist theories stress the significant role of organized interests in the determination of public policy. In this particular case there was an identifiable array of interests seeking to influence policy outcomes. On the whole two distinct groupings of organized interests can be identified, although they were far too fluid, re-grouping from issue to issue, to regard them as competing coalitions.

One grouping, which included various conservative political action committees and foundations such as the Conservative Caucus, the Council for Inter-American Security and the Heritage Foundation, was generally supportive of the administration's policy. Allied with these organizations was the United Nicaraguan Opposition, an umbrella group for the anti-Sandinista forces which sought increased military aid from the USA. At various crucial points the Contras, too, were represented, as their leaders appeared in Washington to lobby Congress. Lobbyists acting on behalf of various Central American governments also sought to influence key congressional votes on military and economic aid. Indeed, an enormous range and variety of organized interests attempted to mobilize political support for the administration's policy towards Central America, because they believed this would be of direct benefit. In return for access and influence a number of groups, such as the Heritage Foundation and the World Anti-Communist League (WACL), sought to promote the administration's policy. Some were exploited as channels for bypassing congressional restrictions on aid and military supplies to rebel forces. The WACL, for instance, is alleged to have been exploited as a mechanism for channeling 'private' but nonetheless 'lethal' aid to the Contra forces.

But there was an equally vocal 'coalition' of organized interests which made every attempt to persuade Congress to block the administration's initiatives on Central America. Church groups, such as the National Conference of Churches, the Office of International Justice and Peace, human rights organizations like the American Civil Liberties Union and Amnesty International, as well as liberal organizations such as the Washington Office on Latin America and the Council on Hemispheric Affairs, mounted very effective campaigns against numerous aspects of the administration's policy. Yet curiously none of these bodies, except perhaps those with religious associations, could in any sense be regarded as powerful actors. Unlike many of the conservative groups, which were backed by corporate wealth, most of these organizations had meagre resources. What made up for their relative weakness in the political process was the ingrained fear among a significant and vocal section of the populace that Reagan's policy was leading to an unwarranted and dangerous military entanglement. This fear was heightened by daily media coverage of American military activities in the region. Such reporting connected in the public mind events in Central America with the early period of the Vietnam War. Indeed, the Vietnam syndrome, despite the administration's attempts to rewrite the lessons of the war, was a major ideological resource for those battling against Reagan's policy. It gave their arguments added legitimacy and in so doing convinced the administration to restrain both its rhetoric and its actions.

Furthermore, the majority of European and Latin American governments refused to offer the administration any political support for its Nicaraguan policy. Particularly after the CIA mining of Nicaraguan harbours in 1984, Reagan came under increasing diplomatic pressure from European and Latin American allies to temper US policy. Such pressure had a marginal impact on policy. Much more significant was the desire to avoid inadvertently offering the major Latin American debtor countries the political pretext for defaulting on their debt repayments; a real possibility had there been a US military intervention in Nicaragua. The White House was therefore obliged to balance the competing demands of its Central American policy and its policy towards international debtors. Such issue-linkage provided the financial establishment and the major US multinational banks with some leverage over the administration's Central American policy. Many viewed that policy as damaging their short-term interests, since it risked creating greater political instability in the region. In fact most banks were so paralysed by the fear of potential default that they had even assisted the Nicaraguans, in defiance of an Executive Order signed by the President in late 1985, with the rescheduling of their external debt.

The national security state and the Iran–Contra scandal

In parallel with its publically declared policy towards Nicaragua the administration also conducted a covert policy from 1983 onwards. Aspects of this
covert policy became public knowledge in 1984 when the CIA admitted a
role in the mining of Nicaraguan harbours. Indeed it was the increasingly
hostile publicity attached to the CIA's covert war that had stimulated the
growing resistance in Congress to the Reagan policy and contributed to the
tightening up of Congressional restrictions (through the Boland amendments) on the use of federal funds to prosecute such activities. When it
became known that the CIA had been conducting its covert activities without informing the Senate Intelligence Committee, as required by law, even
staunch supporters of the President's policy adopted a more critical stance.
Republican Senator Barry Goldwater, in a letter to the Director of the CIA
shortly after the revelations concerning the mining of Nicaraguan harbours
were made public, fulminated: 'I am pissed off ... The President has asked us
to back his foreign policy. Bill, how can we back his foreign policy when we
don't know what the hell he is doing?' (quoted in Foley, 1989, p.11).

But, as the evidence from the Iran–Contra Congressional hearings confirm, such protests merely led to cosmetic changes in the administration's
policy. For members of the NSC staff devised and conducted from the White
House their own secret foreign policy in order to circumvent those Congressional and democratic controls which they believed hampered the successful
realization of the administration's policy objectives with respect to Nicaragua.

From 1984 onwards Lieutenant-Colonel Oliver North, a member of the
President's NSC staff, coordinated a completely secret campaign to supply
the Contra forces with military equipment and funds denied by Congress.
This was done with the express support and assistance of Admiral
Poindexter, then Reagan's Special Assistant for National Security. 'Project
Democracy' as the operation was somewhat ironically entitled, was managed
from the White House without the knowledge of most of the executive
branch including the Secretaries of State and Defense. It embraced a secret
network of private agencies and organizations, and a number of Third World
governments, through which funds and military equipment were supplied
to the Contra forces without implicating the US government in their supply.
By such means North was able to funnel considerable resources to the Contras. But this was in complete contravention of the legal prohibition enacted
by Congress (in the form of the Boland amendment) against any federal
funds being used to support the Contra forces. This deception was compounded doubly by the illegal sale of arms to Iran, in return for the release of
American hostages, and the channeling of the proceeds to Project Democracy. When this became public knowledge in the fall of 1986 the Reagan
administration was plunged into a serious political crisis reminiscent of the
1974 Watergate scandal which had culminated in President Nixon's resignation.

The Iran–Contra affair, as it was christened by the media, represented a
stunning assault on the constitutional principles and democratic practices
which informed American government. Indeed, the actions of those NSC
staff members implicated in the affair demonstrated an astounding level of

contempt for the democratic process. For, as Koh has observed: ' ... all of the NSC's actions during the Iran–Contra affair ran counter to announced US foreign policy objectives and all were conducted without the knowledge of either Congress or virtually all of the executive branch.' (Koh, 1990, p.60.) The affair raised fundamental questions about the formulation and implementation of foreign policy in the Reagan administration. In particular Congress demanded to know just how far the President was implicated in these attempts to subvert the democratic process. The subsequent Tower Commission inquiry and Congressional investigations into the affair absolved the President from any knowledge of the diversion to the Contras of funds acquired from arms sales to Iran. However, these inquiries confirmed the President's failure to assert control over his own NSC staff and the complete autonomy granted them in the determination and execution of policy. Indeed the official reports from these inquiries convey an image of the NSC as almost completely out of control conducting a covert foreign policy, through largely private channels, which at times undermined and ran counter to the established policies of the State Department. Even the President's own account of the affair confirms a policy process in some disarray since '... the only constitutional players in that process — the President, the Vice President and Congress — as well as the only other statutory NSC members, the Secretaries of State and Defense, were almost entirely excluded from decision making.' (Koh, 1990, p.114.) In what must rank as a historic understatement the official (majority) Congressional report on Iran–Contra concluded that the whole episode demonstrated an urgent need for '...a renewal of the commitment to constitutional government and sound processes of decision making.' (Quoted in Koh, 1990, p.21.)

Despite the findings of the Tower Commission and the Congressional inquiry the President survived the affair although his public image was severely discredited. However, more permanent damage was inflicted on the Presidency, for the whole Iran–Contra mess resurrected constitutional issues concerning the rightful role of Congress in the determination of foreign policy. For Congress perceived Iran–Contra not simply as an abuse of executive power but more importantly as a fundamental denial of the tacitly accepted convention that the executive's discretionary powers were subject to legislative supervision. According to Foley: 'The game rules were not breached by the administration's efforts to evade them, but by its conspiracy blatantly to defy them.' (Foley, 1989, p.15.) Certainly in the aftermath of the scandal the administration reiterated, much to Congressional annoyance, that it had not broken the law since Congressional prohibitions, in the form of the Boland amendment, did not apply specifically to the NSC. Moreover, the President's robust talk of executive privilege did little to calm Congressional critics of the abuse of executive authority.

As Koh observes: '...the Iran–Contra affair represented a frontal executive branch assault upon the principle of power sharing that underlies the National Security Constitution.' (Koh, 1990, p.115.) Not surprisingly therefore the political fallout from the scandal continues to shape the politics of executive-legislative relations in respect of foreign and defence policy. This is essentially because there remains a guarded suspicion in Congress that Iran–Contra was not an aberration, or a simple failure of Presidential management, but rather a further blatant episode in the long history of executive attempts since the Vietnam war to neutralize and circumvent the democratic process in the formulation and conduct of national security policy.

Policy as process and outcome

At one level the Reagan administration's policy towards Central America nicely illustrates the classical pluralist image of the policy process. Power was fragmented; there was a plethora of organized interests both within and outside government; and this created complex and dynamic patterns of interaction, among fluid coalitions of competing interests, which resulted in processes of bargaining, compromise and accommodation. Policy was an outcome of these processes in the sense that it was action which commanded some form of tacit consensus among the participants. But policy was never fixed or constant; events and changing circumstances made the policy-making process a continuous rather than a discrete activity. Nor was the process predictable, for new issues arose, political forces regrouped, and new battles were fought. However, although it renders the policy process intelligible, this classical pluralist picture fails to capture one very significant dimension in this particular case.

Clearly the 'state', in the form of the executive branch, was far from being a disinterested arbiter between conflicting interests, as classical pluralist accounts of the policy process suggest. It was very much a dominant actor with its own strong preferences. And those preferences reflected deeply conservative ideological interests, rather than representing public opinion or a societal consensus. Moreover, the 'state' attempted quite successfully to establish and retain control over the policy-making agenda. Indeed one of its greatest successes was in convincing the majority of the public that the problem in Central America was an externally generated one, i.e. of communist expansionism, rather than a consequence of the flagrantly unjust domestic socio-economic structures in all of these nations which would have demanded a quite different policy response. Far from the American 'state' being weak, in the sense of being overwhelmingly constrained or influenced by powerful societal forces, policy-making on Central America seems to indicate that it is a much more autonomous and powerful force in the determination of public policy than pluralist theories admit. Such autonomy is readily confirmed in the revelations of the White House role in the Iran–Contra dealings. This suggests that in this particular case study neo-pluralist accounts of the policy process appear decidedly more appropriate since neo-pluralism stresses the powerful role of the bureaucracy and the White House in shaping the agenda and the processes of public policy-making. Such a conclusion may well become even more apparent in the case of policy-making with respect to the Latin American debt issue.

8.3   Responding to the debt problem

In 1976 Mexico and Brazil owed approximately $56 billion to foreign lenders, of which about half was to multinational banks. Ten years later that figure had reached an astronomical $196 billion, an increase of over 300 per cent. By 1985 Latin America's external debt as a whole stood at a staggering $368 billion. For the United States the problem of Latin American debt is a prime example of what Chapter 7 referred to as an 'intermestic' issue. Indeed it highlights, in a highly pronounced form, the intimate connection between the domestic and the international. In the mid 1980s a loan default by any of the major Latin American debtor nations could have triggered a major financial crisis in the United States with serious consequences for the domestic economy. Here is a major public policy problem created essentially through the independent commercial activities of a handful of US multinational banks which have become overexposed in their lending to Latin America. Since they were also the largest banks in the United States, the financial stability of the entire US banking system became vulnerable to any default on loan payments by the major Latin American debtor nations. By 1984, for instance, the nine major US banks were owed over $42 billion by the four largest debtors, a sum approaching 127 per cent of their total capital. When, in late 1982, Mexico announced that it could not guarantee to make scheduled payments to its American debtors the financial alarm was raised in Washington and New York.

A pragmatic response to Latin American debt

Mexico's potential default presented the Reagan administration with the first key test of its 'free market' approach to the problems of international finance and Third World debt. Since attaining office the new administration had strenuously opposed, on ideological grounds, the provision of taxpayers' money to international financial institutions, such as the World Bank and the International Monetary Fund, in order to alleviate the problems of Latin American indebtedness. However, the Treasury and the Federal Reserve, responsible respectively for general government economic policy and regulation of the private banking sector, were openly concerned by the potential domestic consequences of allowing Mexico to default. As the Treasury Secretary explained to the House Banking Committee in 1982, such a default would lead to a cycle of economic contraction which would create 'Higher unemployment and a reduction in economic activity, with all they entail for city, state and federal budgets ... None of this is in the interest of the US citizen' (quoted in Lever and Huhne, 1985, p.117).

In addition, the Federal Reserve was acutely aware of the potential instability that Mexico's default would provoke in the domestic banking system, which was already suffering from unprecedented levels of bank failures. The President was thus persuaded to endorse a package of temporary crisis measures to assist Mexico. Cohen notes that: 'Like the cavalry of old the US government rushed to the rescue ... quickly providing more than $2.5 billion of emergency assistance' (Cohen, 1985, p.715).

Such action did not break entirely with the administration's ideological commitment to free market principles, for it was frequently reiterated that this was a temporary crisis measure. Moreover, the Federal Reserve and the Treasury forcefully communicated their expectation that private banks should expand their lending to Mexico, and other states, to prevent any further potential defaults. But the banks failed to heed these exhortations and bank lending to Latin America virtually ceased. No bank was willing to risk further exposure and endanger profitability, shareholder confidence and, in the worst possible scenario, its corporate viability. Lack of further funds, however, merely compounded the problems facing the largest borrowers, such as Brazil and Argentina, whose collective situation progressively deteriorated.

By late 1983 the Treasury and Federal Reserve had mounted several 'rescue' operations in response to the inability of both Argentina and Brazil to meet their scheduled loan replacements. For the largest debtors the situation was becoming untenable. The economic recession in Europe and the US had slashed their export earnings, inflation was rampant, and the outflow of resources to pay foreign banks was crippling their domestic economies. Most were reaching a critical situation in which they would be unable even to pay the interest on debt repayments, which had been rescheduled many times. With only emergency relief being offered they formed a 'debtors club', called the Cartegena group, which aimed to bring collective pressure to bear on the US government, international financial institutions and multinational banks to establish a more flexible and realistic policy to ease the debt burden. A veiled threat lay beneath their approaches to the international financial community, namely that a collective default or 'debt strike' might be unavoidable should no effective policy response be forthcoming. This development provoked a fundamental re-examination of the administrations policy.

Within the Reagan administration a variety of prescriptions emerged on what could or should be done. The Treasury, with its responsibility for national economic policy, was acutely aware of the disastrous consequences of any single or collective default. This would instigate a deflationary cycle of credit contraction in the American economy and destabilize the international financial system. The Treasury believed that the way to avoid this was to provide longer-term and more substantial financial aid to the debtor nations, but the major difficulty was how to finance such a package. Bilateral aid from the US would have to be made conditional, since Congress would not sanction it without recognizable political returns for American taxpayers. But the stringent conditions necessary to satisfy Congress would undoubtedly provoke what everyone was attempting to avoid. Politically there were also major problems in formulating an effective policy towards the debtors without the banks taking a key role, since there was mounting opposition in Congress to anything that appeared like a bail-out or a subsidy for the major US banks. Equally, the Treasury was sensitive to the fact that an internationalized solution, which would involve the US providing additional resources to the IMF, the Inter-American Development Bank and the World Bank to loan to the debtors, would not be easily negotiable. For the White House was opposed to expanding the responsibilities of any international agencies since it regarded them as beyond effective US control. Nor could Congress be guaranteed to vote the massive funding required, since it had already blocked an increase in the US contribution to the IMF and the World Bank. The Treasury therefore came to the conclusion that the only politically feasible and rational policy was an internationalized solution, but one in which private banks played a major role. This could be constructed in such a way as to meet the debtor nations' immediate needs, overcome the banks' objections to increased lending to the debtors and marginalize any political opposition in Congress while crucially preventing the nightmare of a collective default. The Treasury set about convincing the White House of its policy proposals.

Among the other major bureaucratic actors there was considerable support for the Treasury view that the US government had to take action on the debt crisis in Latin America. The Federal Reserve, which regulated the private banking system and would have to step in if there were major bank collapses, endorsed the need for government intervention to prevent a major financial crisis. It had already been forced to deal with a mounting number of bank failures, almost a twelve-fold increase between 1974 and 1983, and the debt crisis in Latin America made the twenty four largest US banks extremely vulnerable. If any single one of these collapsed, the Federal Reserve would have few alternatives other than to 'bail out' or even nationalize it, in all but name, otherwise confidence in the whole domestic banking system would quickly vanish. Any 'bail out' would pose intriguing political problems, not least because such a policy would require legitimation in a polity which, as Chapter 6 noted, is fiercely opposed to anything which smacks of public ownership. The Federal Reserve thus supported the Treasury's view that a more interventionary policy had to be adopted with some urgency.

This conclusion was reinforced by the opinions of the Department of Commerce and the Department of State. The Department of Commerce was concerned that any default would lead to a significant downturn in US exports to Latin America, which in the 1980s had become the largest export market for US goods outside Europe. Major defaults would seriously reduce this trade, leading to a loss of jobs and plant closures, particularly in the new sunbelt growth regions which were most dependent on inter-American trade. This undesirable prospect had energized corporate and political forces in those vulnerable areas to lobby Congress and the executive branch to take firmer action to protect their livelihoods. The State Department, however, was less exercised by the domestic implications of potential default than the political and strategic ramifications of simply allowing it to occur. It alerted the White House and Congress to the possible consequences for hemispheric relations of a major default by Latin American states. Among the political casualties would be the move towards democratization in Brazil and Argentina, heightened levels of regional political instability, which could easily be exploited by revolutionary and external forces, and a further erosion of the hemispheric structures of military and political co-operation. As the State Department forcefully argued, the administration could not trade vital hemispheric political relationships for the sake of an ideological attachment to free market principles.

Beyond the executive branch pressure mounted for a more coherent policy towards the debt problem. The consortium of banks implicated in the crisis sought to impress their views on the policy-makers. The nine largest banks in the USA, which were also the most overexposed in Latin America, attempted to convince the administration that only government action would be effective. Moreover, by refusing for their own valid commercial reasons to lend further money to the biggest debtor countries they effectively set the policy agenda, in that they limited the options available to the administration while unintentionally deepening the crisis. This effectively increased pressure on the administration to act.

There were numerous channels through which the banking community obtained access to the key decision makers. Constant personnel interchanges between the major banks and the Federal Reserve and Treasury were important, particularly at senior levels. But there was also the much more institutionalized network of relationships which gives the largest banks privileged access to the state machine. Various committees and advisory groups have been spawned by the Treasury to complement its policy-making particularly with regard to highly technical issues. Such bodies exist to generate co-operative solutions to any policy problems which arise between the largest private banks and the Treasury. Through these formal mechanisms the banks were able to exert influence on the policy-makers. But these larger banks were also able to acquire the support of most of the banking community through the American Bankers' Association (ABA). This was a somewhat unique development since the multinational banks and smaller domestic banks generally have widely divergent interests. Aware of the drastic consequences of a debt strike for the whole domestic banking system, the ABA lent weight to demands for effective government action. The ABA has a clear 'insider group' status with the Treasury and the Federal Reserve; as one politician commented, the Federal Reserve is a 'wholly owned subsidiary of the American Bankers' Association' (quoted in Aronson, 1977, p.55). Transnational contacts among bankers within the global banking community were also exploited to lend support to the arguments by the domestic banking sector. Through the Institute of International Finance, which acts as an international pressure group for the major multinational banks, the international banking community's support for the major American banks' policy with respect to Latin American debtors was communicated directly to the US administration.

Alongside pressure from the banking community, the Department of Commerce and the State Department were subject to considerable lobbying from other organized interests from the corporate world. In particular, the powerful Council of the Americas, which represents the interests of the major US corporate investors in Latin America, has direct links with the key policy-makers. Like the ABA, it is very much an insider group, and as Kryzanek (1985, p.115) indicates, 'works closely with an administration in formulating policy (especially if that administration is Republican)'. Together with the Association of American Chambers of Commerce in Latin America, these two organizations contributed the vital support of the business community to the bankers' call for government action.

Of course, there were also organized interests which lobbied against any government support for the banks. In particular, the AFL-CIO and other union groups protested about subsidies going to multinational banks and companies which only exported US jobs to Latin America. There were also groups, like the Conservative Caucus, which were opposed to any 'bail out' solely on ideological grounds. However, organized opposition was almost totally divided and fragmented. In effect, banking and corporate interests dominated the policy-making arena. Despite this the administration's final policy statements did not wholly reflect their demands.

By 1984 opposition to a more interventionary policy, particularly from within the White House, had been totally marginalized. The President and his closest advisers were thoroughly convinced by the Treasury and corporate analyses of the situation. Nonetheless, the Federal Reserve and the Treasury continued to pressurize banks to step up their lending to Latin American debtors. They even threatened regulatory action against them. As Cohen explains, this largely involved alluding to 'closer scrutiny of their books if they did not go along with fresh loans for countries like Mexico' (Cohen, 1985, p.716). The banks made some compromises and the administration, too, sought to encourage this through loans via the government-owned Export–Import Bank. But events in 1984 and 1985 finally forced the abandonment of the administration's pragmatic approach, and a major new policy initiative was announced in which it warmly embraced economic interventionism. Politically, it was a far from easy task for a President elected on a radical conservative platform to reduce federal government intervention in the economic sphere.

The Baker Plan

Throughout 1984 and 1985 the economic circumstances of most of the large Latin American debtor countries had worsened considerably, as primary commodity prices fell, economic growth declined, foreign investment slowed, and US interest rates remained at a high level. Although they had obtained short-term relief through the rescheduling of debt repayments, this went little way towards alleviating their situation, for the debt crisis involved a phenomenal transfer of resources from Latin America to the USA. Indeed, by 1985 the debtor countries had transferred a staggering $106 billion to Western banks and financial institutions in little more than 4 years. This, the Cartegena group agreed, could not continue without imposing an even more severe and intolerable strain on their domestic economic and political structures. At their meetings in 1984 and 1985, the group adopted a more militant stance. The debt problem was now becoming increasingly politicized, and American policy-makers feared the possibility of radical developments which could dramatically alter the status quo. These fears were fanned in June 1985 by the calls of President Castro of Cuba for the unilateral cancellation of this 'illegitimate debt' (*Keesings Archives*, 1985, p.34156). All this coincided with a number of important political developments in the USA.

Chief among these was that Reagan had been returned for a second term. This led to some key personnel changes, crucial among which was the transfer of Treasury Secretary Donald Regan to the post of Chief Assistant to the President and the appointment of James Baker as the new Treasury Secretary. Debt issues now received a much higher priority in the White House. But also important was the fact that congressional opposition to international measures for dealing with the debt problem, involving increased funding for the IMF or other international financial institutions, had been virtually emasculated. Although Congress was not the central arena in the policy-making process, it did provide a focal point for the rather disparate opposition. But only the most die-hard Republicans and New Right converts could ignore the pressure emanating from the business community as the serious domestic implications of the Latin American debt crisis were gradually understood. A more accommodating domestic political environment, combined with a deteriorating situation in Latin America, provided the Treasury with a politically opportune juncture to unveil a new debt policy initiative.

Following a lengthy period of discussion with experts in the domestic and international financial communities, the new Treasury Secretary proposed, at the IMF–World Bank meeting in Seoul in October 1985, the Baker Plan. This plan was predicated upon considerably expanded US financial support for the IMF, the World Bank and the Inter-American Development Bank as mechanisms for assisting the debtor countries. In return for additional resources these institutions would be required to impose certain conditions on the recipients, which involved a greater opening up of their economies to foreign investment and an increased reliance on private enterprise. In effect the US, through these international financial institutions, was acting to police the debtors and so ensure that there would be no disastrous collapse of the banking system. However, it was not a 'bail out' of the banks. For their part the banks were required to make additional, quite large short-term loans to the major debtors to stave off default. The Baker Plan was therefore very much a 'partnership' between the government and banks

Although the Baker Plan did not resolve the problems of the debtor countries it did provide a temporary alleviation of their situation. Moreover, it established the basis for a new international consensus between multi-national banks, the IMF, and key creditor nations on the subsequent steps necessary for managing the global debt crisis. By the late 1980s the Baker Plan had been replaced by the Brady Plan which adopted a much more radical approach to the debt crisis. It was able to do so by building upon the government–bank partnership nurtured by the Baker Plan.

In attempting to understand the policy-making process which produced the Baker Plan three aspects of the policy remain acutely puzzling. First is the fact that the administration was able to obtain the agreement of the commercial banks, against their individual commercial instincts, to a policy involving even more lending to the major debtor nations. Second, there is the more curious fact that the administration adopted a boldly interventionary policy which ran directly counter to its political and ideological principles. But third is the more intriguing fact that despite the intimate links between government and the commercial banks, the administration did not, to put it crudely, simply translate the banks demands into government policy. These three 'puzzles' raise some interesting questions about the nature of the policy-making process in this particular case and economic policy making more generally.

Explaining debt policy
A classical pluralist account of debt policy would not get very far in explaining the puzzles identified above, for classical pluralists regard policy as the outcome of a competition between organized interests involving bargaining and compromises facilitated by the state. Yet this seems far removed from

what actually occurred on the debt issue. Policy appears to have been decided largely between government experts and private experts. Congress and wider group interests were not noticeably significant determinants of debt policy. Yet certain major organized interests, like the ABA and the multinational banks, were very much a part of the official policy process, since government depended upon them for technical advice, information and the effective implementation of its policies. Certainly in this case the Treasury was aware that any policy would have to gain the assent of at least the major US banks, since they could, by non-co-operation, easily prevent its effective implementation. Equally, the major banks were aware that they depended on government for maintaining a stable domestic and international financial environment which was vital to their efficient operation. They also recognized that the Treasury and the Federal Reserve had regulatory tools which could be used to coerce them. Consequently, a 'partnership' between government and the major banking corporation appears to have been the primary determinant of debt policy. This reflects very much a neo-pluralist account, since it stresses the role of experts in decision-making, the co-option of organized interests into the official policy process, and the marginal role of congressional representatives and the wider public in shaping policy outcomes.

But this neo-pluralist account does not entirely explain all the 'puzzles' of debt policy alluded to above. However, if the debt policy issue is located within the larger structure of US–Latin American relations, then some of these 'puzzles' can be partially resolved. This implies adopting a neo-Marxist explanatory framework. Such an explanation would emphasize the fundamental role of the American 'state' in maintaining the structure of dependence in inter-American relations, since that structure is vital to the health of the US economy. As a hegemonic power, the USA was therefore unavoidably drawn to intervene in the debt problem, despite the ideological commitments of the administration, since it threatened to undermine the exploitative structure of economic relations in the hemisphere. That the Reagan administration did not act solely at the behest of the banks is explicable in terms of America's hegemonic role in this structure, which is to facilitate the expansion and welfare of American capitalism rather than to promote the specific interests of one particular sector of capital such as the banks. This emphasis on ensuring the stability and pursuing the needs of the 'system' is even more evident in the conditionality of aid under the Baker Plan; for the conditions attached to financial aid, such as opening up economies to foreign competition, can be viewed as instruments for enabling the further penetration of American corporate capital throughout Latin America. For neo-Marxists this is a further means by which the structure of dependence is reproduced. While a neo-Marxist account would not deny the interaction between state agencies and the major banking interests in the formulation of debt policy, it would argue that the significance of such interaction to the final policy outcomes is much less than the overriding requirement to keep the structure of dependence in inter-American relations rigidly intact.

It should be apparent from this brief exploration of policy-making in these two case studies that pluralist, neo-pluralist and neo-Marxist theories offer distinctive perspectives on the public policy process. Although philosophically incompatible, they nonetheless provide valuable insights into the nature and determinants of public policy-making, and equally into the functioning of American democracy.

8.4 The policy process and democratic ideals: concluding reflections

Although, over the last two decades, the foreign policy process has experienced an 'explosion' in public participation, this has provoked quite contradictory reactions. Conservatives believe it to be inherently bad, since too much democracy makes it impossible for the executive to pursue a sound and coherent foreign policy which reflects the 'national interest'. As Halle (1978) argues, Americans have failed 'to reconcile mass democracy with the wise conduct of foreign policy'. Many liberals, on the other hand, including the founding father of empirical democratic theory, Robert Dahl (1985) fervently believe that an even more democratic foreign policy process would lead to a much wiser and safer foreign policy. Whatever the merits of these competing views, both recognize that the relationship between democratic ideals and the foreign policy process is fraught with tensions, contradictions and dilemmas. But foreign policy, as Chapter 7 explained, is not unique in this sense, for many of those same tensions and dilemmas are equally evident in almost every single sector of public policy-making. This final section offers some brief reflections on the relationship between democratic ideals and the policy process in the American polity.

One crucial factor which has transformed the relationship between America's democratic aspirations and the policy process is its hegemonic role in the global system. As a hegemonic power, it has certain functions to perform as well as responsibilities to fulfil in maintaining both global stability and the framework of the world capitalist economic order. This imposes certain domestic burdens and costs which many citizens may not wish to bear and therefore actively oppose through the democratic process. Vietnam and Nicaragua are good cases in point here. A constant tension therefore exists between the 'democratic' nature of the political process, which facilitates opposition to executive action, and the perceived 'demands' of being a global power. On the most crucial issues, like the use of force abroad or in crises, the democratic process is often subordinated to the requirements of being a great power. A case in point being the Iran–Contra affair which demonstrated executive contempt for democratic processes which interfered with 'realpolitiks'.

This connects directly to the issue of executive leadership in policy matters. During the Nixon–Kissinger era, power was overwhelmingly concentrated in the White House in the belief that only executive leadership could ensure that the national interest was promoted both at home and abroad. Executive leadership sought to provide a rational strategic approach to the problems that confronted the nation. But such leadership requires presidential primacy, secrecy, resolve and decisivenesss, qualities which cannot flourish in a democratic process predicated on the separation of powers and the requirement to obtain at least a tacit domestic consensus on policy initiatives. This inherent conflict between the desire of Presidents to provide strong leadership and an attachment to democratic values designed to ensure that power is not overly concentrated in any one political institution injects a real dilemma into the policy process. Such a dilemma can never be satisfactorily resolved without compromising either executive leadership or democratic practices.

Democracy implies that public policy outcomes should be perceived as both legitimate but also effective, in terms of achieving specific policy goals. But these requirements are often contradictory, for a policy which the experts in the bureaucracy believe to be the most effective and rational solution to a given problem may conflict with what politicians, the public and organized interests are willing to accept or support. Policy-making on Central America illustrates this contradiction extremely well. This is not an isolated case, however, for on many policy issues there is a visible tension between what commands agreement among the participants in the policy-making process and what is the most rational, efficient and effective course of action to pursue. In an age in which instrumental rationality and efficiency are prized, this dilemma has come increasingly to the fore.

Mention of rationality and efficiency highlights the more pervasive tendency for policy-making, across all issues and policy sectors, to be dominated by experts. This is just as apparent in health policy as it is in defence policy. The two case studies in this chapter provide ample evidence of the role of experts, whether government officials or the representatives of organized interests, in the policy-making process. Yet, as the debt issue demonstrates, the realities of modern international interdependence mean that even when the vital interests of the whole, or significant sections, of the political community may be at risk participation in policy-making is largely restricted to the experts. This raises a crucial dilemma concerning the proper extent of public participation in policy-making, a dilemma which has the most profound implications for democratic practice. Since many policy issues, such as the debt issue, are highly complex there is a real tension in the policy-making process between the emphasis upon expert decision-making and the requirement for effective public participation. Implicit in the attachment to expert decision making is the belief that public participation in the policy process brings with it real dangers, for as Walter Lippmann eloquently phrased it mass opinion 'has shown itself to be a dangerous master of decisions when the stakes are life and death' (Lippmann, 1956, p.24).

Foreign policy-making, as with the making of domestic policy, poses a number of significant challenges to the nature and aspirations of modern American liberal democracy. Writing some years ago, at the height of the Vietnam War, Theodore Lowi posed the question whether 'After twenty years of world leadership ... a pluralistic democracy can adjust to the requirements of its world role' (Lowi, 1969, p.187). In the post-Cold War era in which the United States is consciously reaffirming its role as a hegemonic power in the global system that question still remains unanswered.

References

ARONSON, J.D. (1977) *Money and Power — Banks and the World Monetary System*, London, Sage.

CAPITANCHIK, D. and EICHENBERG, R.C. (1983) *Defence and Public Opinion*, Chatham House Paper No. 20, London, Routledge and Kegan Paul.

COHEN, B.J. (1985) 'International debt and linkage strategies: some foreign policy implications for the United States', *International Organization*, Vol. 39, No. 4, Autumn, pp. 699–728.

DAHL, R. (1985) *Controlling Nuclear Weapons: Democracy versus Guardianship*, New York, Syracuse University Press.

FOLEY, M. (1989) *Mumbling Across the Branches*, International Politics, University of Aberystwyth.

HALLE, L. (1978) 'Foreign policy and the democratic process: the American experience' in Halle, L.J. and Thompson, K.W. (eds) *Foreign Policy and the Democratic Process: the Geneva Papers*, Washington DC, University Press of America.

KEESINGS ARCHIVES (1985) November, p. 33966, December, p. 34032–3.

KOH, H.H. (1990) *The National Security Constitution*, Yale, Yale University Press.

KRASNER, S.D. (1978) *Defending the National Interest — Raw Materials, Investments and US Foreign Policy*, New Jersey, Princeton University Press.

KRYZANEK, M.J. (1985) *US–Latin American Relations*, New York, Praeger.

LEVER, H. and HUHNE, C. (1985) *Debt and Danger — The World Financial Crisis*, Harmondsworth, Penguin.

LIPPMANN, W. (1956) *The Public Philosophy*, New York, Mentor Books.

LIPSET, S.L. (1985) 'The elections, the economy and public opinion: 1984', *Political Science*, Vol. 18, Winter, pp. 28–38.

LOWENTHAL, A.F. (1986) 'Threat and opportunity in the Americas', *Foreign Affairs*, Vol. 64, No. 3, pp. 539–62.

LOWI, T.J. (1969) *The End of Liberalism*, New York, W.W. Norton.

RUBIN, B. (1985) *Secrets of State—the State Department and the Struggle over US Foreign Policy*, New York, Oxford University Press.

SCHNEIDER, W. (1984) 'Public opinion' in Nye, J.S. *The Making of America's Soviet Policy*, New Haven, Yale University Press.

Further reading

COCHRANE, J.D. (1985) 'Perspectives on the Central American crisis', *International Organization*, Vol. 39, No. 4, Autumn.

GLASBERG, D.S. (1989) 'Bank hegemony research and its implications for power structure theory', *Critical Sociology*, Vol. 16, No. 23, pp. 27–49.

LEONARD, T.M. (1985) *Central America and US Policies 1820s–1980s*, Claremont, Cal., Regina Books.

Appendix 1   The Constitution of the United States of America

We the people of the United States, in order to form a more perfect Union, establish Justice, insure domestic Tranquility, provide for the common defence, promote the general Welfare, and secure the Blessings of Liberty to ourselves and our Posterity, do ordain and establish this CONSTITUTION for the United States of America.

ARTICLE I

Section 1. All legislative Powers herein granted shall be vested in a Congress of the United States, which shall consist of a Senate and House of Representatives.

Section 2. The House of Representatives shall be composed of Members chosen every second Year by the People of the several States, and the Electors in each State shall have the Qualifications requisite for Electors of the most numerous Branch of the State Legislature.

No person shall be a Representative who shall not have attained the Age of twenty-five Years, and been seven Years a Citizen of the United States, and who shall not, when elected, be an Inhabitant of that State in which he shall be chosen.

(Representatives and direct Taxes shall be apportioned among the several States which may be included within this Union, according to their respective Numbers, which shall be determined by adding to the whole Number of free Persons, including those bound to Service for a Term of Years, and excluding Indians not taxed, three-fifths of all other persons.)[1] The actual Enumeration shall be made within three Years after the first Meeting of Congress of the United States, and within every subsequent Term of ten Years, in such Manner as they shall by Law direct. The Number of Representatives shall not exceed one for every thirty thousand, but each State shall have at Least one Representative; and until such enumeration shall be made, the State of New Hampshire shall be entitled to chuse three, Massachusetts eight, Rhode Island and Providence Plantations one, Connecticut five, New York six, New Jersey four, Pennsylvania eight, Delaware one, Maryland six, Virginia ten, North Carolina five, South Carolina five, and Georgia three.

When vacancies happen in the Representation from any State, the Executive Authority thereof shall issue Writs of Election to fill such Vacancies.

The House of Representatives shall chuse their Speaker and other Officers; and shall have the sole Power of Impeachment.

Section 3. The Senate of the United States shall be composed of two Senators from each State, chosen by the Legislature thereof,[2] for six Years; and each Senator shall have one Vote.

---

[1] This provision was modified by the Sixteenth Amendment. The three-fifths reference to slaves was rendered obsolete by the Thirteenth and Fourteenth Amendments.

[2] See the Seventeenth Amendment.

Immediately after they shall be assembled in Consequence of the first Election, they shall be divided as equally as may be into three Classes. The Seats of the Senators of the first Class shall be vacated at the Expiration of the second Year, of the second Class at the Expiration of the fourth Year, and of the third Class at the Expiration of the sixth Year, so that one-third may be chosen every second Year; and if Vacancies happen by Resignation, or otherwise, during the Recess of the Legislature of any State, the Executive thereof may make temporary appointments until the next Meeting of the Legislature, which shall then fill such vacancies.

No person shall be a Senator who shall not have attained to the Age of thirty Years, and been nine Years a Citizen of the United States, and who shall not, when elected, be an Inhabitant of that State for which he shall be chosen.

The Vice President of the United States shall be President of the Senate, but shall have no Vote, unless they be equally divided.

The Senate shall chuse their other Officers, and also a President pro tempore, in the absence of the Vice President, or when he shall exercise the Office of President of the United States.

The Senate shall have the sole Power to try all Impeachments. When sitting for that Purpose, they shall be on Oath of Affirmation. When the President of the United States is tried, the Chief Justice shall preside; And no Person shall be convicted without the Concurrence of two-thirds of the Members present.

Judgment in Cases of Impeachment shall not extend further than to removal from Office, and disqualification to hold and enjoy any Office of honor, Trust or Profit under the United States; but the Party convicted shall nevertheless be liable and subject to Indictment, Trial, Judgment and Punishment, according to Law.

Section 4. The Times, Places and Manner of holding Elections for Senators and Representatives, shall be prescribed in each State by the Legislature thereof; but the Congress may at any time by law make or alter such Regulations, except as to the Places of chusing Senators.

The Congress shall assemble at least once in every Year, and such Meeting shall be on the first Monday in December, unless they shall by Law appoint a different Day.[3]

Section 5. Each House shall be the Judge of the Elections, Returns and Qualifications of its own Members, and a Majority of each shall constitute a Quorum to do Business; but a smaller Number may adjourn from day to day, and may be authorized to compel the Attendance of absent Members, in such Manner, and under such Penalties as each House may provide.

Each House may determine the Rules of its Proceedings, punish its Members for disorderly Behaviour, and, with the Concurrence of two-thirds, expel a Member.

Each House shall keep a Journal of its Proceedings and from time to time publish the same, excepting such Parts as may in their Judgment require Secrecy; and the Yeas and Nays of the Members of either House on any

---

[3]See the Twentieth Amendment.

question shall, at the Desire of one-fifth of those Present, be entered on the Journal.

Neither House, during the Session of Congress, shall without the Consent of the other, adjourn for more than three days, not to any other Place than that in which the two Houses shall be sitting.

Section 6. The Senators and Representatives shall receive a Compensation for their Services, to be ascertained by Law, and paid out of the Treasury of the United States. They shall in all Cases, except Treason, Felony, and Breach of the peace, be privileged from Arrest during their Attendance at the Session of their respective Houses, and in going to and returning from the same; and for any Speech or Debate in either House, they shall not be questioned in any other Place.

No Senator or Representative shall, during the Time for which he was elected, be appointed to any civil Office under the Authority of the United States, which shall have been created, or the Emoluments whereof shall have been increased during such time; and no Person holding any Office under the United States, shall be a Member of either House during his Continuance in Office.

Section 7. All Bills for raising Revenue shall originate in the House of Representatives; but the Senate may propose or concur with Amendments as on other Bills.

Every Bill which shall have passed the House of Representatives and the Senate, shall, before it become a Law, be presented to the President of the United States; if he approve he shall sign it, but if not he shall return it, with his Objections to that House in which it shall have originated, who shall enter the Objections at large on their Journal, and proceed to reconsider it. If after such Reconsideration two-thirds of that House shall agree to pass the Bill it shall be sent, together with the Objections, to the other House, by which it shall likewise be reconsidered, and if approved by two-thirds of that House, it shall become a law. But in all such Cases the Votes of both Houses shall be determined by Yeas and Nays, and the Names of the Persons voting to and against the Bill shall be entered on the Journal of each House respectively. If any Bill shall not be returned by the President within ten Days (Sundays excepted) after it shall have been presented to him, the Same shall be a Law, in like Manner as if he had signed it, unless the Congress by their Adjournment prevent its Return, in which Case it shall not be a Law.

Every Order, Resolution, or Vote to which the Concurrence of the Senate and House of Representatives may be necessary (except on a question of Adjournment) shall be presented to the President of the United States: and before the Same shall take Effect, shall be approved by him, or being disapproved by him, shall be repassed by two-thirds of the Senate and House of Representatives, according to the Rules and Limitations prescribed in the Case of a Bill.

Section 8. The Congress shall have Power To Lay and collect Taxes, Duties, Imposts and Excises, to pay the Debts and provide for the common Defence and general Welfare of the United States; but all Duties, Imposts and Excises shall be uniform throughout the United States;

To borrow money on the Credit of the United States;

To regulate Commerce with foreign Nations, and among the several States, and with the Indian Tribes;

To establish an uniform Rule of Naturalization, and uniform Laws on the subject of Bankruptcies throughout the United States.

To coin Money, regulate the Value thereof, and of foreign Coin, and fix the Standard of Weights and Measures;

To provide for the Punishment of counterfeiting the Securities and current Coin of the United States;

To establish Post Offices and post Roads;

To promote the Progress of Science and useful arts, by securing for limited Times to Authors and Inventors the exclusive Right to their respective Writings and Discoveries;

To constitute Tribunals inferior to the supreme Court;

To define and punish Piracies and Felonies committed on the high Seas, and Offenses against the Law of Nations;

To declare War, grant Letters of Marque and Reprisal, and make Rules concerning Captures on Land and Water;

To raise and support Armies, but no Appropriation of Money to that Use shall be for a longer Term than two Years;

To provide and maintain a Navy;

To make Rules for the government and Regulation of the land and naval Forces;

To provide for calling forth the Militia to execute the Laws of the Union, suppress Insurrections and repel Invasions;

To provide for organizing, arming, and disciplining the Militia, and for governing such Part of them as may be employed in the Service of the United States, reserving to the States respectively, the Appointment of the Officers, and the Authority of training the Militia according to the discipline prescribed by Congress;

To exercise exclusive Legislation in all Cases whatsoever, over such District (not exceeding ten Miles square) as may, by Cession of particular States, and the acceptance of Congress, become the Seat of the Government of the United States, and to exercise like Authority over all Places purchased by the Consent of the Legislature of the State in which the Same shall be, for the Erection of Forts, Magazines, Arsenals, dock-Yards, and other needful Buildings; — And

To make all Laws which shall be necessary and proper for carrying into Execution the foregoing Powers, and all other Powers vested by this Constitution in the Government of the United States, or in any Department or Officer thereof.

Section 9. The Migration or Importation of such Persons as any of the States now existing shall think proper to admit, shall not be prohibited by the Congress prior to the Year one thousand eight hundred and eight, but a tax or duty may be imposed on such importation, not exceeding ten dollars for each Person.

The privilege of the Writ of Habeas Corpus shall not be suspended, unless when in Cases of Rebellion or Invasion the public Safety may require it.

No Bill of Attainder or ex post facto Law shall be passed.

No capitation, or other direct Tax shall be laid, unless in Proportion to the Census or Enumeration herein before directed to be taken.[4]

No Tax or Duty shall be laid on Articles exported from any State.

No Preference shall be given by any Regulation of Commerce or Revenue to the Ports of one State over those of another; not shall Vessels bound to, or from one State, be obliged to enter, clear, or pay Duties in another.

No Money shall be drawn from the Treasury, but in consequence of Appropriations made by Law; and a regular Statement and Account of the Receipts and Expenditures of all public Money shall be published from time to time.

No Title of Nobility shall be granted by the United States: And no Person holding any Office of Profit or Trust under them, shall, without the Consent of the Congress, accept of any present, Emolument, Office, or Title, of any kind whatever, from any King, Prince, or foreign State.

Section 10. No State shall enter into any Treaty, Alliance, or Confederation; grant Letters of Marque and Reprisal; coin Money; emit Bills of Credit; make any Things but gold and silver Coin a Tender in Payment of Debts; pass any Bill of Attainder, ex post facto Law, or Law impairing the Obligation of Contracts, or grant any Title of Nobility.

No State shall, without the Consent of the Congress, lay any Imposts or Duties on Imports or Exports, except what may be absolutely necessary for executing its inspection Laws: and the net Product of all Duties and Imposts, laid by any State on Imports or Exports, shall be for the Use of the Treasury of the United States and all such Laws shall be subject to the Revision and Control of the Congress.

No State shall, without the Consent of Congress, lay any duty of Tonnage, keep Troops, or Ships of War in time of Peace, enter into any Agreement or Compact with another State, or with a foreign Power, or engage in War, unless actually invaded, or in such imminent Danger as will not admit of delay.

ARTICLE II

Section 1. The executive Power shall be vested in a President of the United States of America. He shall hold his Office during the Term of four Years, and, together with the Vice President, chosen for the same Term, be elected, as follows

Each State shall appoint, in such Manner as the Legislation thereof may direct, a Number of Electors, equal to the whole number of Senators and Representatives to which the State may be entitled in the Congress; but no Senator or Representative, or Person holding an Office of Trust or Profit under the United States, shall be appointed an Elector.

The Electors shall meet in their respective States, and vote by Ballot for two persons, of whom one at least shall not be an Inhabitant of the same State with themselves. And they shall make a List of all Persons voted for, and of the Number of Votes for each; which List they shall sign and certify, and transmit sealed to the Seat of the Government of the United States,

---

[4]See the Sixteenth Amendment.

directed to the President of the Senate. The President of the Senate shall, in the Presence of the Senate and House of Representatives, open all the Certificates, and the Votes shall then be counted. The Person having the greatest Number of Votes shall be the President, if such Number be a Majority of the whole Number of Electors appointed; and if there be more than one who have such Majority, and have an Equal Number of Votes, then the House of Representatives shall immediately chuse by Ballot one of them for President; and if no Person have a Majority, then from the five highest on the List the said House shall in like Manner chuse the President, but in chusing the President, the Votes shall be taken by States, the Representation from each State having one Vote; A quorum for this Purpose shall consist of a Member or Members from two thirds of the States, and a Majority of all the States shall be necessary to a Choice. In every Case, after the Choice of the President, the Person having the greatest Number of Votes of the Electors shall be the Vice President. But if there should remain two or more who have equal Votes, the Senate shall chuse from them by Ballot the Vice President.[5]

The Congress may determine the Time of chusing the Electors, and the Day on which they shall give their Vote; which Day shall be the same throughout the United States.

No person except a natural born Citizen, or a Citizen of the United States, at the time of the Adoption of this Constitution, shall be eligible to that Office who shall not have attained the Age of thirty-five Years, and been fourteen Years a Resident within the United States.

In Case of the Removal of the President from Office, or of his Death, Resignation, or Inability to discharge the Powers and Duties of the said office, the same shall devolve on the Vice President, and the Congress may by Law provide for the Case of Removal, Death, Resignation or Inability, both the President and Vice President, declaring what Officer shall then act as President, and such Officer shall act accordingly, until the Disability be removed, or a President shall be elected.

The President shall, at stated Times, receive for his Services, a Compensation, which shall neither be increased nor diminished during the Period for which he shall have been elected and he shall not receive within that Period any other Emolument from the United States, or any of them.

Before he enters on the Execution of his Office, he shall take the following Oath or Affirmation: — "I do solemnly swear (or affirm) that I will faithfully execute the Office of President of the United States, and will to the best of my Ability, preserve, protect and defend the Constitution of the United States."

Section 2. The President shall be Commander in Chief of the Army and Navy of the United States, and of the Militia of the several States, when called into the actual Service of the United States; He may require the Opinion in writing, of the principal officer in each of the executive Departments, upon any subject relating to the Duties of their respective Offices, and he shall have Power to Grant Reprieves and Pardons for Offenses against the United States, except in Cases of Impeachment.

---

[5]This paragraph was superseded by the Twelfth Amendment.

He shall have Power, by and with the Advice and Consent of the Senate, to make Treaties, provided two-thirds of the Senators present concur; and he shall nominate, and by and with the Advice and Consent of the Senate, shall appoint Ambassadors, other public Ministers and Consuls, Judges of the supreme Court, and all other Officers of the United States, whose Appointments are not herein otherwise provided for, and which shall be established by Law: but the Congress may by Law vest the Appointment of such inferior Offices, as they think proper, in the President alone, in the Courts of Law, or in the Heads of Department.

The President shall have Power to fill up all Vacancies that may happen during the Recess of the Senate by granting Commissions which shall expire at the End of their next Session.

Section 3. He shall from time to time give to the Congress Information of the State of the Union, and recommend to their Consideration such Measures as he shall judge necessary and expedient; he may, on extraordinary Occasions, convene both Houses, or either of them, and in Cases of Disagreement between them, with Respect to the Times of Adjournment, he may adjourn them to such Time as he shall think proper; he shall receive Ambassadors and other public Ministers; he shall take Care that the Laws be faithfully executed, and shall Commission all of the Officers of the United States.

Section 4. The President, Vice President and all civil Officers of the United States, shall be removed from Office on Impeachment for, and Conviction of, Treason, Bribery, or other high Crimes and Misdemeanors.

ARTICLE III

Section 1. The judicial power of the United States shall be vested in one supreme Court, and in such inferior Courts as the Congress may from time to time ordain and establish. The Judges, both of the supreme and inferior Courts, shall hold their offices during good Behaviour, and shall, at stated Times, receive for their Services a Compensation which shall not be diminished during their Continuance in Office.

Section 2. The judicial Power shall extend to all Cases, in Law and Equity, arising under this Constitution, the Laws of the United States and Treaties made, or which shall be made, under their Authority; — to all Cases affecting Ambassadors, other public Ministers and Consuls; — to all Cases of admiralty and maritime Jurisdiction; — to Controversies to which the United States shall be a Party; — to Controversies between two or more States; — between a State and Citizens of another State;[6] — between Citizens of different States; — between Citizens of the same State claiming Lands under Grants of different States, and between a State, or the Citizens thereof, and foreign States, Citizens or Subjects.

In all Cases affecting Ambassadors, other public Ministers and Consults, and those in which a State shall be a Party, the supreme Court shall have

[6]See the Eleventh Amendment.

original Jurisdiction. In all the other Cases before mentioned, the supreme Court shall have appellate Jurisdiction, both as to Law and Fact, with such Exceptions, and under such Regulations as the Congress shall make.

The trial of all Crimes, except in Cases of Impeachment, shall be by Jury, and such Trial shall be held in the State where the said Crimes shall have been committed, but when not committed within any State, the Trial shall be at such Place or Places as the Congress may by Law have directed.

Section 3. Treason against the United States, shall consist only in levying War against them, or in adhering to their Enemies, giving them Aid and Comfort. No Person shall be convicted of Treason unless on the Testimony of two Witnesses to the same overt Act, or on Confession in open Court.

The Congress shall have power to declare the Punishment of Treason, but no Attainder of Treason shall work Corruption of Blood, or Forfeiture except during the Life of the Person attainted.

ARTICLE IV

Section 1. Full Faith and Credit shall be given in each State to the public Acts, Records, and judicial Proceedings of every other State. And the Congress may by general Laws prescribe the Manner in which such Acts, Records and Proceedings shall be proved, and the Effect thereof.

Section 2. The Citizens of each State shall be entitled to all Privileges and Immunities of Citizens in the several States.

A Person charged in any State with Treason, Felony, or other Crime, who shall flee from Justice, and be found in another State, shall on demand of the executive Authority of the State from which he fled, be delivered up, to be removed to the State having Jurisdiction of the Crime.

No Person held to Service or Labour in one State, under the Laws thereof, escaping into another, shall in Consequence of any Law or Regulation therein, be discharged from such Service or Labour, but shall be delivered up on Claim of the Party to whom such Service or Labour may be due.[7]

Section 3. New States may be admitted by the Congress into this Union; but no new States shall be formed or erected within the Jurisdiction of any other State; nor any State be formed by the Junction of two or more States, or parts of States, without the Consent of the Legislatures of the States concerned as well as of the Congress.

The Congress shall have Power to dispose of and make all needful Rules and Regulations respecting the Territory or other Property belonging to the United States; and nothing in this Constitution shall be so constructed as to Prejudice any Claims of the United States, or of any particular State.

Section 4. The United States shall guarantee to every State in this Union a Republican Form of Government, and shall protect each of them against Invasion; and on Application of the Legislature, or of the Executive (when the Legislature cannot be convened) against domestic Violence.

ARTICLE V

The Congress whenever two-thirds of both Houses shall deem it necessary, shall propose Amendments to this Constitution, or, on the Application of

---

[7]Obsolete. See the Thirteenth Amendment.

the Legislatures of two-thirds of the several States, shall call a Convention for proposing Amendments, which, in either Case, shall be valid to all Intents and Purposes, as part of this Constitution, when ratified by the Legislatures of three-fourths of the several States, or by Conventions in three-fourths thereof, as the one or the other Mode of Ratification may be proposed by the Congress; Provided that no Amendment which may be made prior to the Year one thousand eight hundred and eight shall in any Manner affect the first and fourth Clauses in the Ninth Section of the first Article; and that no State, without its Consent, shall be deprived of its equal Suffrage in the Senate.

ARTICLE VI

All Debts contracted and Engagements entered into, before the Adoption of this Constitution, shall be as valid against the United States under this Constitution, as under the Confederation.

This Constitution, and the Laws of the United States which shall be made in Pursuance thereof; and all Treaties made, or which shall be made, under the Authority of the United States, shall be the supreme Law of the Land; and the Judges in every State shall be bound thereby, any Thing in the Constitution or Laws of any State to the Contrary notwithstanding.

The Senators and Representatives before mentioned, and the Members of the several State Legislatures, and all executive and judicial Officers, both of the United States and of the several States, shall be bound by Oath or Affirmation, to support this Constitution; but no religious Test shall ever be required as a Qualification to any Office or public Trust under the United States.

ARTICLE VII

The Ratification of the Conventions of nine States shall be sufficient for the Establishment of this Constitution between the States so ratifying the Same. Done in Convention by the Unanimous Consent of the States Present the Seventeenth Day of September in the Year of our Lord one thousand seven hundred and eighty seven and of the Independence of the United States of America the Twelfth. In Witness whereof We have hereunto subscribed our Names

Go. Washington
Presid't and depty from Virginia

Delaware	*New York*
Geo: Read	Alexander Hamilton
John Dickinson	
Jaco: Broom	
Gunning Bedford jun	*New Jersey*
Richard Bassett	Wil: Livingston
	David Brearley
	Wm. Paterson
	Jona: Dayton

Maryland
James McHenry
Dani Carroll
Dan: of St. Thos Jenifer

New Hampshire
John Langdon
Nicholas Gilman

South Carolina
J. Rutledge
Charles Pinckney
Charles Cotesworth Pinckney
Pierce Butler

Massachusetts
Nathaniel Gorham
Rufus King

Georgia
William Few
Abr Baldwin

Connecticut
Wm. Saml Johnson
Roger Sherman
Robt. Morris
Thos. Fitzsimons
James Wilson
Thomas Mifflin
Geo. Clymer
Jared Ingersoll
Gouv Morris

Virginia
John Blair
James Madison, Jr.

North Carolina
Wm Blount
Hu Williamson
Richd Dobbs Spaight

Pennsylvania
B. Franklin

Attest:
William Jackson, Secretary

AMENDMENTS[8]

Amendment I
Congress shall make no law respecting an establishment of religion, or pro-hibiting the free exercise thereof; or abridging the freedom of speech, or of the press; or the right of the people peaceably to assemble, and to petition the Government for a redress of grievances.

Amendment II
A well regulated Militia, being necessary to the security of a free State, the right of the people to keep and bear Arms, shall not be infringed.

Amendment III
No Soldier shall, in time of peace be quartered in any house, without the consent of the Owner, nor in time of war, but in a manner to be prescribed by law.

---

[8]The first 10 Amendments were adopted in 1791.

Amendment IV

The right of the people to be secure in their persons, houses, papers, and effects, against unreasonable searches and seizures, shall not be violated, and no Warrants shall issue, but upon probable cause, supported by Oath or affirmation, and particularly describing the place to be searched, and the persons or things to be seized.

Amendment V

No person shall be held to answer to a capital, or otherwise infamous crime, unless on a presentment or indictment of a Grand Jury, except in cases arising in the land or naval forces, or in the Militia, when in actual service in time of War or public danger; nor shall any person be subject for the same offence to be twice put in jeopardy of life or limb, nor shall be compelled in any criminal case to be a witness against himself, nor be deprived of life, liberty, or property, without due process of law; nor shall private property be taken for public use, without just compensation.

Amendment VI

In all criminal prosecutions, the accused shall enjoy the right to a speedy and public trial, by an impartial jury of the State and district wherein the crime shall have been committed, which district shall have been previously ascertained by law, and to be informed of the nature and the cause of the accusation; to be confronted with the witnesses against him; to have the compulsory process for obtaining witnesses in his favor, and to have the Assistance of Counsel for his defence.

Amendment VII

In suits at common law, where the value in controversy shall exceed twenty dollars, the right of trial by jury shall be preserved, and no fact tried by a jury, shall be otherwise reexamined in any Court of the United States, than according to the rules of the common law.

Amendment VIII

Excessive bail shall not be required, nor excessive fines imposed, nor cruel and unusual punishments inflicted.

Amendment IX

The enumeration in the Constitution, of certain rights shall not be construed to deny or disparage others retained by the people.

Amendment X

The powers not delegated to the United States by the Constitution, nor prohibited by it to the States, are reserved to the States respectively, or to the people.

Amendment XI[9]

The Judicial power of the United States shall not be construed to extend to any suit in law or equity, commenced or prosecuted against one of the United States by Citizens of another State, or by Citizens or Subjects of any Foreign States.

Amendment XII[10]

The Electors shall meet in their respective states and vote by ballot for President and Vice President, one of whom, at least, shall not be an inhabitant of the same state with themselves; they shall name in their ballots the person voted for as President and in distinct ballots the person voted for as Vice President, and they shall make distinct lists of all persons voted for as President, and of all persons voted for as Vice President, and of the number of votes for each, which lists they shall sign and certify, and transmit sealed to the seat of government of the United States, directed to the President of the Senate; — The President of the Senate shall, in the presence of the Senate and House of Representatives, open all the certificates and the votes shall then be counted; — The person having the greatest number of votes for President, shall be the President, if such a number be a majority of the whole number of Electors appointed; and if no person have such majority, then from the persons having the highest numbers not exceeding three on the list of those voted for as President, the House of Representatives shall choose immediately, by ballot, the President. But in choosing the President, the votes shall be taken by states, the representation from each state having one vote; a quorum for this purpose shall consist of a member or members from two-thirds of the states, and a majority of all the states shall be necessary to a choice. And if the House of Representatives shall not choose a President whenever the right of choice shall devolve upon them, before the fourth day of March next following, then the Vice President shall act as President, as in the case of the death or other constitutional disability of the President. — The person having the greatest number of votes as Vice President, shall be the Vice President, if such number be a majority of the whole number of Electors appointed, and if no person have a majority, then from the two highest numbers on the list, the Senate shall choose the Vice President; a quorum for the purpose shall consist of two-thirds of the whole number of Senators, and a majority of the whole number shall be necessary to a choice. But no person constitutionally ineligible to the office of President shall be eligible to that of Vice President of the United States.

Amendment XIII[11]

Section 1. Neither slavery nor involuntary servitude, except as a punishment for crime whereof the party shall have been duly convicted, shall exist within the United States, or any place subject to their jurisdiction.

Section 2. Congress shall have power to enforce this article by appropriate legislation.

[9]Adopted in 1798.

[10]Adopted in 1804.

[11]Adopted in 1865.

Amendment XIV[12]

Section 1. All persons born or naturalized in the United States and subject to the jurisdiction thereof, are citizens of the United States and of the State wherein they reside. No State shall make or enforce any law which shall abridge the privileges or immunities of citizens of the United States; nor shall any State deprive any person of life, liberty, or property, without the due process of law; nor deny to any person within its jurisdiction the equal protection of the laws.

Section 2. Representatives shall be apportioned among the several States according to their respective numbers, counting the whole number of persons in each State, excluding Indians not taxed. But when the right to vote at any election for the choice of electors for President and Vice President of the United States, Representatives in Congress, the Executive and Judicial Officers of a State, or the members of the Legislature thereof, is denied to any of the male inhabitants of such State, being twenty-one years of age, and citizens of the United States, or in any way abridged, except for participation in rebellion, or other crime, the basis of representation therein shall be reduced in the proportion which the number of such male citizens shall bear to the whole number of male citizens twenty-one years of age in such State.

Section 3. No person shall be a Senator or Representative in Congress, or elector of President and Vice President, or hold any office, civil or military, under the United States, or under any State, who, having previously taken an oath, as a member of Congress, or as an officer of the United States, or as a member of any State legislature, or as an executive or judicial officer of any State, to support the Constitution of the United States, shall have engaged in insurrection or rebellion against the same, or given aid or comfort to the enemies thereof. But Congress may by a vote of two-thirds of each House, remove such disability.

Section 4. The validity of the public debt of the United States, authorized by law, including debts incurred for payment of pensions and bounties for services in suppressing insurrection or rebellion, shall not be questioned. But neither the United States nor any State shall assume or pay any debt or obligation incurred in aid of insurrection or rebellion against the United States, or any claim for the loss or emancipation of any slave; but all such debts, obligations and claims shall be held illegal and void.

Section 5. The Congress shall have power to enforce, by appropriate legislation, the provisions of this article.

Amendment XV[13]

Section 1. The right of citizens of the United States to vote shall not be denied or abridged by the United States or by any State on account of race, color, or previous condition of servitude.

Section 2. The Congress shall have power to enforce this article by appropriate legislation.

---

[12]Adopted in 1868.

[13]Adopted in 1870.

Amendment XVI[14]

The Congress shall have power to lay and collect taxes on incomes, from whatever source derived, without apportionment among the several States, and without regard to any census or enumeration.

Amendment XVII[15]

The Senate of the United States shall be composed of two Senators from each State, elected by the people thereof, for six years, and each Senator shall have one vote. The electors in each state shall have the qualifications requisite for electors of the most numerous branch of the State legislatures.

When vacancies happen in the representation of any State in the Senate, the executive authority of such State shall issue writs of election to fill such vacancies: Provided, That the legislature of any State may empower the executive thereof to make temporary appointments until the people fill the vacancies by election as the legislature may direct.

This amendment shall not be so construed as to affect the election or term of any Senator chosen before it becomes valid as part of the Constitution.

Amendment XVIII[16]

Section 1. After one year from the ratification of this article the manufacture, sale or transportation of intoxicating liquors within, the importation thereof into, or the exportation thereof from the United States and all territory subject to the jurisdiction thereof for beverage purposes is hereby prohibited.

Section 2. The Congress and the several States shall have concurrent power to enforce this article by appropriate legislation.

Section 3. This article shall be inoperative unless it shall have been ratified as an amendment to the Constitution by the legislatures of the several States, as provided in the Constitution, within seven years from the date of the submission hereof to the States by the Congress.

Amendment XIX[17]

The right of Citizens of the United States to vote shall not be denied or abridged by the United States or by any State on account of sex.

Congress shall have power to enforce this article by appropriate legislation.

Amendment XX[18]

Section 1. The terms of the President and Vice President shall end at noon on the 20th day of January, and the terms of Senators and Representatives at noon on the 3d day of January, of the years in which such terms would have ended if this article had not been ratified; and the terms of their successors shall then begin.

[14]Adopted in 1913.

[15]Adopted in 1913.

[16]Adopted in 1919. Repealed by the Twenty-first Amendment.

[17]Adopted in 1920.

[18]Adopted in 1933.

Section 2. The Congress shall assemble at least once in every year, and such meeting shall begin at noon on the 3d day of January, unless they shall by law appoint a different day.

Section 3. If, at the time fixed for the beginning of the term of the President, the President elect shall have died, the Vice President elect shall become President. If a President shall not have been chosen before the time fixed for the beginning of his term, or if the President elect shall have failed to qualify, then the Vice President elect shall act as President until a President shall have qualified; and the Congress may by law provide for the case wherein neither a President elect nor a Vice President elect shall have qualified, declaring who shall then act as President or the manner in which one who is to act shall be selected, and such person shall act accordingly until a President or Vice President shall have qualified.

Section 4. The Congress may by law provide for the case of the death of any of the persons from whom the House of Representatives may choose a President whenever the right of choice shall have devolved upon them, and for the case of the death of any of the persons from whom the Senate may choose a Vice President whenever the right of choice shall have devolved upon them.

Section 5. Sections 1 and 2 shall take effect on the 15th day of October following the ratification of this article.

Section 6. This article shall be inoperative unless it shall have been ratified as an amendment to the Constitution by the legislatures of three-fourths of the several States within seven years from the date of its submission.

Amendment XXI[19]

Section 1. The eighteenth article of amendment to the Constitution of the United States is hereby repealed.

Section 2. The transportation or importation into any State, Territory, or possession of the United States for delivery or use therein of intoxicating liquors, in violation of the laws thereof, is hereby prohibited.

Section 3. This article shall be inoperative unless it shall have been ratified as an amendment to the Constitution by conventions in the several States, as provided in the Constitution, within seven years from the date of the submission hereof to the States by the Congress.

Amendment XXII[20]

Section 1. No person shall be elected to the office of the President more than twice, and no person who has held the office of President, or acted as President, for more than two years of a term to which some other person was elected President shall be elected to the office of the President more than once. But this Article shall not apply to any person holding the office of President when this Article was proposed by the Congress, and shall not prevent any person who may be holding the office of President, or acting as President, during the term within which this Article becomes operative from

[19]Adopted in 1933.

[20]Adopted in 1951.

holding the office of President or acting as President during the remainder of such term.

Section 2. This article shall be inoperative unless it shall have been ratified as an amendment to the Constitution by the Legislatures of three-fourths of the several States within seven years from the date of its submission to the States by Congress.

Amendment XXIII[21]

Section 1. The District constituting the seat of Government of the United States shall appoint in such manner as the Congress may direct:

A number of electors of President and Vice President equal to the whole number of Senators and Representatives in Congress to which the District would be entitled if it were a State, but in no event more than the least populous State; they shall be in addition to those appointed by the States; but they shall be considered, for the purposes of the election of President and Vice President, to be electors appointed by a State; and they shall meet in the District and perform such duties as provided by the twelfth article of amendment.

Section 2. The Congress shall have power to enforce this article by appropriate legislation.

Amendment XXIV[22]

Section 1. The right of citizens of the United States to vote in any primary or other election for the President or Vice President, for electors for President or Vice President, or for Senator or Representative in Congress, shall not be denied or abridged by the United States or any State by reason of failure to pay any poll tax or other tax.

Section 2. The Congress shall have power to enforce this article by appropriate legislation.

Amendment XXV[23]

Section 1. In case of the removal of the President from office or his death or resignation, the Vice President shall become President.

Section 2. Whenever there is a vacancy in the office of the Vice President, the President shall nominate a Vice President who shall take the office upon confirmation by a majority vote of both houses of Congress.

Section 3. Whenever the President transmits to the President pro tempore of the Senate and the Speaker of the House of Representatives his written declaration that he is unable to discharge the powers and duties of his office, and until he transmits to them a written declaration to the contrary, such powers and duties shall be discharged by the Vice President as Acting President.

Section 4. Whenever the Vice President and a majority of either the principal officers of the executive departments or of such other body as Congress may by law provide, transmit to the President pro tempore of the Senate and

[21]Adopted in 1961.

[22]Adopted in 1964.

[23]Adopted in 1967.

the Speaker of the House of Representatives their written declaration that the President is unable to discharge the powers and duties of his office, the Vice President shall immediately assume the powers and duties of the office as Acting President.

Thereafter, when the President transmits to the President pro tempore of the Senate and the Speaker of the House of Representatives, his written declaration that no inability exists, he shall resume the powers and duties of his office unless the Vice President and a majority of either the principal officers of the executive department or of such other body as Congress may by law provide, transmit within four days to the President pro tempore of the Senate and the Speaker of the House of Representatives their written declaration that the President is unable to discharge the powers and duties of his office. Thereupon Congress shall decide the issue, assembling within 48 hours for that purpose if not in session. If the Congress, within 21 days after receipt of the latter written declaration, or, if Congress is not in session, within 21 days after Congress is required to assemble, determines by two-thirds vote of both houses that the President is unable to discharge the powers and duties of his office, the Vice President shall continue to discharge the same as Acting President; otherwise the President shall resume the powers and duties of his office.

Amendment XXVI[24]
Section 1. The Right of Citizens of the United States, who are eighteen years of age or older, to vote shall not be denied or abridged by the United States or by any State on account of age.

Section 2. The Congress shall have power to endorse this article by appropriate legislation.

---

[24] Adopted in 1971.

Appendix 2 Presidents, Elections and Congresses, 1789–1990

Year	President	Congress	House Majority party		House Minority party		Senate Majority party		Senate Minority party	
1789–1797	George Washington	1st	38	Admin	26	Opp	17	Admin	9	Opp
		2nd	37	Fed	33	Dem-R	16	Fed	13	Dem-R
		3rd	57	Dem-R	48	Fed	17	Fed	13	Dem-R
		4th	54	Fed	52	Dem-R	19	Fed	13	Dem-R
1797–1801	John Adams	5th	58	Fed	48	Dem-R	20	Fed	12	Dem-R
		6th	64	Fed	42	Dem-R	19	Fed	13	Dem-R
1801–1809	Thomas Jefferson	7th	69	Dem-R	36	Fed	18	Dem-R	13	Fed
		8th	102	Dem-R	39	Fed	25	Dem-R	9	Fed
		9th	116	Dem-R	25	Fed	27	Dem-R	7	Fed
		10th	118	Dem-R	24	Fed	28	Dem-R	6	Fed
1809–1817	James Madison	11th	94	Dem-R	48	Fed	28	Dem-R	6	Fed
		12th	108	Dem-R	36	Fed	30	Dem-R	6	Fed
		13th	112	Dem-R	68	Fed	27	Dem-R	9	Fed
		14th	117	Dem-R	65	Fed	25	Dem-R	11	Fed
1817–1825	James Monroe	15th	141	Dem-R	42	Fed	34	Dem-R	10	Fed
		16th	156	Dem-R	27	Fed	35	Dem-R	7	Fed
		17th	158	Dem-R	25	Fed	44	Dem-R	4	Fed
		18th	187	Dem-R	26	Fed	44	Dem-R	4	Fed
1825–1829	John Quincy Adams	19th	105	Admin	97	Dem-J	26	Admin	20	Dem-J
		20th	119	Dem-J	94	Admin	28	Dem-J	20	Admin
1829–1837	Andrew Jackson	21st	139	Dem	74	Nat R	26	Dem	22	Nat R
		22nd	141	Dem	58	Nat R	25	Dem	21	Nat R
		23rd	147	Dem	53	AntiMas	20	Dem	20	Nat R
		24th	145	Dem	98	Whig	27	Dem	25	Whig
1837–1841	Martin Van Buren	25th	108	Dem	107	Whig	30	Dem	18	Whig
		26th	124	Dem	118	Whig	28	Dem	22	Whig
1841	William H. Harrison									
1841–1845	John Tyler	27th	133	Whig	102	Dem	28	Whig	22	Dem
		28th	142	Dem	79	Whig	28	Whig	25	Dem

Year	President	Congress	House Majority party	House Minority party	Senate Majority party	Senate Minority party
(1845–1849)	James K. Polk	29th	Dem 143	Whig 77	Dem 31	Whig 25
		30th	Whig 115	Dem 108	Dem 36	Whig 21
1849–1850	Zachary Taylor	31st	Dem 112	Whig 109	Dem 35	Whig 25
1850–1853	Millard Fillmore	32nd	Dem 140	Whig 88	Dem 35	Whig 24
1853–1857	Franklin Pierce	33rd	Dem 159	Whig 71	Dem 38	Whig 22
		34th	Rep 108	Dem 83	Dem 40	Rep 15
1857–1861	James Buchanan	35th	Dem 118	Rep 92	Dem 36	Rep 20
		36th	Rep 114	Dem 92	Dem 36	Rep 26
1861–1865	Abraham Lincoln	37th	Rep 105	Dem 43	Rep 31	Dem 10
		38th	Rep 102	Dem 75	Rep 36	Dem 9
1865–1869	Andrew Johnson	39th	Union 149	Dem 42	Union 42	Dem 10
		40th	Rep 143	Dem 49	Rep 42	Dem 11
1869–1877	Ulysses S. Grant	41st	Rep 149	Dem 63	Rep 56	Dem 11
		42nd	Rep 134	Dem 104	Rep 52	Dem 17
		43rd	Rep 194	Dem 92	Rep 49	Dem 19
		44th	Rep 169	Dem 109	Rep 45	Dem 29
1877–1881	Rutherford B. Hayes	45th	Dem 153	Rep 140	Rep 39	Dem 36
		46th	Dem 149	Rep 130	Dem 42	Rep 33
1881	James A. Garfield	47th	Rep 147	Dem 135	Rep 37	Dem 37
1881–1885	Chester A. Arthur	48th	Dem 197	Rep 118	Rep 38	Dem 36
1885–1889	Grover Cleveland	49th	Dem 183	Rep 140	Rep 43	Dem 34
		50th	Dem 169	Rep 152	Rep 39	Dem 37
1889–1893	Benjamin Harrison	51st	Rep 166	Dem 159	Rep 39	Dem 37
		52nd	Dem 235	Rep 88	Rep 47	Dem 39
1893–1897	Grover Cleveland	53rd	Dem 218	Rep 127	Dem 44	Rep 38
		54th	Rep 244	Dem 105	Rep 43	Dem 39
1897–1901	William McKinley	55th	Rep 204	Dem 113	Rep 47	Dem 34
		56th	Rep 185	Dem 163	Rep 53	Dem 26

Appendix 2 Presidents, Elections and Congresses, 1789–1990 (continued)

Year	President	Congress	House Majority party		House Minority party		Senate Majority party		Senate Minority party	
1901–1909	Theodore Roosevelt	57th	Rep	197	Dem	151	Rep	55	Dem	31
		58th	Rep	208	Dem	178	Rep	57	Dem	33
		59th	Rep	250	Dem	136	Rep	57	Dem	33
		60th	Rep	222	Dem	164	Rep	61	Dem	31
1909–1913	William Howard Taft	61st	Rep	219	Dem	172	Rep	61	Dem	32
		62nd	Dem	228	Rep	161	Rep	51	Dem	41
1913–1921	Woodrow Wilson	63rd	Dem	291	Rep	127	Dem	51	Rep	44
		64th	Dem	230	Rep	196	Dem	56	Rep	40
		65th	Dem	216	Rep	210	Dem	53	Rep	42
		66th	Rep	240	Dem	190	Rep	49	Dem	47
1921–1923	William G. Harding	67th	Rep	301	Dem	131	Rep	59	Dem	37
1923–1929	Calvin Coolidge	68th	Rep	225	Dem	205	Rep	51	Dem	43
		69th	Rep	247	Dem	183	Rep	56	Dem	39
		70th	Rep	237	Dem	195	Rep	49	Dem	46
1929–1933	Herbert Hoover	71st	Rep	267	Dem	167	Rep	56	Dem	39
		72nd	Dem	220	Rep	214	Rep	48	Dem	47
1933–1945	Franklin D. Roosevelt	73rd	Dem	310	Rep	117	Dem	60	Rep	35
		74th	Dem	319	Rep	103	Dem	69	Rep	25
		75th	Dem	331	Rep	89	Dem	76	Rep	16
		76th	Dem	261	Rep	164	Dem	69	Rep	23
		77th	Dem	268	Rep	162	Dem	66	Rep	28
		78th	Dem	218	Rep	208	Dem	58	Rep	37
1945–1953	Harry S. Truman	79th	Dem	242	Rep	190	Dem	56	Rep	38
		80th	Rep	245	Dem	188	Rep	51	Dem	45
		81st	Dem	263	Rep	171	Dem	54	Rep	42
		82nd	Dem	234	Rep	199	Dem	49	Rep	47
1953–1961	Dwight D. Eisenhower	83rd	Rep	221	Dem	211	Rep	48	Dem	47
		84th	Dem	232	Rep	203	Dem	48	Rep	47
		85th	Dem	233	Rep	200	Dem	49	Rep	47
		86th	Dem	283	Rep	153	Dem	64	Rep	34

Year	President	Congress	House Majority party		House Minority party		Senate Majority party		Senate Minority party	
1961–1963	John F. Kennedy	87th	263	Dem	174	Rep	65	Dem	35	Rep
1963–1969	Lyndon B. Johnson	88th	258	Dem	177	Rep	67	Dem	33	Rep
		89th	295	Dem	140	Rep	68	Dem	32	Rep
		90th	247	Dem	187	Rep	64	Dem	36	Rep
1969–1974	Richard M. Nixon	91st	243	Dem	192	Rep	57	Dem	43	Rep
		92nd	254	Dem	180	Rep	54	Dem	44	Rep
1974–1977	Gerald R. Ford	93rd	239	Dem	192	Rep	56	Dem	42	Rep
		94th	291	Dem	144	Rep	60	Dem	37	Rep
1977–1981	Jimmy Carter	95th	292	Dem	143	Rep	61	Dem	38	Rep
		96th	280	Dem	155	Rep	58	Dem	41	Rep
1981–1989	Ronald Reagan	97th	243	Dem	192	Rep	53	Rep	47	Dem
		98th	269	Dem	166	Rep	54	Rep	46	Dem
		99th	253	Dem	182	Rep	53	Rep	47	Dem
1989–	George Bush	100th	255	Dem	177	Rep	54	Dem	46	Rep
		101st	261	Dem	177	Rep	55	Dem	45	Rep

Abbreviations:

Admin	= Administration supporters
AntiMas	= Anti-Masonic
Dem	= Democratic
Dem-R	= Democratic Republican
Fed	= Federalist
Dem-J	= Jacksonian Democrats
Nat R	= National Republican
Opp	= Opponents of administration
Rep	= Republican
Union	= Unionist

Index

Note: Sub-entries are in alphabetical order, except where chronological order is significant.